Reflections on *The World Café*

We are deeply grateful for the reflections of key colleagues around the world who have reviewed advance copies of this book and offered their diverse perspectives on its relevance for our readers.

After all these years, I can still remember my first World Café! Our success with the "Commons Café" would not have been possible without this groundbreaking work.

**Sharif Abdullah, founder,
the Commonway Institute, and author of
*Creating a World that Works for All***

———

World Café conversations are one of the best ways I know to truly enhance knowledge sharing and tap into collective intelligence. The few simple principles in this book can lead to conscious conversations with the power to change not only the individuals who participate, but also our collective future.

**Verna Allee, author of *The Knowledge
Evolution* and *The Future of Knowledge***

———

The wisdom of many voices speaks from these pages! May we take seriously their invitation to call forth what has heart and meaning in our world through conversations that matter.

**Tom Atlee, founder, The Co-Intelligence
Institute, and author of *The Tao of Democracy***

———

The capacity to see the world of the "other" sounds simple, but it is not. Yet it is the core of creating a new human history together. The World Café and this book serve as an inspiration to help make that possible.

**Lic. Esteban Moctezuma Barragan,
Mexico's former Minister of
Social Development**

———

The prevailing wisdom is that talk is cheap and that it's a poor, timid substitute for action. This warm and inviting book demonstrates that conversation *is* action, because it is the wellspring from which relationships and trust are generated and informed decisions grow.

**Thomas F. Beech, President and CEO,
Fetzer Institute**

The challenge of leadership in these times of breathtaking speed and exhausting complexity is to find creative ways to embrace the future, and let go of the past. World Café dialogue provide us the opportunity to do just that.

**Paul Borawski, Executive Director
and Chief Strategic Officer,
American Society for Quality**

———

Understanding the World Café's fascinating model of a living social system is essential for the understanding of life and leadership in human organizations.

**Fritjof Capra, author of *The Web of Life*
and *The Hidden Connections***

———

The World Café couldn't be more timely. It offers inspiration and practical guidance to those who want to convene groups—even very large groups—for conversations that stimulate hope, creativity, and collective commitment.

**Laura Chasin, founder and Director,
Public Conversations Project**

———

This book and the stories in it offer hope for addressing complex challenges and provide methods for strengthening family and community relationships. It is truly a work of art and a very important contribution.

**Rita Cleary, co-founder,
Visions of a Better World Foundation**

———

World Café conversations touch the heart of what "human being" or "being human" means. By cherishing and including diverse voices, this book models the very nature of collective knowledge that is the heart of the World Café approach to dialogue.

**Sara Cobb, Director, Institute for Conflict
Analysis and Resolution, George Mason
University, and former Executive Director,
Program on Negotiation, Harvard Law School**

The invention of the World Café approach to constructive conversation is a tremendous step forward. If it can be applied widely there is a good chance that this world will be a much happier and more productive place.

Napier Collyns, co-founder, Global Business Network

What a great piece of work and contribution to the world! *The World Café* gives you the confidence to begin a new way of learning together—creating a safe environment to surface important questions and to make a real difference.

Kevin Cushing, CEO, AlphaGraphics, Inc.

This book lives its message of dialogue—with multiple voices that increase our mutual intelligence through its broad and deep insights into the magic of collective wisdom.

Leif Edvinsson, Professor of Intellectual Capital, University of Lund, Sweden

---

Those of us who help lead cities and local communities must bring the World Café, with its creative way of having productive conversations, into our public discourse.

Ed Everett, City Manager, Redwood City, California

The World Café is a practical, robust, and resilient approach for engaging with complex but important questions—creating outcomes that are seen as having deep legitimacy and therefore are more likely to be acted upon.

Martin Fischer, Senior Leadership Advisor, British National Health Service

---

The World Café is a powerful process for catalyzing conversations that matter—and that can heal. This book shows you how to use that process—and then watch the sparks fly!

Mark Gerzon, President, Mediators Foundation, and author of *Leading Beyond Borders: Tools for Transforming Conflict Into Synergy*

In this groundbreaking book, Juanita Brown and the World Café community offer the world a gift: a simple, brilliant, beautiful process for creating quality conversations about important issues, during one of the most divisive times in our history.

Sandy Heierbacher, Director, National Coalition for Dialogue & Deliberation

---

The World Café is a remarkably efficient and natural way for "the system to see (and hear) itself"—a critical capacity in our complex world. It has helped our SoL community work on important current issues and build relationships that last for years.

C. Sherry Immediato, Managing Director and President, Society for Organizational Learning (SoL)

In the decade of dilemmas ahead we need more conversations that matter and fewer speeches that don't. We need to learn in new ways. *The World Café* is an immediate and practical resource for that learning.

Bob Johansen, Senior Vice President and Distinguished Fellow, Institute for the Future

---

The World Café works like the window of a cathedral whose light reminds people to tap into their innate sources of natural wisdom. This book is a living story with many profound insights. It helps us create lives that matter through conversations that live.

Rev. Jan Willem Kirpestein, founder, and Johan Bontje, Senior Advisor, Encounter of Worldviews Foundation, The Netherlands

---

The principles for hosting strategic conversations shared in this book have been the foundation of our Executive MBA program. Why? Because they work!

Robert Lengel, Associate Dean for Executive Education and Director of the Center for Professional Excellence, University of Texas, San Antonio

The World Café is such a dynamic process that I thought it would be impossible to portray what actually goes on in this verbal whirlwind of ideas and collective thinking. Yet this book captures the essence of this critical approach to "learning how to learn."

Wit Ostrenko, President and CEO, Tampa Bay Museum of Science and Industry

———

The way *The World Café* brings to light the fundamental importance of conversation as a core process is both inspiring and exciting. It demonstrates that we are all more dependent than ever on listening and open conversation.

Mike Pfeil, Vice President, Corporate Communications, Altria Group, Inc.

———

If you are asking yourself: "What might I do to promote breakthrough thinking?"—here's an approach that provides the essential ingredients. It's practical, engaging, and applicable anywhere in the world.

Marjorie Parker, co-founder, Norwegian Center for Leadership Development, and author of *Creating Shared Vision*

———

This is a simple yet revolutionary, elegant yet practical way of digging deep and thinking big together.

Vicki Robin, co-founder, Conversation Cafes and Let's Talk America; and co-author of *Your Money or Your Life*

———

The World Café is an innovative social technology that can access collective wisdom. It is a must-read and a must-practice for all researchers and practitioners of social transformation and organizational change.

Claus Otto Scharmer, Senior Lecturer, MIT Sloan School of Management and co-author of *Presence: Human Purpose and the Field of the Future*

———

The World Café contains an astounding cornucopia of dialogic treasures, enabling us to appreciate and explore the ecology of systemic ideas and principles at the core of this important work.

Fred Steier, former President, American Society for Cybernetics

I love the way this book weaves in the scientific theory behind how dialogue and the World Café operate. The diverse voices who speak here also offer hope that we may yet evolve into true stewards of each other, all life, and the planet.

Barbara Waugh, co-founder, e-Inclusion; Director, University Relations, Hewlett-Packard; and author of *The Soul in the Computer*

———

We have used Café dialogues at our international and regional conferences with 1000 people and with small gatherings of 50. All come away with a deep and fulfilling connection to one another while having "conversations that matter."

Rose Welch, Community Network and International Conference Director, Institute of Noetic Sciences

———

Conversations, circles, and community are the cutting edge of the 21st century, and *The World Café* provides a map to this uncharted territory. If you want to know where we're headed, as a society and as a global culture, read this book!

Justine and Michael Toms, co-founders, New Dimensions World Broadcasting Network

———

The future performance of our organizations is directly related to the quality of conversations that happen there. The World Cafe gives us proven ingredients to cook up conversations that count. It is a must read for anyone aspiring to leadership in the 21st century.

Eric Vogt, President, International Corporate Learning Association (InterClass)

———

The World Café has been a key format in our international Systems Thinking conferences. It is an amazingly effective way to overcome the barriers that separate us and release our collective wisdom in service of more informed, more creative action.

Ginny Wiley, President, Pegasus Communications

The World Café

The World Café

Shaping Our Futures Through Conversations That Matter

Juanita Brown

with

David Isaacs

and

The World Café Community

BK

BERRETT–KOEHLER PUBLISHERS, INC.
San Francisco

Berrett-Koehler Publishers, Inc.
235 Montgomery Street, Suite 650
San Francisco, CA 94104-2916
Tel: (415) 288-0260   Fax: (415) 362-2512   www.bkconnection.com

Ordering Information
Quantity sales. Special discounts are available on quantity purchases by corporations, associations, and others. For details, contact the "Special Sales Department" at the Berrett-Koehler address above.
Individual sales. Berrett-Koehler publications are available through most bookstores. They can also be ordered directly from Berrett-Koehler: Tel: (800) 929-2929; Fax: (802) 864-7626; www.bkconnection.com
Orders for college textbook/course adoption use. Please contact Berrett-Koehler: Tel: (800) 929-2929; Fax: (802) 864-7626.
Orders by U.S. trade bookstores and wholesalers. Please contact Publishers Group West, 1700 Fourth Street, Berkeley, CA 94710. Tel: (510) 528-1444; Fax (510) 528-3444.

Berrett-Koehler and the BK logo are registered trademarks of Berrett-Koehler Publishers, Inc.
The World Café and the World Café logo are trademarks of Whole Systems Associates.

Printed in the United States of America
Berrett-Koehler books are printed on long-lasting acid-free paper. When it is available, we choose paper that has been manufactured by environmentally responsible processes. These may include using trees grown in sustainable forests, incorporating recycled paper, minimizing chlorine in bleaching, or recycling the energy produced at the paper mill.

Library of Congress Cataloging-in-Publication Data
Brown, Juanita, 1944–
    The world café : shaping our futures through conversations that matter / by Juanita Brown and David Isaacs.
      p. cm.
    Includes bibliographical references and index.
    ISBN-13: 978-1-57675-258-6
    1. Group facilitation. 2. Communication in social action. 3. Conversation—Social aspects. I. Isaacs, David, 1938– II. Title.

HM751.B76 2005
302.3'46—dc 22   2004040973

First Edition
10 09 08 07 06   10 9 8 7 6 5 4 3

Interior Design: Laura Lind Design   Cover Design: Karen Marquardt
Copy Editor: Sandra Beris   Proofreader: Lunaea Weatherstone
Production: Linda Jupiter, Jupiter Productions   Indexer: Medea Minnich
Illustrations: see page 226

To our loving parents and families, who have helped to shape who we are as people and professionals.

And to the World Café community for teaching us about the magic of collective wisdom and how it can express itself in so many practical ways.

CONTENTS

We Can Be Wise Only Together

By Margaret J. Wheatley

Author of four groundbreaking books, *Leadership and the New Science, A Simpler Way, Turning to One Another,* and *Finding Our Way,* Meg Wheatley is a consultant, speaker, and president of the Berkana Institute, a nonprofit foundation dedicated to developing life-affirming leadership around the globe. In this reflection on the power of conversation and collective wisdom Meg shares her perspective on the unique contribution of the World Café to our common future.

In this troubling time when many people are so disconnected from one another, I keep searching to find those ideas, processes, and behaviors that can restore hope for the future. The World Café does just that. The stories told in these pages by its practitioners from all over the world demonstrate that it is possible for people to find meaning, even joy, in working together. And that through our conversations, as we work together, we discover a greater wisdom that reveals our path forward.

The World Café reintroduces us to a world we have forgotten. This is a world where people naturally congregate because we want to be together. A world where we enjoy the age-old process of good conversation, where we're not afraid to talk about things that matter most to us. A world where we're not separated, classified, or stereotyped. A world of simple greeting, free from technology and artificiality. A world that constantly surprises us with the wisdom that exists not in any one of us but in all of us. And a world where we learn that the wisdom we need to solve our problems is available when we talk together.

This world has been forgotten by us, but it has never abandoned us. For several years, David Isaacs, co-originator of the Café process, has said that our work is to remember this world, that we don't need to create it. From what I observe in many places, however, it appears that our memory of how to work together in healthy, productive ways has been nearly extinguished by the creeping complexity of group work, facilitation techniques, obscure analytic processes, and our own exhaustion. People are more polarized, more overwhelmed, more impatient, more easily disappointed in others, and more withdrawn than ever. We're frustrated by the increasing number of problems that confront us and our impotence to resolve even the most simple ones. And no sane person wants to participate in yet another meeting or get involved with yet another problem-solving process, because these things only increase our frustration and impotence.

Perhaps the most pernicious consequence of this memory loss is our growing belief that humans are a difficult, self-serving species and that we cannot trust each other. As this negative belief grows stronger, we remove ourselves and focus only on work that we can do on our own. We pay attention to the work in front of us, and thus lose any appreciation of the whole system. Isolated and alone, we lose courage and capacity; our work loses meaning and we end up with unending fatigue and loneliness.

The World Café process reawakens our deep species memory of two fundamental beliefs about human life. First, we humans want to talk together about things that matter to us. In fact, this is what gives satisfaction and meaning to life. Second, as we talk together, we are able to access a greater wisdom that is found only in the collective.

I can't

The World Café in Action

As you read the stories and counsel in this book, you will see these two beliefs brought to life in the Café process. In order to provoke your exploration of them, I'd like to underline some of the dimensions of the Café process that bring these beliefs into vibrant, healthy reality.

Belief in Everybody

The World Café is a good, simple process for bringing people together around questions that matter. It is founded on the assumption that people have the capacity to work together, *no matter who they are.* For me, this is a very important assumption. It frees us from our current focus on personality types, learning styles, emotional IQ—all the popular methods we currently use to pre-identify and pre-judge people. Each of these typologies ends up separating and stereotyping people. This is not what was intended by their creators, but it is what has happened.

The Café process has been used in many different cultures, among many different age groups, for many different purposes, and in many different types of communities and organizations. *It doesn't matter who the people are—the process works.* It works because people *can* work well together, *can* be creative and caring and insightful when they're actively engaged in meaningful conversations around questions that count. I hope that these stories inspire us to move away from all the categories and stereotypes we currently use about who should be involved, who should attend a meeting—all the careful but ill-founded analysis we put into constructing the "right" group. We need to be focused on gathering the real diversity of the system, but that's quite different from being absorbed with these other sorting devices.

Diversity

It's important to notice the diversity of the places and purposes for which the World Café is used, and the diversity of participants who are encouraged to attend World Café gatherings. These pages contain a rich illustration of a value I live by: *we need to depend on diversity.* Including diversity well is a survival skill these days, because there's no other way to get an accurate picture of any complex problem or system. We need many eyes and ears and hearts engaged in sharing perspectives. How can we create an accurate picture of the whole if we don't honor the fact that we each see something different because of who we are and where we sit in the system? Only when we have many different perspectives do we have enough information to make good decisions. And exploring our differing perspectives always brings us closer together. One Café member said it well: "You're moving among strangers, but it feels as if you've known these people for a long time."

Invitation

In every World Café, there's a wonderful feeling of invitation. Attention is paid to creating hospitable space. But the hospitality runs much deeper. It is rooted in the host's awareness that everyone is needed, that anyone might contribute something that suddenly sparks a collective insight. Café facilitators are true hosts—creating a spirit of welcome that is missing from most of our processes. It's important to notice this in the stories here, and to contrast it with your own experience of setting up meetings and processes. What does it feel like to be truly wanted at an event, to be greeted by meeting hosts who delight in your presence, to be welcomed in as a full contributor?

Listening

When people are engaged in meaningful conversation, the whole room reflects curiosity and delight. People move closer physically, their faces exhibit intense listening, and the air becomes charged with their attention to each other. A loud, resonant quiet develops, broken by occasional laughter. It becomes a challenge to call people back from these conversations (which I always take as a good sign).

Movement

In the World Café process, people generally move from table to table. But it's much more than physical movement. As we move, we leave behind our roles, our preconceptions, our certainty. Each time we move to a new table, we lose more of ourselves and become bigger—we now represent a conversation that happened among several people. We move away from a confining sense of self and our small certainties into a spaciousness where new ideas can reveal themselves. As one participant describes it: "It's almost as if you don't know where the thought came from because it has merged so many times that it has been molded and shaped and shifted with new dimensions. People are speaking for each other and using words that started somewhere else that they hadn't thought of before."

We also move into a greater awareness as we look for connections amongst the conversations, as we listen to voices other than our own. Patterns become apparent. Things we couldn't see from our own narrow perspective suddenly become obvious to the entire group.

Good Questions

World Café dialogues, like all good conversations, succeed or fail based on what we're talking about. Good questions—ones that we care about and want to answer—call us outward and to each other. They are an invitation to explore, to venture out, to risk, to listen, to abandon our positions. Good questions help us become both curious and uncertain, and this is always the road that opens us to the surprise of new insight.

Energy

I've never been in a World Café that was dull or boring. People become energized, inspired, excited, creative. Laughter is common, playfulness abounds even with the most serious of issues. For me this is proof positive of how much we relish being together, of how wonderful it is to rediscover the fact of human community. As one host from a very formal culture says: "My faith in people has been confirmed. Underneath all the formal ways of the past, people really want to have significant conversations. People everywhere truly love to talk with each other, learn together, and make a contribution to things they care about."

Discovering Collective Wisdom

These are some of the Café dimensions that bring out the best in us. But this is only half the story. World Café conversations take us into a new realm, one that has been forgotten in modern, individualistic cultures. It is the realm of collective intelligence, of the wisdom we possess as a group that is unavailable to us as individuals. This wisdom emerges as we get more and more connected with each other, as we move from conversation to conversation, carrying the ideas from one conversation to another, looking for patterns, suddenly surprised by an insight we all share. There's a good scientific explanation for this, because this is how all life works. As separate ideas or entities become connected to each other, life surprises us with emergence—the sudden appearance of new capacity and intelligence. All living systems work in this way. We humans got confused and lost sight of this remarkable process by which individual actions, when connected, lead to much greater capacity.

To those of us raised in a linear world with our minds shrunken by detailed analyses, the sudden appearance of collective wisdom always feels magical. I am fascinated by the descriptions given by Café participants of this emergence. Here are a few quotes from them. Notice how unusual these descriptions are:

> "The magic in the middle."
> "The voice in the center of the room."
> "The magic in experiencing our own and other people's humanity around whatever the content is."
> "Something coming to life in the middle of the table."
> "What joins us together—a larger whole that we always knew was there, but never really appreciated."

For me, the moments when collective wisdom appears are always breathtaking. Even though I know such wisdom is bound to appear, I'm always stunned with delight when it enters the room. And the appearance of such wisdom is a huge relief. We actually *do* know how to solve our problems! We can discover solutions that work! We've just been looking in the wrong places—we've been looking to experts, or external solutions, or to detailed, empty analyses. And all this time, the wisdom has been waiting for us, waiting for us to enter into meaningful conversations and deeper connections, waiting for us to realize that we can be wise only together.

One last comment. One of the wonderful things about this book is that it is designed to give an enticing taste of a World Café experience; as much as is possible, it embodies what it describes. In these pages, we are introduced to many strangers, diverse people we don't know who may be doing work very different from our own. They relay stories of their many experiences in using the World Café. Their stories are compelling, and it's possible to feel as if we're sitting with them at an intimate café table, exchanging tales, learning from each other, moving closer. Then our gifted host, Juanita, enters and warmly invites us to another level of learning. She speaks in the World Café voice, inviting, curious, inquiring. With her guidance, we can see things that weren't clear, or discover concepts and tips that we can use in our own work. And as stories and learnings weave together, we can begin to notice patterns and insights that weren't available to us before we opened the book. In the end, we too may experience broader insight, wider wisdom, and the magic of collective thinking.

I hope you will enjoy this book for all that it offers. I hope you will read it, savor it, use it, and begin to host Café conversations yourself. If enough of us do so, we can reintroduce many people to a world where people enjoy working together, where collaborative conversation yields true insight and new possibilities for action, where work and life are revived with meaning and possibility. In this way, we truly can restore hope to the future.

INTRODUCTION

Beginning the Conversation:
An Invitation to the World Café

There you go

Iam a child of the sixties. During that time of social and political upheaval, many of us were determined to *tell it like it is,* to see beneath the surface of things to what really mattered. That inner fire that fueled my early years as a social change activist is now tempered by a compassion born of more than thirty years of working intimately with the dilemmas and paradoxes of personal and institutional change in corporate settings. My self-righteousness and certainty have slowly given way to a humility developed out of a growing sense that there are many ways to tell it like it is—that any story worth telling can be experienced from multiple perspectives. It is with this awareness that I share with you the story of the learning journey from which the World Café has emerged and continues to evolve.

When I was growing up in suburban South Miami, Florida, our living room and dinner table were always alive with conversations. These weren't just any kind of conversations. They were passionate discussions about big questions—justice, democracy, and civil rights. From conversations like these in homes and churches, the civil liberties movement in Florida was nurtured and grew into a force for decency and fairness at a time of great turmoil in the South.

I remember, too, the spirited conversations we had at my adopted grandmother's home in southern Mexico when I was a teenager. Trudi Blom had been exiled from Europe during World War II, and there, in the remote state of Chiapas, she founded a global center for dialogue and action on environmental issues—much before it was fashionable to talk about sustainability. At her long dining room table, anthropologists, writers, scientists, and local travelers joined together for delicious meals with Lacandon Maya rain forest people and Chamula highland Indian guests. The diversity of the group always contributed to learning, discoveries, and connections that never could have been anticipated. Today, half a century later, the Na-Bolom Center still serves as a place where diverse people and perspectives meet in dialogue around the dining room table.

During my early years as a community organizer with Cesar Chavez and the farmworkers' movement, it was in the thousands of informal meetings—conversations among those seated on tattered couches in ramshackle homes and labor camps—that small miracles occurred. Through dialogue and reflection, the underlying assumptions that had kept farmworkers stuck for generations began to shift. As workers shared tortilla and bean suppers, they also shared the *if-onlys* of their lives and imagined the impossible. With practice, they began to ask the *what-if* questions. And from the *what-ifs* came the *why-nots!*

Over the last quarter-century, my life has taken me to large corporations as a strategist and thinking partner with senior executives as they struggle to embrace the challenges of the knowledge era. In this world, my language and descriptions have changed to those of strategic dialogue and conversation as a core business process. My community-organizing emphasis has evolved to focus on and embrace the informal communities of practice that are the home for social processes of new learning and knowledge creation. But the essential threads of my life remain unbroken. It is still my deepest belief that it is through conversations around questions that matter that powerful capacities for evolving caring community, collaborative learning, and committed action are engaged—at work, in communities, and at home.

Conversations That Matter

Through our conversations the stories and images of our future emerge, and never has this process been more critical. We now have the capacity, through neglect of the planetary commons on which our lives depend, to make this precious earth, our home, uninhabitable. We now have the capacity, through escalating violence and weapons of mass destruction, to make our precious human species, along with many others, extinct. Yet this is also a moment of opportunity. We are connected as never before in webs of communication and information-sharing through the Internet and other media that make our collective predicament visible on a much larger scale than we could have imagined only a few years ago. And for the first time, we now have the capacity for engaging in connected global conversations and action about what is happening and how we choose to respond—conversations that are not under the formal aegis of any one institution, government, or corporation. It is time for us to engage in those conversations more intentionally. Our very survival as a human community, both locally and globally, may rest on our creative responses to the following questions:

> *How can we enhance our capacity to talk and think more deeply together about the critical issues facing our communities, our organizations, our nations, and our planet?*

> *How can we access the mutual intelligence and wisdom we need to create innovative paths forward?*

This book is the story of a personal and collective journey shaped by these questions. It is a story in which I have been an active participant, along with my partner, David Isaacs, and a lively global community of inquiry and practice. It is the story of the discovery and evolution of the World Café, a simple yet powerful conversational *process* for fostering constructive dialogue, accessing collective intelligence, and creating innovative possibilities for action, particularly in groups that are larger than most traditional dialogue approaches are designed to accommodate.

Anyone interested in creating conversations that matter can engage the World Café process, with its seven core design *principles* to improve people's collective capacity to share knowledge and shape the future together. World Café conversations simultaneously enable us to notice a deeper living *pattern* of connections at work in our organizations and communities—the often invisible webs of conversation and meaning-making through which we already collectively shape the future, often in unintended ways.

COLLECTIVE
INTELLIGENCE

Living
Network
PATTERN

Café
Conversational
PROCESS

Integrated Design
PRINCIPLES

WORLD
CAFÉ

Engaging the World Café *process, principles, and pattern* in practical ways empowers leaders and others who work with groups to intentionally host World Café and other types of dialogue as well as to create dynamic networks of conversation and knowledge-sharing around an organization's real work and critical questions.

How Does a World Café Dialogue Work?

Café conversations are designed on the assumption that people already have within them the wisdom and creativity to confront even the most difficult challenges. The process is simple, yet it can yield surprising results. The innovative design of the World Café enables groups—often numbering in the hundreds of people—to participate together in evolving rounds of dialogue with three or four others while at the same time remaining part of a single, larger, connected conversation. Small, intimate conversations link and build on each other as people move between groups, cross-pollinate ideas, and discover new insights into questions or issues that really matter in their life, work, or community. As the network of new connections increases, knowledge-sharing grows. A sense of the whole becomes increasingly strong. The collective wisdom of the group becomes more accessible, and innovative possibilities for action emerge.

In a Café gathering people often move rapidly from ordinary conversations—which keep us stuck in the past, are often divisive, and are generally superficial—toward *conversations that matter,* in which there is deeper collective understanding or forward movement in relation to a situation that people really care about. The seven World Café design principles, when used in combination, also create a kind of "conversational greenhouse," nurturing the conditions for the rapid propagation of actionable knowledge. These design principles are not limited to a formal Café event. They can also be used to focus and enhance the quality of other key conversations—enabling you to draw on the talent and wisdom of your organization or community to a greater extent than generally occurs with more traditional approaches.

World Café conversations simultaneously create a lived experience of how we naturally self-organize to think together, strengthen community, share knowledge, and ignite innovation. They allow us to see more clearly the importance of conversation as a living force so we can become more intentional about engaging its power. Café conversations demonstrate one innovative way to put living systems theory into practice.

The World Café, both as a designed conversational process and as a deeper living systems pattern, has immediate, practical implications for meeting and conference design, strategy formation, knowledge creation, rapid innovation, stakeholder engagement, and large-scale change. Experiencing a Café conversation in action also helps us make personal and professional choices about more satisfying ways to participate in the ongoing conversations that help shape our lives.

The World Café Goes Global

Since its inception in 1995, tens of thousands of people on six continents have participated in World Café dialogues in settings ranging from crowded hotel ballrooms holding twelve hundred people to cozy living rooms with just a dozen folks present. In a global consumer products company, executives from more than thirty nations used the Café process to integrate a new worldwide marketing strategy. Mexican government and corporate leaders have applied the World Café to scenario planning. Leaders from local communities representing more than sixty countries participated in Café dialogues during the Stockholm Challenge, which offers a Nobel-style prize for those creating technology for the common good.

Faculty members in the United States and Europe are creating virtual, online Knowledge Cafés to conduct distance learning programs. In New Zealand and the United States, the World Café has inspired the creation of local venues for hosting Café conversations on key issues related to business futures, sustainable development, and community collaboration. The World Café has supported Conversation Cafés, Commonway Cafés, and Let's Talk America, key citizen initiatives that invite diverse groups to explore contemporary issues. Local churches and schools have used the World Café process on a smaller scale to build community and access the wisdom of their members.

> The World Café can make a special contribution when the goal is the focused use of dialogue to foster productive relationships, collaborative learning, and collective insight

Whether in business, government, health, education, NGO, or community settings, the World Café can make a special contribution when the goal is the focused use of dialogue to foster productive relationships, collaborative learning, and collective insight around real-life challenges and key strategic questions. This is especially true when working with groups that are larger than most traditional dialogue circles are designed to accommodate.

A Community of Inquiry and Practice

The global World Café learning community—as well as this book—have evolved as colleagues from around the world experiment, document their work, share ideas, and learn from each other about the theory and practice embodied in the Café conversation approach.

I will serve as the primary narrator and your host for weaving together the stories, reflections, and conversations among World Café pioneers and others as we share with you our discoveries and the questions at the edge of our "not knowing." In the Perspectives & Observations sections I'll share my own personal aha's and insights, and introduce you to others who are contributing to our learning.

All pioneering ventures are incomplete, reflecting the particular interests and ways of seeing of those who have been part of the journey, and who make the initial maps of the territory. I am but one among many colleagues who are furthering key aspects of this work. Yet I hope your travels with me through these pages will provide glimpses that stimulate new conversations about where to focus special attention and care in your own organizations and communities.

The research for this book and for my own earlier Ph.D. on the World Café (Brown, 2001) was conducted in the spirit of Appreciative Inquiry, an approach to organizational learning and development originated by David Cooperrider and his colleagues at Case Western University (Cooperrider and Srivastva, 1987; Cooperrider and others, 2003; Whitney and Trosten-Bloom, 2003). Appreciative Inquiry deliberately focuses attention on what works, what brings life and vitality to an experience, and what's possible for its evolution. However, keep in mind that the same challenges that come up in any group can arise in a World Café conversation. At the same time, the World Café's focus on intimate exchange, disciplined inquiry, cross-pollination of ideas, and possibility thinking tends to create psychological safety and lessen inappropriate grandstanding and people's attachment to their own points of view. The very design of Café conversations often makes these common challenges easier to deal with than in many group settings.

What You'll Find Inside

Chapter 1 calls on insights from thought leaders across disciplines to reveal the critical but often invisible role of conversation in shaping our lives and our futures. Chapter 2 invites you to consider a new perspective on conversation as a core process—a fundamental means through which groups and organizations adapt to changing circumstances and co-create the knowledge necessary for success. It also briefly introduces the seven core design principles that are central to understanding the World Café approach to dialogue.

Chapters 3 through 9 share the seven core World Café design principles, with each chapter focusing on one of them. The stories that open these chapters reveal the creativity and imagination with which Café hosts from around the world are using these principles to foster conversations that matter. These real life "learning stories," including the hosts' dilemmas and discoveries, form the heart of the book. More than any abstract treatise, teaching, or training manual, they provide innovative ideas for how to craft a World Café approach adapted to your unique situation. Each chapter then grounds these experiences in a discussion of both the conceptual underpinnings of each design principle and their general application in a wide variety of settings.

Chapter 10 focuses on the practicalities of Café hosting that have not been covered in detail in the earlier exploration of the seven guiding principles. This chapter is designed to stand alone as a World Café hosting guide to help you plan Café dialogues in diverse settings. If you want an initial overview of the specifics of Café hosting, this is the place to start. It provides the information needed for someone with previous group experience to host a successful Café, particularly if you have attended a World Café dialogue yourself.

Chapter 11 begins with several short stories that illustrate ways leaders are using World Café approaches as part of their own conversational leadership—the capacity to engage the collaborative intelligence of their organizations and communities to meet real-life challenges. These form the backdrop for our exploration of both the organizational infrastructures and personal capabilities that conversational leaders can develop in order to nurture greater business and social value using dialogue as a core process.

Chapter 12 highlights the societal implications and the promise inherent in embracing and acting on the insights and practical experiences explored throughout the book. You are encouraged to become a part of the dialogue and deliberation community, sharing your insights and discoveries as you make your own unique contribution to creating a culture of dialogue wherever you may find yourself.

In the epilogue, octogenarian Anne Dosher, Ph.D., the elder of the World Café, shares the questions that have informed her own life's journey and why she has committed her remaining years to nurturing a culture of dialogue. Peter Senge, senior lecturer at the MIT Sloan School of Management and founding chair of the Society for Organizational Learning, then offers an afterword based on our experience together in hosting World Café gatherings with key global leaders.

If you want to learn more about other forms of dialogue, as well as key initiatives that are also making wonderful contributions to the field of dialogue and deliberation, take a look at "Resources and Connections" at the back of the book. And although this book is not an academic treatise, enough reference material has been included in the text to support you in "following the trail" to the conceptual foundations of the World Café and related areas of interest.

How to Engage with What's Here

Having a common architecture as this book unfolded has allowed diverse contributions in a shared framework, enabling you to engage with the material based on your own reading style and preferences. Each chapter begins with a quotation, an illustration, and a question that illuminate the essence of that chapter, so if you look only at the chapter openers you'll gain an overview of the book's main themes. Each chapter's learning stories highlight the way the chapter's core ideas are being put into real-world practice. These stories, although simply "snapshots in time" that continue to unfold, enable you to appreciate the many ways you might introduce and engage Café conversations in your own life and work. In the "Perspectives & Observations" sections that follow, I, as your host, will share multidisciplinary insights from leading edge thinkers as they inform our exploration of dialogue and Café learning. At the end of each chapter, you'll find "Questions for Reflection," a

> Each chapter's learning stories highlight the way the chapter's core ideas are being put into real-world practice

series of questions to consider as you convene and host conversations that matter.

We've purposely included multiple voices and modes of expression as well as graphic illustrations to illuminate key ideas. We've also used the following terms—World Café, Café conversation, and Café dialogue—interchangeably throughout the text to describe the World Café process. In addition, you'll find Café names like Knowledge Café, Leadership Café, Strategy Café, and others that illuminate the many ways people are naming and adapting the basic World Café pattern and process in ways that meet their unique needs and constituencies.

Although this book is not a how-to manual or a detailed recipe for creating a World Café event, you'll find both key ingredients and practical ideas for hosting conversations that matter in many different organizational and community settings. We've discovered that one of the strengths of the World Café approach is its simplicity and versatility. In fact, if you have experience leading or working with groups, a careful reading of the stories that begin each chapter along with a close review of chapter 10 will likely give you enough information to get started. The seven World Café design principles and varied hosting practices you'll find here can be helpful in convening conversations for many different purposes, whether you use the Café format or not. Even if you are not planning to host Cafés personally, the book will provide you with enough perspective to determine if this approach is right for your own organization's meetings, conferences, or retreats.

As I mentioned earlier, "Questions for Reflection," posed at the end of each chapter, encourage you to consider your own experience and process of discovery about conversations that matter. Take a moment to ask yourself these questions now:

▶ *What drew me to this book?*

▶ *If I think of this book as a personal conversation with the authors, how will that affect how I approach what they have to share with me?*

> *What question, if I explore it during my time with this book, could make the most difference in my life and work?*

There is ample room for noting your own thoughts and reflections. Imagine yourself in a Café dialogue and think of these pages as Café tablecloths. Notice what connects to your personal experience and your own process of discovery. Jot down your insights about where to focus special attention and care as you engage conversations that matter in your own organization or community. Consider your own questions. Add your voice to the conversation.

In one of his wonderful poems, the Spanish poet Antonio Machado reminds us, "We make the path by walking on it." By joining us on the path that David and I, with the World Café community, are walking, we hope you will find yourself as intrigued as we are by both the power of conversation and the promise of the World Café. We hope you'll find the value generated from Café conversations around the world as an encouraging sign for the future.

Welcome to the World Café!

Seeing the Invisible: Conversation Matters!

It's never enough just to tell people about some new insight.

Rather, you have to get them to experience it in a way

that evokes its power and possibility. Instead of pouring

knowledge into people's heads, you need to help them grind

a new set of eyeglasses so they can see the world in a

new way.

—John Seely Brown, *Seeing Differently: Insights on Innovation*

What if humans are in conversation

the way fish are in water?

DISCOVERING THE WORLD CAFÉ: THE INTELLECTUAL CAPITAL PIONEERS

As Told By

David Isaacs

David Isaacs, my partner in life and work, is a co-originator of the World Café. In this story he shares the serendipity surrounding the birth of the World Café and its community of practice, along with our early musings about what was at play in Café dialogues. Our initial Café experience also set the stage for unexpected discoveries about the powerful role that conversation plays in shaping our futures.

January 1995. It is a very rainy dawn at our home in Mill Valley, California. A thick mist hangs over Mt. Tamalpais as I look out beyond the massive oak tree that borders the patio outside our living room. We have twenty-four people arriving in half an hour for the second day of a strategic dialogue on intellectual capital. Juanita and I are hosting the gathering in collaboration with Leif Edvinsson, vice president of intellectual capital for the Skandia Corporation in Sweden. This is the second in a series of conversations among the Intellectual Capital Pioneers—a group of corporate executives, researchers, and consultants from seven countries who are at the leading edge of this inquiry.

The field of intellectual capital and knowledge management is still in its infancy. No books have yet been written. No maps exist. We're making them as we go. Last evening we were in the midst of exploring the question: *What is the role of leadership in maximizing the value of intellectual capital?*

Juanita is worried. As she sets out the breakfast and prepares the coffee, she's concerned about how we can create the right setting for the day's agenda if the pouring rain continues and no one can go outside on the patio to visit when they arrive. Then I have an idea. "Why don't we set up our TV tables in the living room and just have people get their coffee and visit around the tables while we're waiting for everyone to arrive? We'll then put away the tables and begin with our normal dialogue circle."

Juanita breathes a sigh of relief. As we set out the small tables and white vinyl chairs, our interactive graphics specialist, Tomi Nagai-Rothe, arrives and adds, "Those look like café tables. I think they need some tablecloths!" She improvises, draping white sheets of easel paper over each of the paired TV tables. Now it's getting kind of playful. We've stopped worrying about the rain, which is coming down in sheets. Juanita decides we need flowers on the café tables, and goes for small vases downstairs. In the meantime, Tomi adds crayons to each of the tables, just like those in many neighborhood cafés. She makes a lovely sign for our front door—*Welcome to the Homestead Café*—playing off our address, Homestead Boulevard, which is actually a narrow road up the side of a mountain.

Just as Juanita places the flowers on the tables, folks begin to arrive. They are delighted and amused. As people get their coffee and croissants, they gather in informal groups around the café tables and begin to talk about last night's question. People are really engaged. They begin to scribble on the tablecloths. Juanita and I have a quick huddle and decide that, rather than have a formal dialogue circle to open the gathering, we will simply encourage people to continue to share what's bubbling up from their conversations that could shed light on the essence of the relationship between leadership and intellectual capital.

Forty-five minutes pass and the conversation is still going strong. Charles Savage, one of our members, calls out, "I'd love to have a feel for what's happening in the other conversations in the room. Why don't we leave one host at the table and have our other members travel to different tables, carrying the seed ideas from our conversation and connecting and linking with the threads that are being woven at other tables?" There's consensus that the suggestion seems like fun. After a few minutes of wrap-up, folks begin to move around the room. One host remains at each table, while the others each go to a different table to continue the conversations.

This round lasts another hour. Now the room is really alive! People are excited and engaged, almost breathless. Another person speaks up. "Why don't we experiment by leaving a new host at the table, with the others traveling, continuing to share and link what we're discovering?"

And so it continues. The rain falling, hard. People huddling around the TV tables, learning together, testing ideas and assumptions together, building new knowledge together, adding to each other's diagrams and pictures and noting key words and ideas on the tablecloths. Juanita and I look up and realize that it is almost lunchtime. We have been participating in the café conversations ourselves and the hours have passed as if they were minutes.

The energy in the room is palpable. It is as if the very air is shimmering. I ask the group to wrap up their conversations and gather around a large rolled-out piece of mural paper that Tomi has placed on the rug in the middle of the living room floor. It looks, in fact, like a large café tablecloth spread on the floor. We invite each small group to put their individual tablecloths around the edges of the larger cloth and then take a "tour" to notice patterns, themes, and insights that are emerging in our midst.

As Juanita and I watch our collective discoveries and insights unfold visually on the large mural paper in the center of the group, we know something quite unusual has happened. We are bearing witness to something for which we have no language. It is as if the intelligence of a larger collective Self, beyond the individual selves in the room, had become visible to us. It feels almost like "magic"—an exciting moment of recognition of what we are discovering together that's difficult to describe yet feels strangely familiar. The café process somehow enabled the group to access a form of collaborative intelligence that grew more potent as both ideas and people traveled from table to table, making new connections and cross-pollinating their diverse insights.

. . .

After that breakthrough meeting, David and I, along with Finn Voldtofte, a close colleague from Denmark who had participated in that initial gathering, spent the next day trying to understand what had happened. We looked at each of the components of the day, examining how it had contributed to the living knowledge that emerged. We considered what had occurred when people entered the house and saw the colorful and inviting Homestead Café in our living room. Was there something about the café itself as an archetype—a familiar cultural form around the world—that was able to evoke the immediate intimacy and collective engagement that we experienced? Did the positive associations that most people make with cafés support the natural emergence of easy and authentic conversation that had happened, despite the lack of formal guidelines or dialogue training among the participants?

We considered the role and use of questions to engage collaborative thinking. Was there something in the way we had framed the conversation around a core question that participants cared about—"What is the relationship between leadership and intellectual capital?"—that affected the quality and depth of collective insight? Then there was the cross-pollination of ideas across groups. Did carrying insights from one group to another enable the emergence of an unexpected web of lively new connections among diverse perspectives? We mused on the function of people writing on their tablecloths and later contributing their collective insights to the common tablecloth as we explored our discoveries together. What was the importance, if any, that people could literally see each other's ideas on their tablecloths, similar to a hurried sketch or an idea scribbled on a napkin?

As we tried to illuminate our experience, we were reminded of how many new ideas and social innovations have historically been born and spread through informal conversations in cafés, salons, churches, and living rooms. We realized that what we had experienced in the café conversation in our living room was perhaps a small-scale replica of a deeper living pattern of how knowledge-sharing, change, and innovation have always occurred in human societies. We recalled the salon movement that gave birth to the French Revolution, as well as the sewing circles and committees of correspondence that foretold America's independence. Finn reminded us of the widespread network of study circles that fostered the social and economic renaissance in Scandinavia during the early twentieth century, and we realized that David's and my early experiences with social movements, including the farmworkers, followed the same pattern of development. Founders of major change efforts often say, "Well, it all began when some friends and I started talking."

The evolving web of conversations in our living room seemed to allow us to experience directly the often invisible way that large-scale organizational and societal change occurs—what we have since come to call "nature's strategic planning process." Are we as human beings so immersed in conversation that, like fish in water, conversation is our medium for survival and we just can't see it? Had we somehow stumbled onto a set of principles that made it easier for larger groups to notice and access this natural process in order to develop collaborative intelligence around critical questions and concerns? Might this awareness support leaders in becoming more intentional about fostering connected networks of conversation focused on their organization's most important questions?

> Are we as human beings so immersed in conversation that, like fish in water, conversation is our medium for survival and we just can't see it?

Out of this conversation, the image of the World Café emerged as a central metaphor to guide our nascent exploration into the possibilities that we had tapped into that rainy day. Many of us who were at that initial gathering began to experiment with the simple process that we had discovered. We began to host World Café conversations in a variety of settings and to share our learnings with each other as we went.

And then from a completely unexpected source, it became clear to me just how much conversation matters. *It matters a lot.*

Knowing Together and Bringing Forth a World

I was serving as co-faculty for a living systems seminar sponsored by the Berkana Institute, which supports new forms of leadership around the world. Fritjof Capra, the noted physicist and living systems theorist, who was also on the faculty, was giving a talk about the nature of knowledge. In his measured, professorial style, Fritjof began to share surprising ideas from the work of two Chilean scientists—evolutionary biologist, Humberto Maturana, and cognitive scientist, Francisco Varela. I won't be able to do full justice to the range and subtlety of their groundbreaking research, but I'd like to share one key aspect of it with you because I think it has direct relevance for how people see the world and how we choose to live in it.

Maturana and Varela's work reaffirms that as a species we humans have evolved the unique capacity for talking together and for making distinctions of meaning in language. This human gift for living in the braided meanings and emotions that arise through our conversations is what enables us to share our ideas, images, intentions, and discoveries with each other. Since our earliest ancestors gathered in circles around the warmth of a fire, conversation has been our primary means for discovering what we care about, sharing knowledge, imagining the future, and acting together to both survive and thrive.

People in small groups spread their insights to larger groups, carrying the seed ideas for new conversations, creative possibilities, and collective action. This systemic process is embodied in self-reinforcing, meaning-making networks that arise through the interactions that conversation makes possible. Maturana and Varela point out that because we live in language—and in the sophisticated coordination of actions that language makes possible—we "bring forth a world" through the networks of conversation in which we participate (1987, p. 234). We embody and share our knowledge through conversation. From this perspective, conversations *are* action—the very lifeblood and heartbeat of social systems like organizations, communities, and societies. As new meanings and the coordinated actions based on them begin to spread through wider networks, the future comes into being. However, these futures can take many alternative paths. In a provocative seminar that Maturana later gave at the Society for Organizational Learning, he brought this message home:

All that we humans do, we do in conversation. . . . As we live in conversation new kinds of objects continue to appear, and as we take these objects and live with them, new domains of existence appear! So here we are now, living with these very funny kinds of objects called firms, companies, profit, incomes, and so on. And we are very attached to them. . . . Just the same, we are not necessarily stuck in any of the objects we create. What is peculiar to human beings is that we can reflect and say, "Oh, I'm not interested in this any more," change our orientation, and begin a new history. Other animals cannot reflect, as they do not live in language. We are the ones who make language and conversation our manner of living. . . . We enjoy it, we caress each other in language. We can also hurt each other in language. We can open spaces or restrict them in conversations. This is central to us. And we shape our own path, as do all living systems (Maturana and Bunnell, 1999, p. 12).

Thus, from the perspective of human evolution, conversation is not something trivial that we engage in among many other activities. Conversation is the core process by which we humans think and coordinate our actions together. The living process of conversation lies at the heart of collective learning and co-evolution in human affairs. *Conversation is our human way of creating and sustaining—or transforming—the realities in which we live.*

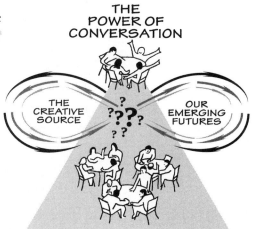

Vicki Robin, my dear friend and colleague, is the founder of Conversation Cafés, an innovative small group dialogue approach that invites citizens to gather in cafés and other public places to explore key societal questions. Recently, she shared with me a vivid reflection of how this often invisible process works in everyday life.

We talk to ourselves in our minds about our past, present, and future. Out of this self-talk, we talk with others about our pasts, present, and futures, generating personal and shared possibilities though lively exchanges of ideas and feelings. We each then carry the meanings and possibilities we've created into other conversations at home, at work, at church, in boardrooms, and bedrooms, and halls of power everywhere. A daughter talks to her father about her concerns for the future . . . and company policy changes. A father talks to his daughter about his concerns for her future . . . and a new life path unfolds, later impacting thousands. Line workers talk with their bosses . . . and a plant is redesigned. Citizens testify at public hearings . . . and new priorities for society emerge. We speak our world into being. A buzz develops—a kind of overtone of resonant ideas carried through multiple conversations—that tells us what's on our collective mind. Some among us put words on this buzz and new possibilities for us as a whole begin to enter our language, the vehicle of meaning-making. We see ourselves in their descriptions—"Ah," we think, "I never saw that, but yes, that is true." We talk about it . . . shaping again what we collectively imagine for ourselves. Our conversations shape the spirit and substance of our times.

We each then carry the meanings and possibilities we've created into other conversations

Another colleague shared with me a wonderful story that provides a powerful example of the way we can shape the future through conversation. The story began with a dinner conversation among four friends over steak and Chianti at the home of a young businesswoman in Munich and evolved, in just a few weeks, into one of the largest mass movements in Germany since the end of World War II.

Over dinner, the four friends decided it was time for them to step out from the "silent majority" and show their repudiation of the rising number of neo-Nazi attacks on foreigners. By the time dessert was over, each agreed to call several friends and colleagues and share the idea of creating a silent candlelight vigil to bear witness to these injustices. Their first gathering drew one hundred friends to a popular downtown bar, each of whom agreed to call ten others to encourage a larger turnout for a second event. Within days the "candlelight conversation" spread across the city through circles of acquaintances in businesses, schools, churches, and civic groups. The original group of friends—and the nation as a whole—were stunned when four hundred thousand people turned out in Munich for the vigil.

Inspired by the Munich gathering, citizens in other cities held conversations and created vigils over the following weeks. Over five hundred thousand turned out in Hamburg, two hundred thousand in Berlin, and one hundred thousand or more in Frankfurt, Nuremberg, and other cities. Many smaller towns joined in what became a national dialogue on the acceptability of neo-Nazi behavior. The seemingly endless chains of flickering candlelight became a powerful symbol of the nation's collective commitment, born in conversation, to turn the tide against such behavior (Kinsler, 1992). And this happened prior to widespread use of the Internet!

Conversation as a Generative Force

I was excited to discover Maturana and Varela's work on the power of conversation to shape our future and to encounter vivid examples of this power in action. For the first time, I could see that leading edge thinkers with backgrounds completely different from our own were discovering what David and I had intuitively sensed from our lived experience with social movements as well as with our early World Café experiments. As we looked at the picture painted by both scholars and practitioners in other fields of endeavor, a fascinating pattern began to emerge. Although their perspectives on the importance of conversation may have made up only a single piece in the larger puzzle each was exploring in his or her own work, when taken together these insights began to reveal the critical role of conversation in shaping our lives. I'd like to share a collage of these ideas to give you a flavor of what we noticed as we literally put the pieces together on a large wallboard. Please take a few minutes to read carefully, on the following pages, what these thought leaders from different fields have to say. I think you'll find their ideas illuminating.

CONVERSATION MATTERS!

Learning Organizations

True learning organizations are a space for generative conversations and concerted action which creates a field of alignment that produces tremendous power to invent new realities in conversation and to bring about these new realities in action.

> Fred Kofman and Peter Senge
> "Communities of Commitment"
> *Organizational Dynamics*

Politics

Democracy begins in human conversation. The simplest, least threatening investment any citizen can make in democratic renewal is to begin talking with other people, asking the questions and knowing that their answers matter.

> William Greider
> *Who Will Tell the People?*

Strategy

Strategizing depends on creating a rich and complex web of conversations that cuts across previously isolated knowledge sets and creates new and unexpected combinations of insight.

> Gary Hamel
> "The Search for Strategy"
> *Fortune*

Information Technology

Technology is putting a sharper, more urgent point on the importance of conversations. Conversations are moving faster, touching more people, and bridging greater distances. These networked conversations are enabling powerful new forms of social organization and knowledge exchange to occur.

> Rick Levine and others
> *The Cluetrain Manifesto*

Education

Within communities that foster human growth and development, change seems to be a natural result of constructing meaning and knowledge together—an outgrowth of our conversations about what matters. Leaders need to pose the questions and convene the conversations that invite others to become involved. . . . In social systems such as schools and districts, one good conversation can shift the direction of change forever.

> Linda Lambert and others
> *The Constructivist Leader*

The Knowledge Economy

Conversations are the way workers discover what they know, share it with their colleagues, and in the process create new knowledge for the organization. In the new economy, conversations are the most important form of work . . . so much so that the conversation is the organization.

> Alan Webber
> "What's So New About the New Economy?"
> *Harvard Business Review*

Family Therapy

Our capacity for change lies in "the circle of the unexpressed," in the capacity we have to be "in language" with each other and, in language to develop new themes, new narratives, and new stories. Through this process we co-create and co-develop our systemic realities.

> Harlene Anderson and Harold Goolishian
> "Human Systems as Linguistic Systems"
> *Family Process*

Leadership

Talk is key to the executive's work . . . the use of language to shape new possibilities, reframe old perspectives, and excite new commitments . . . the active process of dialogue, and the caring for relationships as the core foundation of any social system.

Suresh Srivastva and David Cooperrider
Appreciative Management and Leadership

Executive Development

As the new business landscape continues to emerge, and new forms of organization take shape, our ability to lead will be dependent upon our ability to host and convene quality conversations.

Robert Lengel, Ph.D., Director
Center for Professional Excellence
University of Texas at San Antonio
Executive MBA Program

Futures Research

Conversation is the heart of the new inquiry. It is perhaps the core human skill for dealing with the tremendous challenges we face. The culture of conversation is a different culture, one that can make a difference to the future of the world. If we combine conversations that really matter . . . with the interactive reach of the Internet, we have a powerful force for change from the ground up.

Institute for the Future
In Good Company:
Innovation at the Intersection of
Technology and Sustainability

Collective Intelligence

Dialogue is the central aspect of co-intelligence. We can only generate higher levels of intelligence among us if we are doing some high quality talking with one another.

Tom Atlee, Co-Intelligence Institute
The Tao of Democracy

Consciousness Studies

I'm suggesting that there is the possibility for a transformation of the nature of consciousness, both individually and collectively, and that whether this can be solved culturally and socially depends on dialogue. That's what we're exploring.

David Bohm, *On Dialogue*

Evolutionary Biology

Our human existence is one in which we can live whatever world we bring about in our conversations, even if it is a world that finally destroys us as the kind of being that we are. Indeed, this has been our history since our origins as languaging beings—namely, a history or creation of new domains of existence as different networks of conversation.

Humberto Maturana and Gerda Verden-Zöller
The Origin of Humanness in the Biology of Love

Conflict Resolution, Global Affairs

The reality today is that we are all interdependent and have to coexist on this small planet. Therefore, the only sensible and intelligent way of resolving differences and clashes of interests, whether between individuals or nations, is through dialogue.

His Holiness the Fourteenth Dalai Lama
"Forum 2000" Conference, Prague

What We View Determines What We Do

What if you began to shift your lens to see the power and potential of the conversations occurring in your own family, organization, community, or nation? What if you believed and acted as if your conversations and those of others really mattered? What difference would that make to your daily choices as a parent, teacher, line leader, meeting planner, organizational specialist, community member, or diplomat?

We live inside the images we hold of the world

As Maturana and Varela point out, we live inside the images we hold of the world. It can be disturbing to "see differently" and to contemplate the practical implications of changing our lenses (Lakoff, 2003; Morgan, 1997). Yet as Noel Tichy, head of the University of Michigan's Global Leadership Program, told me many years ago, "What we view determines what we do." How we view the world around us, and how we act based on those images, can make all the difference.

As we enter a time in which the capacity for thinking together and creating innovative solutions is viewed as critical to creating both business and social value, many of us still live with the idea that "talk is cheap," that most people are "all talk and no action," and that we should "stop talking and get to work." Lynne Twist, a social entrepreneur who has raised millions for improving life in developing nations, has a different perspective—one that you might want to play with as you read the stories and reflections that follow. "I believe," she said, "that we don't really live in the world. We live in the conversation we have about the world. . . . And over *that* we have absolute, omnipotent power. We have the opportunity to shape that conversation, and in so doing, to shape history" (Toms, 2002, pp. 38–39). As your host I invite you, just for the time you are reading this book, to put on a new set of glasses. See with new eyes the conversational landscape that has been here all along awaiting our personal attention and care. And begin to live a different future.

Consider the conversations you are currently having in your family, your organization, or your community. To what degree do they create frustration and fragment efforts or offer new insights and ways to work collectively?

If you were to accept the perspective that conversation really is a core process for accessing collective intelligence and co-evolving the future, what practical difference would that make in how you approached conversations, particularly in situations you care about?

Pick one upcoming conversation that matters in your own life or work. What one specific thing might you do or what one choice might you make that would improve the quality of that conversation?

TWO

Conversation as a Core Process:
Co-Creating
Business and Social Value

*Managing in the new economy requires not just change
programs but a changed mindset. . . . Conversations are the
way workers discover what they know, share it with their
colleagues, and in the process create new knowledge for the
organization. In the new economy, conversations are the
most important form of work.*

—Alan Webber, "What's So New About the New Economy?"
Harvard Business Review

What if conversation

is how things get done?

The following two stories offer real-life examples of how leaders in very different settings are using the World Café to create business and social value through fostering conversations that matter.

CREATING A CULTURE OF DIALOGUE: MUSEUM OF SCIENCE AND INDUSTRY, TAMPA BAY

As Told By

Wit Ostrenko and Fred Steier

Wit Ostrenko is the president of the Museum of Science and Industry (MOSI) of Tampa Bay, Florida. Fred Steier, Ph.D., is professor of communication at the University of South Florida and a research fellow at MOSI's Center for Learning. MOSI is a major regional science center that receives eight hundred thousand visitors per year. This is the story of how the museum has been using World Café conversations and conversational leadership as cornerstones in its efforts to redefine the relationship between the institution and its internal and external communities.

We've designed MOSI to be a center for learning conversations. We don't want it to be a one-way, don't-touch-anything science center, so we've struggled with what hands-on learning really means, both for our visitors and for ourselves. How do we learn together as families and as communities? For us, our best learning has been embedded in conversations—with the board, the staff, the larger community, and other science museums and associations.

The very nature of the museum is like a World Café, and each of our exhibits is like a Café table. Most people visit the exhibits in small groups, so there's already informal conversation and collective discovery happening right there on the spot. Then, as people go from one exhibit to another, talking to others they don't even know, they become part of a lively web of conversations and share ideas, just like in an actual World Café event. And because we have many seniors as well as children visiting the museum, the conversations become intergenerational—they naturally cross-pollinate ideas by learning with and from each other.

But our use of the World Café is not only metaphorical. We use the Café process to engage with many of our key issues. We find the Café approach so useful with our internal staff, our professional community, and the public that the Café principles have become an integral part of our thinking about who we are as a community institution.

The first Café we held was at a board retreat. People came with the expectation that it would be another boring board meeting. But at the end, several people said, almost apologetically, that *this was the first time they'd really talked with each other.* The World Café built

28   The World Café

relationships—not only between individual board members but also between the museum and the board as representatives of the community we serve.

So often boards are given the assignment simply to raise money. But the best fundraising comes from talking together and understanding the reason for doing it. For example, it came out during our Board Café that there were no scholarships available to enable the community's blue collar families to visit our museum. They're not poor, but spending $14.95 for adults and another $10.00 for kids is really cost-prohibitive, so they're not coming as often as we would like. It became a fundraising priority to help blue collar and other low-income families. As a result of ideas generated in that Board Café, we're halfway to raising a million-dollar endowment to provide full access to our museum to anyone who doesn't have the ability to pay.

We use our Café conversations to generate what we call "actionable knowledge." For us, this means that we intend for whatever emerges from a Café to be something that can be put into practice. For example, in the middle of 2003 we realized we weren't going to make our budget. We couldn't afford the staff we had, and we were going to have to make several cuts. So, we brought a group of about thirty staff people together and held a World Café to figure out what to do.

The objective of the Café was to generate new revenue-producing programs, with the goal of raising $175,000. We had no preconceived ideas of how to do this. During the Café, we came up with roughly $188,000 worth of new net revenue ideas. One of the wilder ideas was a Yu-Gi-Oh tournament. Nobody had ever heard of Yu-Gi-Oh except for a couple of the parents on our staff who knew how popular the game is because their kids watch it on television. They were the ones who encouraged the rest of the group to say yes to it. We put the stamp of approval on it, along with the other key ideas, right then and there. Do you know what? By putting our key ideas into practice, we ended fiscal year 2003 in the black by $267,000!

So where is the leadership in that kind of situation? The leaders at that Café weren't those with formal management titles, but rather anyone with great ideas for how to produce the most net revenue in a manner that is consistent with our mission and values. There were some real heroes that day! The Café conversations allowed people to contribute whom others don't normally see because they work nights and weekends or lead trips. All of a sudden one of these "invisible" people would put forth a great idea that everyone rallied around. It was very gratifying, and has helped build the feeling of MOSI as a collaborative community that includes our board and staff.

It's starting to become a habit with us to recognize when there is an issue that we need to work through together in a more dialogic manner. We've also noticed that our people get better and better results as they get more experience in using the Café process. We've discovered that we can learn to be better Café contributors. As we get more practice, we generate more actionable knowledge and collective wisdom. For example, our Cafés are helping us generate creative program ideas that we anticipate will bring us $750,000 in net income this fiscal year. That's unheard of for a public institution in an uncertain economy.

The Café is also enabling us to explore the relationship between play and learning that is at the core of MOSI's mission. That kind of creativity and playing with ideas is now happening in other settings, so even when we are not in a Café setting, people still behave in "Café fashion." For example, in a particularly innovative use of the World Café, we've held a number of Café conversations to engage visitors or potential visitors—including senior citizens, members of our minority communities, and children—in codesigning exhibit experiences. This use of the World Café really builds community, and the groups that help in the design process have a greater sense of ownership—the exhibits are truly "theirs." Thus, instead of MOSI being a kind of dictator of community values around science, it is becoming more of a partner with community members in discovering the collective knowledge and interests in science that people didn't even realize counted as knowledge.

We're now reaching out to the associations we belong to beyond our local area. For example, Wit hosted a large four-hundred-person Café with members of the Giant Screen Theater Association, and another with the international board of the Association of Science and Technology Centers. In both cases, World Café conversations helped us identify and prioritize key issues and what actionable steps we're going to take to address those issues. Café conversations are like a positive virus spreading out way beyond where we began!

• • •

It's Win-Win All the Way: Sanofi-Synthelabo

As Told By

Yvon Bastien

I was looking for a way to engage all of our people in thinking about the future of our business. I'd tried several different approaches, but they just weren't bringing out our people's best thinking. I was searching for something that connected the heart, the mind, and the bottom line. It seemed to me that Café conversations combined those three elements, and I decided to experiment with them.

> Yvon Bastien has served as the president and general manager of Sanofi-Synthelabo, Canada, a Paris-based global pharmaceutical company focused on the research, discovery, and development of innovative medicines to treat many diseases. Sanofi-Synthelabo affiliates operate in over one hundred countries worldwide. This is the story of how Café conversations have helped Sanofi-Synthelabo, Canada, create sustainable business value.

We were in the midst of planning a celebration of our first $100 million in sales, a big achievement! I asked David Isaacs to come to Toronto to host a Café conversation with our sixteen-person design team in order to plan for our January strategy event. We wanted to create both a celebration of our success and a strategic conversation about the future of our business with all of our Canadian employees. At the end of the Design Team Café, David asked the group, "Well, what do you think?" And they replied, "Oh, it's great. Café conversations are powerful for a small group of 10 or 20, but they will never work with 250 people." David assured them that a Café dialogue could work even better with a lot of people, so we decided to try it, although there were some who were still skeptical.

As it turned out, the January Strategy Café Conversation and Celebration was extremely successful in generating key ideas for moving the business ahead. Something about the World Café approach helped people drill through the formal layers of their professional titles and bring more of their whole person to the conversation. I could see it in people's eyes and body language at the small tables. Afterwards, many people were excited by what had occurred at the January Café, and they began to go out and host Café conversations themselves on all kinds of business questions. We counted seventeen Café dialogues in the months following that first experience! It was a bit clumsy at first, since we were learning as we went—it was a real challenge to craft the questions, use reflection in a more disciplined way, and give space for real dialogue. But several of us sensed that we were on to something, and I used my "executive privilege" as the president to encourage it to continue.

Then I decided to push the envelope a little bit further and ask, "What if we were to do our long-range plan using Café conversations?" David was instrumental at that point in encouraging us to explore this possibility. We invited twenty or thirty people—the whole senior team, as well as younger leaders who had not been asked to contribute in this way before—and convened a number of Café conversations focused on the long-range plan. We took our time, but we did it. And it was a success! Our Café work generated innovative but realistic action ideas for the strategic plan, as well as the collective commitment to make them happen.

Next I said, "We did a three-year plan using Café conversations—what if we used it for next year's budget?" At that point, some people thought I was taking this Café idea too far! But others, including the director of finance, said, "Well, let's try it." And so we based the following year's budget on the selection of priority action ideas from our Café conversations, which we then grounded in our projected return on investment and return on effort. To our surprise, we discovered that the Café conversation process was quite well-suited to this purpose. You see, in a way, the structure of the World Café obliges you to create a clean slate—a zero-based mentality—that's not encumbered by preconceived ideas. You can then select the ideas that have the most promise and link them to the hard-nosed accounting requirements.

To me, it was critical that our Café conversations be directly focused on business needs and results. But the business is linked to the other worlds we live in—not just the organization but also our families and our communities. I saw our Café conversations as the glue that could hold these aspects together. So we began to experiment with Café conversations in areas where we had important stakeholder relationships. For example, our VP of sales and marketing hosted Café conversations with our business partners. And we did another long-range plan using Café dialogues where we pushed the envelope even further by inviting other external stakeholders—physicians, pharmacists, representatives from the Stroke Recovery Association, and even patients.

These Café conversations have helped us recognize that we don't work for ourselves alone. A special moment occurred during the whole-group conversation at the end of one of our Strategy Cafés when a person from the Stroke Recovery Association said, "You have a great product that prevents strokes. Why can't a part of your larger mission be to stand for *no more strokes* in all of Canada?" The room just lit up. It was like a volcano. All of a sudden, there was a feeling of "Oh, yes, that's it!" Now we're seeing patients, physicians, and hospitals as directly linked to our contribution to society. So, beginning to engage corporate social responsibility in a more focused way is an important outcome from this work.

For the last several years, we've been in hypergrowth mode, with double-digit increases. We're consistently surpassing the expectations of the corporation. I can't say if that is the direct result of our Café conversations or the result of other things we've also been doing, many of which have come from our Café work. But here's what I can say: the World Café has been very essential, very unique, because it's the only process I've found that consistently connects intellect and emotion to a business frame of reference. That's a key strategic business advantage.

For a businessperson, the numbers are the measure of success. If we don't have the numbers, that's the end of the conversations. But if we don't have the conversations, that's the end of the numbers. It's a paradox. The numbers are only the outcome of actions that you've taken upstream, where the pulse of the organization lives. You need to look at how alive the organization is, how people interact and talk with each other—their relationships. That is a key part of the value-producing capacity of the organization. It's very difficult for people to measure that, since the only tool they have to measure is the numbers.

But there are other indicators. I know we're succeeding when I see people more engaged in our business decisions, taking risks, getting the issues on the table, not being afraid to speak and to take action. For example, if you look at the first Café conversation versus the tenth one, you can see a huge evolution in confidence—a knowledge that whatever the issue is, we're going to solve it.

Of course, there are always challenges. I think there's great value in the kind of thinking and knowledge that Café conversations generate. But at the same time, we need better ways to move between the discovery part of a Café conversation and the action-planning part. We need to make sure when moving into the implementation phase that we leaders don't go back to our old control mode of doing things.

For me, Café conversations are an act of respect for our people and their capacity to contribute. A Café dialogue is like the on-ramp to a freeway—you enter into the flow of the traffic by contributing to the conversation and suddenly you're on the highway of the natural evolution of the business. Deep down, I believe that Café conversations are a carrier of life. I like to see people coming to life—and me coming to life at the same time—all around our business. It serves the individual, it serves the community, and it serves the shareholders. It's win-win all the way.

. . .

When Tom Johnson first walked in the door of our home, I must admit I'd stereotyped him. I assumed he'd be focused only on the numbers. After all, he was a famous professor of accounting history and had written a seminal book on management accounting, *Relevance Lost,* which had an impact on measurement systems around the world (1991). However, when he began to speak as part of the opening circle at the intellectual capital dialogue where the World Café was born, I was dumbfounded. He was searching, he said, for a new way to think about performance, measurement, value creation, and results. Tom was concerned that leaders were using his writings on activity-based costing as one more management tool to drive short-term financial targets rather than to nurture sustainable business and social value.

Tom challenged the group with the following set of questions: *Is it the financial and performance targets or the relationships among people and their patterns of working and thinking together that produce the outcomes we value? If organizations are living systems, then what core processes can an organization utilize that mirror nature's patterns? Where do you as a leader place intention and attention in a living system?* These powerful questions struck a chord with the other participants at that initial World Café and have continued to resonate in our thinking and research into the role of conversation as a core process.

On Means and Ends

With his colleague Anders Bröms of Sweden, Tom later wrote another seminal book, *Profit Beyond Measure,* focused on these questions (2000). Based on extensive research, it encouraged leaders to shift their attention from a focus on management exclusively by results (MBR) toward "management by means" (MBM)—the relationships and processes that shape the organization's capacity to learn, adapt to changing circumstances, and create the knowledge necessary for its long-term performance. Tom and Anders point out that because we've separated the ends (financial targets and performance objectives) from the means (the processes and practices used to create them), ends have come to seem more concrete, more "real," and therefore, more valuable than means. In contrast, Tom and Anders show how means and ends co-evolve simultaneously. "The task of managers," they argue, "is to stop treating results as a target one reaches by aiming better. Instead, results are an outcome that emerges spontaneously from mastering practices that harmonize with the patterns inherent in the system itself. In other words, manage the means, not the results. *Means are ends in the making*" (2000, p. 50, italics mine).

Tom Johnson's work has greatly informed our thinking about the role of conversation as a core process, a fundamental "means" by which relationships are built, knowledge is shared, and value is created. As we explored this thinking with Tom and his wife, prominent educator Elaine Johnson, we began to see how the World Café can help make this natural process more tangible and real, and therefore more actionable. In Elaine's words, "What we're saying is that conversation is the essential, fundamental, and indispensable means. But *how* these conversations are viewed and structured will lead to different outcomes." Tom adds, "If conversation is seen as a core means for creating organizational performance, then how leadership works with conversation will be a key factor in determining how well the organization does. If people say, 'Conversation means shut up and don't speak until you're spoken to, or don't talk until the boss authorizes you to,' that will lead to one set of results, and if the conversations occur more along the lines of the World Café principles, that will lead to a different set of results."

We've developed a simple picture to depict one way of visualizing this core process of value creation at work.

As our living tree, A Core Process for Value Creation, illustrates, questions that matter stimulate

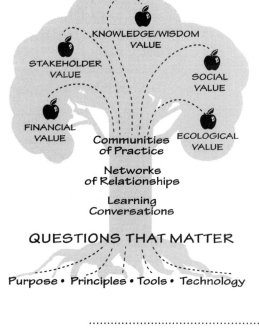

A CORE PROCESS FOR VALUE CREATION

KNOWLEDGE/WISDOM VALUE

STAKEHOLDER VALUE

SOCIAL VALUE

FINANCIAL VALUE

ECOLOGICAL VALUE

Communities of Practice

Networks of Relationships

Learning Conversations

QUESTIONS THAT MATTER

Purpose • Principles • Tools • Technology

learning conversations. These conversations, in turn, strengthen the networks of relationships and communities of practice through which an organization creates the fruits of its labors. The main challenge is that this core process is generally invisible, unfocused, and rarely used intentionally by leaders as a means to create sustainable business and social value.

Start Talking and Get to Work

For most leaders, accepting the centrality of human conversation as a key organizational means for achieving desired results entails a profound shift of mind—from seeing conversation as a peripheral activity to seeing conversation as one of the organization's most valued assets. Experiencing a World Café conversation makes it easier to visualize your whole organization or community as a dynamic, naturally occurring "Café," so you can work more intentionally with the often invisible conversational and social networks underlying organizational performance.

Stop for a moment. Pause, as Peter Senge of MIT and I have in Café gatherings with key executives, to consider the practical implications of the following question: *If critical organizational knowledge really does get created through networks of conversation and personal relationships, what does that mean in practical terms for strategy evolution, for training and development, for technology infrastructures, for the physical design of workplaces and spaces, and for your own action choices as an organizational member or leader?*

I'll never forget the booming voice of a six-foot-four Texan, the head of global operations for a major multinational auto manufacturer who was responsible for more than fifty thousand employees. As he contemplated the implications of this shift in point of view, his voice rang out, "Damn! Do you know what I've gone and done?" All eyes turned in his direction. I held my breath. "I've just gone and reorganized my entire global operation. I've broken up the learning communities and ongoing conversations that have gotten built up over the years. It's going to take us a *long time* to recover from this!" His heartfelt comment stimulated a lively conversation about what leaders could do to work more effectively with conversation as a core process in their own organizations.

The Relationship Between Talk and Action

One of the most important shifts required in this new way of viewing conversation is to re-evaluate our traditional view that talk and action are separate activities. We had a fascinating conversation with Café hosts in Denmark that explored this question. One participant suggested that we consider revising our traditional views of talk and action, seeing them as a single integrated whole rather than as separate activities. *What if, when conversations are highly energized and relevant, you are already in the action phase? What if it's not talking and discovery followed by action planning and implementation in the linear way we in the West think about it?*

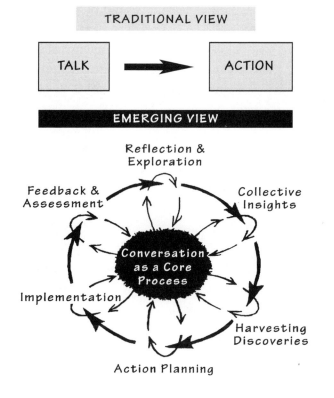

THE RELATIONSHIP BETWEEN TALK AND ACTION

As he suggested, perhaps the whole process is part of a single action cycle—reflection/insight/harvesting/action planning/implementation/feedback—in which conversation is a lively core process every step of the way. We're discovering that when people care about the questions they are working on and when their conversations are truly alive, participants naturally want to organize themselves to do whatever has to be done, discovering who cares about what and who will take accountability for next steps. Perhaps my eighty-four-year-old mom said it best when she shared a fundamental insight from her lifetime of organizational work. "You see," she mused, "conversation *is* action. You can think things and you can feel things but it doesn't become 'real' until you express it. Then it begins to germinate. Other people hear it, other people begin to feel it, you share ideas together—and if it's important enough, relevant action becomes just a natural thing that happens."

The World Café is designed primarily to generate collective knowledge-sharing, webs of personal relationships, and new possibilities for action. A Café dialogue sets the stage for more traditional forms of action planning, which often occur during the same session but at a later point in time. Yvon Bastien, of Sanofi-Synthelabo, Canada, raises an important question for leaders who are reconceiving the dichotomy between talk and action and are harnessing conversation as a core process: "How can we invent conversational processes for ongoing action planning and implementation that generate the same energy and spirit as the World Café generates for strategic thinking and collective insight?" This is a question that those who believe we need to "*start* talking and get to work" can profitably explore as we consider how to develop innovative conversational processes that are alive throughout the whole action cycle—from initial exploration through implementation.

> A Café dialogue sets the stage for more traditional forms of action planning

Doorways to Dialogue:
Entering a Common Courtyard

The World Café is not the only doorway to the type of dialogue that enables us to tap into the power of conversation as a core process for generating innovative possibilities and bringing forth new futures. The image I hold of this rich territory comes from my experience as a teenager living with my adopted grandmother in a colonial town in Chiapas, Mexico. When you entered the home through the large carved wooden door, the first thing you saw was a large central courtyard with vivid bougainvillea, lush flowers, and verdant trees in big clay pots with a large fountain in the center. You could enter the central courtyard by going through any of the multiple arched entryways that surrounded this open, flower-filled space in the middle of the house.

For me, entering the space of authentic dialogue is like entering this central courtyard in the spacious home of our common humanity. The World Café is only one valuable doorway into this central courtyard of collective possibility. Strategic dialogues, indigenous councils, salons, wisdom circles, citizens' deliberative councils, women's circles, study circles, Bohmian dialogue groups, Appreciative Inquiry, Open Space, Future Search, public deliberation models, and other conversational modalities from many cultures and historical periods have contributed to and draw on this life-affirming experience. Information on many of these is listed in "Resources and Connections," which you'll find at the back of this book. I encourage you to seek out a variety of dialogue approaches. Find the doorways to dialogue that best connect to your personal life experiences, your needs, and your own unique path of contribution. Then use your creativity and imagination to become a conversation host in your own life and work.

For the rest of our time together, we'll be focusing on the theory and practice behind the World Café. The seven World Café design principles, which we introduce on the following page and explore in the chapters that follow, provide one easy-to-use approach to engaging the power of conversations that matter, whether or not you ever decide to host a formal World Café event.

Cultivating Conversation as a Core Process

The following set of seven integrated World Café design principles has been developed over the years as a means of intentionally harnessing the power of conversation for business and social value. Here's a quick overview of each principle:

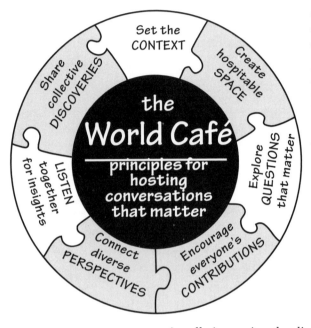

Set the context: Clarify the purpose and broad parameters within which the dialogue will unfold.

Create hospitable space: Ensure the welcoming environment and psychological safety that nurtures personal comfort and mutual respect.

Explore questions that matter: Focus collective attention on powerful questions that attract collaborative engagement.

Encourage everyone's contribution: Enliven the relationship between the "me" and the "we" by inviting full participation and mutual giving.

Cross-pollinate and connect diverse perspectives: Use the living-system dynamics of emergence through intentionally increasing the diversity and density of connections among perspectives while retaining a common focus on core questions.

Listen together for patterns, insights, and deeper questions: Focus shared attention in ways that nurture coherence of thought without losing individual contributions.

Harvest and share collective discoveries: Make collective knowledge and insight visible and actionable.

These simple principles, *when used in combination,* provide useful guidance for anyone seeking creative ways to foster authentic dialogue in which the goal is thinking together and creating actionable knowledge.

Think about the conversations taking place in your organization or community. To what extent do members actively consider and work with conversation as a core process for creating business or social value?

If you began to consider conversation a fundamental means for co-creating value in your organization, what specific implications would it have for how you do your own work?

What are some practical ways you can imagine to raise people's awareness, in your family, your organization, or your community, about the power of conversation as a key means for creating valued outcomes—whether those be tangible outcomes, like new ideas, or intangible ones, like trust, respect, and a feeling of inclusion?

THREE

PRINCIPLE 1
Set the Context

All thinking and learning takes place in a context. The mind always seeks context in order to create meaning.

—Ed Clarke, Ph.D., educator and author of
Designing and Implementing an Integrated Curriculum

What if context is like the
banks of a river through which
collective meaning flows?

DE CONGRESO A CONVERSACIÓN (FROM CONFERENCE TO CONVERSATION): MEXICO'S NATIONAL FUND FOR SOCIAL ENTERPRISE

As Told By

Carlos Mota Margain

Carlos Mota Margain, a long-time colleague, has introduced Café approaches to a variety of corporate, non-profit, university, and government settings in Mexico on issues as diverse as scenario planning, visioning, youth development, and multi-stakeholder engagement. Setting the appropriate context within which the Café's purpose and process will unfold enables members to join together within a common frame of reference. This is the tale of Carlos's collaboration in creating the context for a major government forum on social and economic development.

I'm happy to share my experience with you because it was a positive outcome from what seemed, at the beginning, to be a big challenge. I was contacted by Laura Certucha, director of planning for the National Fund for Social Enterprise (FONAES), part of our Ministry of Economy. FONAES is a key player helping to create the emerging "social economy" in Mexico—that is, an economy that considers social and community needs as well as purely economic factors for improving the lives of our people, especially those who are most disadvantaged. Such factors include microenterprises, cooperatives, and other local development efforts.

Laura was planning an official *congreso*, a major conference, on the emerging social economy. The original purpose of the conference was to bring leading experts from around the world together to share their research and experience on the social economy with key government officials, mainly from the Ministry of Economy and the Ministry of Social Development. I've attended many *congresos* in Mexico. They are mostly very formal and highly structured official events with keynote speakers or a panel of experts. Sometimes there are questions and answers, but it is generally a one-way information-sharing opportunity with little real interchange between speakers and members of the audience or among the participants themselves.

During my conversations with Laura about how we could understand the deeper opportunities for the social economy at this key moment in Mexico's history, we came up with an idea. Why not shift the context of this event from presentation to exploration? Why not move it from being a *congreso*, a formal conference, toward becoming a *foro*, a more interactive forum, where we could be in real learning conversations—everyone together? Yes, new ideas could come from international experts. But we could then use the wisdom and experience of all of the three hundred participants to consider our unique Mexican reality and context. Everyone could imagine together what kind of innovations could happen to create a new economy that includes social as well as economic interests.

In my heart I wanted to help create an event that was truly alive—alive in itself, not just in the transmission of ideas and knowledge from the few to the many. Of course, we had to get the approval for this shift from the key directors of FONAES. To our delight, they said yes! However, I think people were still quite concerned because it had never been done that way before. We needed to find a way for key people to experience this new "Café way" of being together. So I suggested to Laura that we first host a mini–World Café with the twelve top FONAES executives. In this three-round mini-Café, we focused on the best possibilities for the overall future of FONAES that this *foro* could help achieve. Well, many interesting ideas were brought forward in that mini-Café. We documented the key insights and circulated them to the twelve senior executives. That raised the overall energy and excitement for the *foro* at the most senior level. We had built a good working relationship with the senior leaders of the event, but there was still *a lot* of detailed work to do!

We learned that it takes careful planning—and time—to meet the challenge of changing from traditional ways of doing things. Our core design team met twice a week over a four-month period. We didn't mind the hard work, though. It was fun and exciting to try this new way of being together at an official gathering.

The first thing was to develop the invitation list. Once we had shifted our thinking away from the original concept of one-way information-sharing by experts, it changed our thinking about appropriate participants. In order to have the quality of rich conversation and creative thinking we wanted, we would need to invite not only the key stakeholders from government but also businesspeople, farmers, representatives of NGOs, researchers, educators—a microcosm of the whole society! That was important because we realized that no single stakeholder group by itself can bring forth innovative solutions to complex social issues.

We also had to create a unique invitation that would signal that this was going to be a different kind of meeting—a special gathering where everyone was going to contribute their unique perspectives on the possibilities for the social economy of Mexico. We sent a very personal and warm invitation to each potential guest. In the invitation we shared the forum's purpose: "To create a space for reflection, for the exchange of national and international experiences, and for the generation of knowledge that will promote and focus efforts for the social economy both in Mexico and around the world."

We also created a special symbol to represent the different kind of process we hoped to use at the gathering. The symbol was designed to show that the knowledge could come from many sources, but that the sparks of innovation and wisdom would be discovered in the middle of the conversation as a whole.

We were surprised at how rapidly people responded. Often in Mexico an officially delivered invitation is expected for these types of gatherings, but our personal and warm approach, even in the e-mailed invitations, seemed to be attractive to many people, including key representatives from the World Bank, the Mondragon Cooperatives from Spain, and PlaNet Finance from France.

Knowledge from Many Sources

Another big thing we did was to set the unique context of the gathering in advance for the experts, so they understood they were coming not just to give their speeches and leave but as learners and contributors for the entire meeting. I think this surprised many, in a good way.

Then we needed to negotiate the parameters of the event. I suggested that we run the entire forum in a Café format. The director of FONAES felt that might be too great a departure from how things were normally done. The compromise was to have the keynote speeches in the mornings in a normal auditorium-style setting. We'd then arrange the speakers from the morning keynotes in a small dialogue circle with a moderator and have them engage, in front of the audience, around what they'd learned from each other. That dialogue circle among the experts would be the bridge to the afternoon Café conversations among all the participants. After lunch we'd move to a different nearby room—our World Café—where everybody together would explore key questions based on the morning's input.

The questions we used at the Café were also very important for helping people understand the context in which we were working together. We actually had a short workshop for the core planning team on framing powerful questions. That was important internally at FONAES in order to reshape the context from traditional expert presentations to a focus on questions that would enable all participants to contribute their knowledge and experience. For example, one of the questions was, *Beyond academic or technical definitions, what is the true meaning, for you, of a social economy?* We sent the Café questions to keynote speakers and other presenters in advance. This helped clarify the framework in which they would share their own reflections in their morning keynote addresses as well as in the circle dialogues among key speakers and presenters prior to each afternoon's Café.

We had some real challenges in making the physical environment suitable for this kind of conversational gathering. First we had to change hotels, since we needed flexible space—both for the Café conversations and for hosting the learning exhibits of various social economy projects, which were designed to provide food for thought and stimulate more informal conversations. Second, hotels in Mexico only have banquet tables that seat ten, so we had to rent special small tables. Then there were other details, like getting the colored markers and the small flower vases and the flowers. These may seem like little things, but you have to understand that we were dealing with a Mexican government institution. The FONAES finance department had never *heard* of a conference with small tables, little vases with flowers, special white-paper tablecloths, and cups with markers for hundreds of people! It was an ongoing negotiation, but they were great and in the end most everything was approved.

The day of the event arrived. What we said to open the Café was as important, I think, as all the advance work we had done to set a different context. We found that it's necessary to help people know what's the appropriate "Café way" of being and learning together. Otherwise, everyone will revert to their traditional ways of doing things. I reminded people about the invitation they had received—that they had been invited to participate in a conversation, not just to listen to presentations. I also told them that in a Café dialogue everyone is equal, no one is higher or lower in status, and every idea is a valid contribution. I said that every person had something valuable from his or her experience to share—even though there might be rural farmers sitting next to very well-known government officials and key business executives. After I gave the explanation of how we were going to work together, I asked everyone to move to a new table so we could make sure we had a good mix of life experience and perspectives at each table. FONAES representatives served as the initial hosts to welcome people to their tables and to make everyone feel comfortable.

I think people were a little nervous in the beginning. The first round of the Café started out a bit slowly and hesitantly . . . but only for a few minutes. Soon people started to engage very openly, and a lively exchange of ideas began. When it was time to move into the second round, you could feel that people were very curious about what would happen next. They liked moving around the room and meeting new people.

After three rounds of conversation, we opened a plenary session in which we invited the members to share not only their findings but also their feelings—what the conversation had meant to them personally. There were many heartfelt expressions, particularly from rural people who were surprised they could talk so easily with top officials. And the more senior officials from government and business said they learned so much from people they normally would not have the chance to be in that kind of conversation with. Changing the context so that everyone was equal without authority or rank really worked!

By the end of the second day's World Café, it was as if we were cultivating one big garden, with the ideas from participants and experts as the nutrients we were putting into the soil and the seeds we were planting. By the third afternoon's Café, a change seemed to come over the group. They became much more reflective than before. There was an unusual feeling of aliveness, momentum, and depth. For example, the whole room would fall silent as people took in what one member of the group was saying. The mood changed from just being, "Oh, wow, this is fun and exciting," to a deeper contemplation of the real meaning of what each person was saying and the possibilities it might offer for the future. Those were the moments of magic for me.

What were the outcomes of taking the risk and shifting the context of this gathering from the traditional way? First of all, it created a very different atmosphere from that of most *congresos*. It was very warming to my heart to see the honest way people appreciated this opportunity to develop new ideas and insights that they could use to improve their own distinctive endeavors and to collaborate for the common good of Mexico. I could imagine the powerful impact of these three hundred people each taking just one key discovery about the emerging social economy into their own networks of relationships and institutions.

In terms of practical outcomes, the director of FONAES told the group that the insights from these conversations were going to help create the agenda and focus for the organization's efforts over the coming year. In addition, a second international *foro* has been scheduled to build on our original findings and insights. One of the experts who attended, Marcos de Castro Sanz, president of the Confederation for the Social Economy of Spain, said this was such a different and useful learning experience that he'd like to bring the Café format to his Spanish colleagues for engaging this kind of multisector thinking and dialogue on other key development issues.

My key discovery from this World Café experience? It's amazing what can happen when you shift the context to provide simple interactive formats for diverse stakeholders to really talk together as equals across traditional boundaries. It felt like a big challenge at first, but it was worth the risk! Seeing people from such different social and economic backgrounds creating ideas *together* for Mexico's future was deeply rewarding.

· · ·

Perspectives & Observations

It was Eric Vogt, a pioneer in developing online learning communities, who first showed David and me the importance of context in providing the framework in which individual and collective meaning-making unfolds. A number of years ago, Eric called me from his home in Cambridge, Massachusetts. He had recently read an article that I had written with David on building organizations as learning communities (Brown and Isaacs, 1995). He excitedly told me, "We *have* to meet and visit. Our values and thinking are so complementary!" Only later did we both realize that we'd *already* met and visited together—as teenagers more than thirty years earlier, dancing in the courtyard of my adopted grandmother's home in Chiapas, Mexico, where Eric's father was head of the Harvard Anthropology Project. It's a small world!

Eric had recently written an article on organizational learning entitled "Learning Out of Context" (1995). It included a very simple but key idea (left) that allowed David and me to visualize and illustrate the role of *context* in holding, surrounding, and informing both the *content* and the *process* of a great conversation.

The Role of Context

Context is the situation, frame of reference, and surrounding factors that, in combination, help shape the ways we make meaning of our experiences. Most of us are not used to thinking consciously about context even though its presence is critical for our minds to create patterns of understanding (Johnson, 2001). We become confused and uncomfortable when the relation between the larger context and the content we are exploring or the process that's being used is unclear.

Setting the context involves intentionally creating the flexible boundaries in which the group's collaborative learning unfolds. I often like to imagine context as the banks of a river that help channel the flow of meaning without controlling it. In planning for a conversation that matters, the Café host and planning team play a key role as architects of context by helping to focus (but not control) the *content* as well as providing support to shape the *process* of the dialogue—not only in advance of but also during the gathering.

The nested-bowl illustration on the previous page has helped us evolve our thinking about the elements of contextual architecture that are involved in shaping an effective Café conversation. We are finding that setting an appropriate context for Café conversations requires paying attention to three key elements: *purpose, participants, parameters*. At first glance, these three elements may seem rather simple. However, each of these contextual elements builds on and relates to the others, creating a whole system that surrounds and informs the conversation. They are an essential part of bringing "coherence without control" to the conversational experience.

The amount of time and attention Café hosts pay to these contextual elements is usually proportional to the size and complexity of the gathering. Carlos's Mexican *foro* was a large event requiring considerable up-front planning as well as context setting at the event itself. For a smaller Café gathering, all three elements might be addressed in a single design conversation. Hosts have found, however, that it's important to consider each of these elements in planning a Café gathering, even if only briefly. Aspects of these elements can then be introduced as part of the contextual framework at the event itself.

Once you've hosted a number of Cafés or other collaborative conversations, each of these aspects of setting the context becomes

ELEMENTS OF CONTEXT

PURPOSE

PARTICIPANTS

PARAMETERS

SETTING THE CONTEXT

more intuitive as you call on learnings from previous gatherings. In addition, the next two chapters, "Create Hospitable Space" (chapter 4) and "Explore Questions That Matter" (chapter 5), introduce two complementary Café principles that build on and enhance the effectiveness of the initial contextual architecture.

Because context can be an amorphous concept, I'll use Carlos's Mexican *foro* as the example throughout this chapter to ground our exploration of contextual architecture. Where appropriate, I've illuminated key points in small exhibits that compare the original *congreso* concept with the *foro* approach that Carlos and his colleagues actually used. Both Carlos and another World Café colleague, Arian Ward, have helped develop simple yet practical ways to shape the context for a Café conversation in order to increase the likelihood of accessing living knowledge and breakthrough thinking. David and I are grateful for their insight, commitment, and collaboration.

Clarify the *Purpose*

Clarifying the purpose includes several elements.

Understand the Current Situation

Clarifying the relevant aspects of the larger situation in which you are hosting a learning conversation is a powerful initial step in defining the overall purpose of the Café. There may be social, economic, political, organizational, community, or even interpersonal factors. Ask yourself, *What is the real-life situation or need that makes this conversation relevant, and why is it important?* For Carlos and the *foro* planning team, the complex realities of Mexico's current socioeconomic situation, coupled with the need to seek the broadest range of creative new thinking for the nation's social economy, helped guide the design of the event. When they assessed Mexico's current realities and needs, it revealed the value of engaging the knowledge and experience not only of traditional experts but also of multisector stakeholders who could provide a rich set of perspectives. The resulting shift—from presentation-based *congreso* to conversational *foro*—reflected this understanding of the current reality and larger needs that made the event important.

Explore Your Own Design Assumptions

In addition to articulating your beliefs or assumptions about the nature of the current situation, it is useful to explore your assumptions about how people create knowledge together. This can make a big difference in how you articulate the purpose of the event, determine if a Café is the appropriate approach, and frame the invitation to the participants. For example, in the Mexican case, although all agreed that Mexico was experiencing complex socioeconomic challenges that required a thoughtful response, the design team tested their traditional beliefs about the role of experts in shaping that response. The conference planners began to see knowledge creation as a social and community endeavor—not the sole purview of experts—and one in which conversation is a core process. The event, therefore, was crafted with this assumption at its core.

The World Café is grounded in a growing body of research about the social nature of learning (Allee, 2002; Lambert and others, 1995; Sandow and Allen, 2004; Wenger, 1998; Wenger and others, 2002). As the planning team's design partner, Carlos helped the team see the creative opportunities in exploring their early assumptions in order to determine the appropriateness of a Café approach for accessing the collective intelligence of the entire conference community. Chapter 10 gives additional information on when (and when not) to choose the World Café.

DESIGN ASSUMPTIONS

Congreso

▶ Mexico is facing complex socioeconomic challenges.

▶ Formal presentations of a situation analysis by Mexican and international experts to government officials can provide the most relevant data for effective planning and decision making.

▶ The role of the nonpresenting participants is to become more informed about the best thinking in the field.

Foro

▶ Mexico is facing complex socioeconomic challenges.

▶ Diverse voices create a richer situation analysis by bringing new insight to planning and decision making around complex issues.

▶ People want to contribute their knowledge, learn together, and make a difference.

▶ Each participant in the conversation has expertise and can make a unique contribution.

Articulate the "Big Why"

A clear purpose provides a kind of North Star—the deeper intention that guides the design of the Café. It is what determines your criteria for success. One way to consider the purpose of the Café is simply to ask, *Why are we bringing people together? What need (or needs) will this conversation fulfill?* At times, creating a special name for your World Café dialogue can help signal its broad purpose—for example, Leadership Café, Strategy Café, Product Development Café, or simply Discovery Café. In Carlos's story, the purpose evolved from providing expert information on the social economy to creating a collaborative space for exchanging national and international experiences and for generating knowledge that could focus large-scale efforts on behalf of the social economy, both in Mexico and beyond.

> A clear purpose provides a kind of North Star— the deeper intention that guides the design of the Café

Clarify Possible Outcomes

A Café is purposely designed to avoid predetermined outcomes. However, illuminating the most exciting possibilities and considering the possible outcomes or success criteria that matter most for achieving your purpose can be important aspects of shaping a Café conversation. For example, *tangible outcomes* might include discovering new strategic directions, considering innovative program or policy options, or illuminating new business opportunities for a specific product.

However, Café conversations are generally *not* focused, at least initially, on finding an immediate answer or a solution. Often the most powerful Café outcome is discovering the right questions to ask in relation to a critical issue, or simply creating the opportunity to think and explore your situation together with others for the first time. These and other *intangible outcomes*—like building new relationships, sharing knowledge, and providing opportunities for contribution by those traditionally excluded from decision making—often have great payoffs that create long-term value.

Congreso

- FONAES is positioned as a key actor in the global exchange on Mexico's new social economy.
- State-of-the-art knowledge is brought to Mexico by international experts.
- Government representatives are provided with relevant data for future planning.

Foro

- FONAES is positioned as a global convener and host, creating a space for reflection, exploration, exchange of experiences, and generation of knowledge to promote and focus efforts on behalf of the social economy in Mexico and beyond.
- Expertise is used to stimulate multistakeholder dialogue and access collective wisdom for future decision making.
- All participants become co-learners and contributors.

Determine the Right *Participants*

Diversity of thought and experience is perhaps the single most important criterion for gaining new insight and accessing collective wisdom. For this reason, the participants you invite are a key part of setting the context in which innovative possibilities will unfold. Often in designing a Café, the participant group is already defined from the outset. However, it is always useful to ask, *Who else do we want to join this conversation in order to help us achieve our purpose? What additional perspectives might contribute valuable insights? Who could receive real benefit by being a part of the conversation?* We often neglect to invite participants who will (a) likely be affected by the outcomes of the conversation or (b) have unique or different perspectives to offer. These are key voices to include in any Café conversation, and are useful to consider when exploring who should be invited. For example, in hosting a Café on the future of education in a local community, one Café design team decided to invite not only teachers, parents, and school administrators but also students of all ages who would be affected by their decisions.

STAKEHOLDERS/PARTICIPANTS

Congreso

- Presenters and panelists: international experts.
- Audience: Mexican government officials from key government ministries.

Foro

- Everyone is a participant; international experts act as conversation catalysts and learning partners.
- Representatives of a cross section of Mexican society participate, including government officials, NGOs, social-cooperative enterprises, businesses of varied sizes (rural and urban), legislators, educators, researchers, and students.

Be Creative with *Parameters*

Finally, parameters are the third element of contextual architecture.

Clarify Your Learning Approach

Traditional meeting approaches focused on PowerPoint presentations and speeches are often ill-suited for enabling people to think together intelligently about complex challenges and questions. Yet as Carlos found out, with courage and creativity it's often possible to design a powerful new learning context from quite traditional beginnings. The Café format is adaptable enough that you can often integrate it into more traditional meeting formats and environments. But it is important to consider how far you can push the design parameters. In Carlos's case, the planning group's willingness to stretch the parameters of a traditional conference model resulted in a very different and innovative framework for eliciting individual and collective meaning. At the same time, it still retained many traditional meeting structures, such as the keynote presentations in the morning. Determining the overall learning and conversational approach, as well as clarifying the ways a Café conversation can contribute, helps you set the context by framing the major design elements of the gathering you are hosting.

LEARNING APPROACH

Congreso

▶ Auditorium style.

▶ Formal keynote presentations.

▶ Expert panels.

▶ Written questions from audience with verbal responses by presenters or panelists.

Foro

▶ Auditorium-style formal presentations.

▶ Dialogue circles among presenters with moderator.

▶ Café conversations focused on core questions eliciting everyone's contribution, including experts as participants and FONAES execs as table hosts.

▶ Each day's Café insights are fed into next day's conversations via overnight summaries, shared by Economic Ministry representative.

▶ Daily Cafés create an evolving/deepening collaborative dialogue around key themes.

Determine Pre-Event Activities

Although the FONAES gathering involved very detailed advance planning, even when hosting a two- or three-hour Café it's important to pay attention to key aspects that will make it a successful event. For example, framing and issuing the invitation, whether via mail, phone, e-mail, or fax, is a key aspect of setting the appropriate pre-event context for the gathering. It helps set the expectation in advance that this will be a different kind of meeting where everyone will have an active opportunity to contribute. Carlos's story details some of the other types of pre-event activities that proved essential to shaping the context in which the *foro* unfolded, including sending a personal invitation to each guest that explained the forum's purpose, creating a special symbol to represent the different kind of process they hoped to use at the gathering, and clarifying to the experts what would be expected of them. As a host, use your imagination to determine which pre-event activities are needed for planners, presenters (if they will be included), and participants to enter the gathering with a common set of expectations and sense of positive anticipation regarding the purpose and process.

PRE-EVENT ACTIVITIES

Congreso

▶ Periodic planning meetings.

▶ Formal invitations and presenter scheduling.

▶ Formal meeting space is secured.

Foro

▶ Core planning team is formed to do detailed design—reflecting diverse perspectives and based on agreements on how to interact.

▶ A mini-Café is held with FONAES execs about best possibilities.

▶ Personal invitations are sent to everyone, which explain the new conversational context.

▶ Workshop is held on framing Café questions.

▶ Early attention is paid to negotiating resources, venue, physical layout, Café setup, and supplies.

▶ Presenters are briefed on Café questions and process, and their role as learning partners.

Consider Post-Event Follow-Up

Often the form of the follow-up is determined at the Café event itself. However, thinking in advance about what kind of follow-up might occur is an important parameter to consider in setting the context, because it can affect how you frame the invitation and set the context during the gathering itself. For example, if you know that participant insights will become part of a longer-term development process, it might be important to share that in your initial invitation. Follow-up needs or plans can also determine the manner in which you document the Café. In the case of the *foro*, although a number of key next steps emerged in the moment based on the group's Café conversations, resources were dedicated in advance to create a follow-up government publication detailing the presentations and outputs from the event.

POST-EVENT FOLLOW-UP

Congreso

▶ Government creates documentation of presentations.

▶ Possible follow-up *congreso* is considered.

Foro

▶ Government publishes presentations, learnings from expert dialogue circles, and summary of Café insights.

▶ Next steps emerge from Café dialogues, including possible regional Cafés.

▶ Interim discoveries are scheduled to feed into a follow-up *foro*.

▶ Virtual learning exchange among experts is facilitated by FONAES.

Find the Appropriate Location

We'll talk in much more depth about creating hospitable spaces for authentic conversation in the following chapter. We've found this to be one of the most essential parameters to work with early on because most conference and retreat venues, as well as meeting rooms in organizations, are poorly equipped to accommodate conversation-based processes. In Carlos's case, simply finding a hotel ballroom was not sufficient. He needed a hotel that could accommodate large auditorium presentations while simultaneously having enough flexible space to host both World Café conversations and participant exhibitions in order to stimulate new thinking and breakthrough possibilities.

Secure Needed Resources and Setup

Important parameters include time, budget, equipment, furnishings, and supplies. These might seem like obvious considerations, yet what appears simple often requires unexpected negotiations to stretch these parameters in order to create a conversational context where people can think together in new ways. As the following exhibit demonstrates, Carlos's *foro* required a quite different set of resources than the *congreso* that had been originally considered.

RESOURCES AND SETUP

Congreso

▶ Setup is for for formal auditorium presentations and lectures.

▶ Chairs are placed in rows.

▶ Time is set for Q&A from audience at plenary sessions.

Foro

▶ Setup is for formal auditorium presentations, dialogue circles, and Café conversations.

▶ Budget is allocated for rental of small tables, tablecloths, butcher paper, markers, and flowers on each table.

▶ Appropriate time is set aside each afternoon for Café conversations.

Set the Context at the Event

We'll talk in more depth about the role of the Café host, as well as specific Café etiquette, in chapter 10. We've found, however, that since Café conversations are a departure from traditional meeting experiences, it is important to reset the context during the event—often at several junctures. This includes clarifying the situation or issue that has brought the group together—the "Big Why" of the Café. It also includes highlighting the interactive learning orientation in which this new type of conversational process will take place. As you can see from Carlos's story, the initial introduction of the Café process at the event can have a significant impact on the way the conversational vessel is shaped for individual and collective meaning to emerge.

CONTEXT SETTING AT THE EVENT

Congreso

▶ Purpose is clear, but overall process context is not emphasized.

▶ Participants are instructed to write questions after formal presentations for presenter response.

Foro

▶ The purpose and process are reiterated throughout the event.

▶ Participants are reminded that they are invited to participate in authentic and active conversation rather than be a passive audience.

▶ The experts' analysis is framed as a resource to provide food for thought.

▶ There is an invitation to engage in a different way of talking and listening with new people.

▶ Everyone's experience and ideas are considered a valuable contribution to the whole.

▶ Café etiquette is explained, and how everyone will work together.

▶ FONAES reps act as table hosts, welcoming a diverse mix of sectors and participants to each table.

▶ Café questions are shaped so that all can contribute.

Often, in addition to sharing Café etiquette, as Carlos did, Café hosts begin with a brief table conversation and whole-group sharing among participants focused on the following question: *Recall a time when you had a great conversation where real learning or new insight occurred—what enabled that to happen?* In this way, members have the opportunity to participate in setting the emotional context and framework to support innovative thinking.

Setting the context—at the planning stage, during the event itself, and in positioning whatever follow-up will occur (or not) as a result of the conversation—can make or break a collaborative inquiry. Becoming a creative "architect of context" at every stage of conversational design and implementation is an art, not only for World Café hosts but for anyone seeking to create effective conditions for authentic dialogue.

Think about a meeting, conference, or gathering you've attended that went really well. What was it about how the context was set—either prior to or at the event itself—that contributed to its effectiveness?

Consider an upcoming gathering you are planning. Based on the three key elements of context setting that we've explored in this chapter, what might you pay more attention to in your planning that would help set a conversational tone and invite a greater diversity of perspectives toward the outcomes you are seeking?

How might you set the context at the event itself to help people feel comfortable moving into this more collaborative and conversational way of learning together?

FOUR

PRINCIPLE 2
Create Hospitable Space

The idea is to create a physical space that enables you to move around in that space, and to create a social space that encourages you to swap and share and help each other. If you can design the physical space, the social space, and the information space together to enhance collaborative learning, then that whole milieu turns into a learning technology. People just love working there and they start learning with and from each other.

—John Seely Brown, former chief scientist, Xerox Corporation

What if we create environments that
nurture authentic conversation?

DOES NOT
EXIST, YOU
FUCKING IDIOTS!!!

A SYSTEM THINKING TOGETHER:
THE PEGASUS SYSTEMS THINKING IN ACTION CONFERENCE

As Told By

David Isaacs

David Isaacs, a co-originator of the World Café, has collaborated with corporate, community, government, health, and educational leaders to craft strategic conversations around a wide variety of key issues affecting the future. In this story he focuses on creating hospitable space for collaborative dialogue in a very large group setting.

The annual Systems Thinking in Action (STA) conference, hosted by Pegasus Communications, focuses on innovative applications of systems thinking, organizational learning, and new forms of leadership. It attracts about one thousand participants from around the world. The title of that year's conference was "Learning Communities: Building Enduring Capability." To our surprise, the conference coordinator, LeAnne Grillo, called us and asked, "How would you like to do a keynote Café with the whole conference in the hotel ballroom focused on collective processes of learning and knowledge creation?"

Well, that phone conversation created quite a buzz in our office! Juanita, our colleague Nancy Margulies, and I could hardly imagine what it would be like to create a Café for 1,000 people from more than twenty countries. The largest Café we had done up to that point was for 250 people. How would we scale it up to more than four times that size, and still create a welcoming, intimate Café learning environment for people from diverse professional backgrounds and cultures?

Would it be possible, in the confines of a ninety-minute session, for so many people to explore core questions about the social nature of learning? Could we move beyond a focus on individual contributions and help people appreciate the phenomenon of collective intelligence—a "system thinking together"—in that large a group? Our challenge was to create the environment for this experience to happen. Nancy is a gifted graphic artist, illustrator, and designer. Juanita is great at conceptual stuff. And I've learned over the years how to make people feel comfortable together. So the three of us began to imagine and play with what might be possible when we combined our skills.

Here's what actually happened when we got to the conference. We took one look at the large, sterile, hotel ballroom and thought about how we could transform it into a warm, friendly Café environment for a thousand people—all in the mere forty-five minutes we would have during the break between sessions. We arranged for the hotel to get small, round cocktail tables for four (no small feat in a banquet-oriented hotel). Conference volunteers rounded up red-checkered tablecloths, small vases, and fresh red-and-white carnations for each table. We put white paper sheets over the tablecloths, just like in many cafés, and left a small container of colored markers to use for doodling.

While we couldn't get rid of the raised stage, we did manage to have the speaker's podium removed. We replaced it with a round café table next to a special type of overhead projector that Nancy could use for prepared graphics as well as for real-time visual recording of the whole-group conversations. Her drawings of the audience's contributions would be projected onto huge video screens so that everyone's comments could be seen as well as heard. We brought in palm trees and other greenery to give the room a warmer, more natural feel. And in a stroke of luck, we discovered an inexpensive way to project different colored designs on the huge blank walls. When the lights were dimmed, this gave the effect of walking into an intimate jazz café.

But we realized that creating a welcoming, hospitable environment for such a large group extended beyond the physical setup of our keynote Café. We wanted to create a different feel for the conference as a whole. Our keynote session was on the afternoon of the second day. In order to get people into the Café mood ahead of time, we arranged to have the coffee break areas also set up with a Café theme: red-checkered cloths on the serving tables, as well as on café tables in the foyers nearby. Nancy made beautiful silk banners with different quotes on them, such as this one from Martin Buber: "All real living is meeting." These were hung in the break area, making it look like an art show rather than just a regular get-your-coffee-quick place. We tried to create many subtle signals that something different and interesting was happening here.

When it came time to transform the ballroom, Nancy put colorful signs outside in the hallways that said *No Entry (Yet!), Café Under Construction.* We had a quick meeting with the volunteers, hotel crew, and technicians—everybody involved in the setup. We told them it was important that we all think of ourselves as the co-hosts for this gathering and that in the next forty-five minutes we were going to transform this traditional hotel ballroom into a welcoming World Café. Prior to our keynote, the ballroom had been divided into three formal meeting rooms, so we had our work cut out for us. We put upbeat jazz on the sound system and literally took the walls down. It was amazing to watch the transformation. I'll never forget it.

Nancy had created hand-drawn, whimsical overheads with quotes from well-known scientists and others that gave a flavor of the key ideas that underpinned our work:

> ▶ *Intelligence emerges as the system connects to itself.*

> ▶ *In life, the issue is not control but dynamic interconnectedness.*

> ▶ *The real voyage of discovery lies not in seeking new land-scapes but in having new eyes.*

Nancy had also made a colorful *Welcome to the World Café* overhead that would be shown on the large video screen at the front of the room.

When the transformation was complete, we opened all the ballroom doors simultaneously. There to greet each guest was a volunteer host shaking hands and extending a welcome. Posters at each entryway invited folks to sit with people they didn't know, to welcome each other, and to start getting acquainted. Michael Jones, a gifted musician, played mellow piano music, creating a warm neighborhood café atmosphere. We dimmed the ballroom lights slightly so that our projected designs could be seen all over the room, giving it a warm, intimate feeling even in such a huge space. The *Welcome to the World Café* sign appeared on one large video screen, while the scientists' quotes alternated on the other. As hundreds of people streamed into the ballroom, our Café was coming to life!

It was fascinating to notice the shift of collective energy from previous plenary sessions held in this very same room. We could feel the playfulness and curiosity as people began to gather at the small round tables. They immediately began talking with each other. The buzz of conversation filled the room as everyone got settled.

In an effort to reinforce our role as Café hosts rather than traditional presenters, I opened the gathering by welcoming this group from twenty-seven different countries with their own words for "welcome." I wanted people to see that we were, indeed, a *World* Café, representing almost every continent on the globe. We were a microcosm of the whole system. Perhaps, if we were lucky that day, we would see and experience ourselves as a system thinking together.

Part of creating a hospitable space for everyone to contribute was clarifying how to treat each other well in a Café dialogue. Without doing any formal dialogue teaching or lengthy presentation of guidelines, Nancy briefly shared a few pointers (left) on Café etiquette.

As people began to explore the first question together, the room came alive! When it was time for the first twenty-minute round to come to a close, I decided to try an experiment. I quietly raised my hand and signaled to the tables closest to me to do the same. As people noticed what was happening, a wave of hands began to rise throughout the huge ballroom and in less than sixty seconds the entire room fell silent. We all laughed as I asked the participants to notice how they collectively already knew what to do.

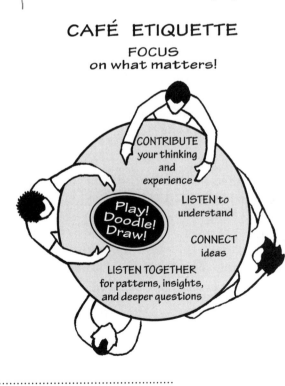

CAFÉ ETIQUETTE

FOCUS
on what matters!

CONTRIBUTE your thinking and experience

Play! Doodle! Draw!

LISTEN to understand

CONNECT ideas

LISTEN TOGETHER for patterns, insights, and deeper questions

Then I asked people to begin the second round of conversation by moving to another Café table in their general vicinity. The host who remained at the table would share the essence of their conversations from the notes and drawings on their tablecloths, and travelers would link and connect ideas they were bringing from their own previous table conversations. It was absolutely astounding to watch the 750 travelers at 250 tables say goodbye to their table hosts, pick up their books, bags, and materials, and quickly move to surrounding tables where they were welcomed as guests by their new hosts. Self-organized hosting works!

For the second and final round, I encouraged people to notice the patterns, themes, and deeper questions that were emerging from their mutual listening and from the cross-pollination of new ideas being shared. Now there were four different conversations linked at each table, greatly increasing the number of connections and possible new insights.

I put up my hand again as the round ended. As before, a wave of silence swept the room. Now the room seemed to be filled with a special kind of focused energy. It was palpable. I asked people to notice what it felt like to experience a whole system thinking together about questions it cared about. Instead of normal, small-group report-outs, Juanita and I stepped down into the audience for a "conversation of the whole." We gave a moment of silence and asked people, as they offered their key insights, to imagine themselves thoughtfully contributing to weaving a connected "knowledge web" together. During this entire period, Nancy was creating visual images of what was unfolding. As a way of ending, we asked people to turn to one other person and share a seed idea that they wanted to take home, plant, and allow to grow.

Amazingly, all of this happened in just one and a half hours. When the session was over and people began to leave, volunteers with brightly wrapped boxes were at all the doors, giving each person a gift—a large, colorful poster that Nancy, Juanita, and I had created. This *Map of the Territory* summarized the assumptions underlying the World Café and included key conceptual quotes, interdisciplinary contributions, simple guidelines for Café hosting, and ways to find additional resources.

Even though the Café was over, it seemed that people didn't want to leave. The hotel staff kept trying to get people to move along because they had to redo the ballroom and put up the wall dividers again for the next session, but it was hard to get people to stop talking.

What did I learn from this little experiment about creating hospitable space for large-group dialogue and learning? I discovered the importance of creating a welcoming and informal environment, which included this:

- *Setting up the room to look like an actual café*
- *Naming the Café (in this case, Knowledge Café) to reflect our purpose*
- *Having the intimacy of small table conversations in a larger common space, and making sure each table felt connected to the larger whole*
- *Using art, music, and greenery*

- *Having volunteers act as greeters and hosts*
- *Using the language of "hosts, travelers, and guests" during the Café rounds to encourage a spirit of mutual hospitality and friendship*
- *Encouraging living systems images through the use of metaphors, such as planting seeds and cross-pollinating ideas*
- *Going out into the audience to be with the participants during the conversation of the whole*
- *Wearing informal yet appropriate attire*
- *Using hand-drawn graphics rather than PowerPoint presentations*
- *Giving gifts to each participant*

These may seem like simple things, but they are rarely done in the context of supporting collaborative intelligence and knowledge evolution in organizations. Creating a safe, inviting, and informal space is one way of encouraging more generative conversations to emerge. There is something about the physical and social environment of a café that evokes more authentic conversations, even across cultures—conversations that are more creative, playful, curious, intimate, and honest than those in most formal business meetings and off-site retreats. We took a step in that direction in our World Café keynote session and we're learning more all the time.

· · ·

Perspectives & Observations

Before the birth of the World Café, I'd never thought much about hosting. However, for Joy Anderson, a lively social entrepreneur who uses Café-style conversations to welcome new colleagues into her network, hosting is a way of life. As we sat in our hilltop living room where the World Café was discovered, Joy told me that as a young child she learned from her parents, two Lutheran ministers, that among many early peoples, offering food and shelter to travelers was a sacred obligation and a matter of mutual survival.

Travelers brought not only small gifts from their own lands but also their personal stories, news from their travels, and novel ideas to the tables of their hosts. Joy offered a wonderful perspective that her father, Herbert Anderson, shared one Christmas on the spirit of

Christian hospitality. He described hospitality as a stance of openness toward new people and ideas, a lens that reflects our experience in hosting Café conversations. "Hospitality," he said, "is the act of affirming gifts in others. It is entertaining ideas that enable us to see life in a new way. When we offer hospitality to the stranger or a guest, we welcome something new, unfamiliar, and unknown into our lives that has the potential to expand our world." Our own emphasis on encouraging people to serve as Café table hosts who welcome travelers as guests or "ambassadors of meaning" for each progressive round of conversation draws on the same spirit of welcome, inclusiveness, novelty, and mutual contribution that lies at the heart of hosting and the creation of hospitable space the world over.

> Hospitality is the act of affirming gifts in others

In his wonderful book *The Great Good Place* (1989), sociologist Ray Oldenburg focuses on the importance of informal gathering places for the development of innovative ideas, democratic practice, and community life throughout history. His insights on what he calls "the third place" are critical to our understanding of Café conversations and why they work. According to Oldenburg, the third place is a locale that exists apart from the "womb" of private family space and the "rat race" of the workaday world. Such places—including cafés—provide neutral ground where people of diverse perspectives and backgrounds can come together in an inclusive way. They offer hospitality. They are upbeat, and at times, playful. They accept and welcome newcomers and lively conversation, which helps maintain their vitality. In fact, it is the quality of the conversation itself that is the defining characteristic of third places. As Jaida N'ha Sandra puts it in *The Joy of Conversation* (1997), a fascinating history of salons and their role in social innovation, the point of creating hospitable space is to encourage the quality of conversation for which salons have become famous as incubators of new thinking.

For most people, the idea of creating hospitable space is not actually foreign or new. But what is exciting and novel is the intentional creation of these environments for our conversations at work. As one executive said to me, "You know, this is so obvious and so important. These are the everyday human things we pay attention to when we're having a gathering or welcoming guests in our home, but we just don't think about how important they are when we're thinking together with our colleagues about key issues." Another added, "Our workplaces, and many hotels and conference centers, aren't designed to create the right environments for the kind of strategic thinking and quality conversation that is so important for the future of our business. Boardrooms and conference rooms are so sterile and cold. And those big tables are barriers too. It's something we're going to need to pay a lot more attention to as leaders if we want to support knowledge-sharing and get the best results."

Transforming Traditional Meeting Spaces

What do these insights from our traditions of human community as well as our Café discoveries tell us about the value of creating hospitable space to catalyze collaborative conversation? In his provocative work *Shared Minds*, Michael Schrage, a former research fellow at MIT's Media Lab, points out that the physical setup of most meetings actually subverts collaborative effort by focusing on deadening one-way presentations that "subsidize the excesses of individual communication at the expense of collaborative community" (1990, p. 122).

The physical setup of most meetings actually subverts collaborative effort by focusing on deadening one-way presentations

Schrage focuses on creative ways to make meeting environments more dynamic and interactive, including creating informal meeting environments, introducing collaborative technology tools, and creating common spaces that enable people to see each other's ideas visually in real time. (The paper tablecloths used for drawing key ideas provide this opportunity in Café conversations.) Schrage concludes that "in many respects it's easier to get results by changing the meeting environment than by trying to persuade people to behave differently" (1990, p. 122).

Like Schrage, Roslie Capper of New Zealand knows that environments matter, and she put that knowledge into practice. While others in the field were thinking about the process and the content of the conversations they were hosting, Roslie was thinking about the physical and psychological context that could nurture these deeper conversations. "What really gave me pause was the time I went to a conference on creating a sustainable future," Roslie told us. "The speakers were honoring the natural world in a hotel ballroom with no natural light, no plants, and no fresh air!"

First introduced to the World Café at an International Women's Dialogue, Roslie had a dream: "I wanted to design a venue that would intentionally support the kind of thinking together that I had seen in Café conversations and in dialogue circles," says Roslie. With seed funding from friends, family, and associates, she created TOTEM, a business and meeting center on Auckland's waterfront. It was designed with curved walls and a huge glass roof over the large circular reception area where people could gather and mix informally. Art reflecting New Zealand's multicultural heritage was placed throughout the building. Roslie had comfortable furniture designed in natural, vibrant colors. The meeting spaces were outfitted with lots of small round tables with comfy chairs of the right size for supporting Café dialogues and other interactive processes. An Italian cappuccino machine in the business lounge enabled people to enjoy serving themselves and naturally begin conversations with people they hadn't met before—making new friends. "We adopted the motto *Connections Made Easy*," says Roslie, "which is very similar to what happens in a Café conversation. For us, TOTEM has been the embodiment of the Swedish term for business, *närings liv,* that I learned from David Isaacs. In English it means 'nourishment for life.' The goal of TOTEM? To nourish life while connecting people and ideas in unexpected ways."

People began to recognize that something different was happening at TOTEM. Roslie shares that "little by little we began to provide organizations with thinking partners to help them create strategic conversations at TOTEM using what we might call the deeper World Café philosophy and principles even when it wasn't the full Café process itself." Rosalie's dream is to have TOTEM meeting venues in every major city in the world to help demonstrate the importance of paying attention to the subtle, sometimes invisible, aspects of conversational environments in order to support new ways of thinking and being together in the service of things we care about.

Michael Schrage's insights and Roslie's experiment with TOTEM mirror our own discoveries in creating interactive Café environments to support collaborative work. Edna Pasher, a Café pioneer from Israel who has worked with key leaders there, points out, "You have to design the communications environment if you want it to work. You have to be an architect of the knowledge ecology." It seems like common sense, doesn't it? But perhaps that's what Café conversations help us do—remember common sense and put it into practice.

Creative Approaches to Designing Café Learning Environments

In talking with Café hosts around the world, the power and importance of creating a conversational environment that looks, to the degree possible, like an actual café is one of our most interesting discoveries. Yet the range of creativity among World Café hosts is amazing. There are many exciting ways to create hospitable space and evoke those intangible human qualities that make Café dialogues most effective. As a World Café host, you're limited only by your imagination.

For example, Andrea Dyer, an organizational learning consultant who has used Café methods in a range of settings, describes the Café environment she created at a global strategy event for a major multinational corporation that involved representatives from over thirty countries. "We had people take pictures of sunrises in their home countries and send them in advance," says Andrea. "And we had them take pictures of their families. We had a gallery in the hallway coming into the room. We changed the artwork over the three days. We also put the graphic murals from the whole-group conversations into the art gallery every day."

(continued on p. 73)

BUILDING ON TRADITIONS OF DIALOGUE: SAUDI ARAMCO

As Told By

Bronwyn Horvath, Ed.D.

S audi Aramco is a fully integrated oil company with opera-tions in exploration, production, refining, and marketing. We have over fifty thousand employees and an additional one hundred thousand outside contractors, representing fifty-four different nationalities. Our operations include remote out-posts in the Rub-al-Khali desert and offshore platforms in the Arabian Gulf. We also build schools and roads, run hospitals, and support residential communities the size of small towns. We maintain a fleet of planes and helicopters that rival some national carriers.

> Bronwyn Horvath is the Leadership Forum facilitator for Saudi Aramco, Saudi Ara-bia's national oil company. The World Café has been used with groups of over seven hundred people to bridge organizational hierar-chies and build on Arab soci-ety's historical traditions of dialogue. This story shows that hospitable space can be created in a way that suits any culture.

As you can imagine, one of the greatest challenges for any company of this size is effective communication. We'd been strug-gling with the question of how to promote broad information-sharing, let alone meaningful dialogue, at this level of complexity.

Then the senior vice president of Saudi Aramco's Engineer-ing and Operations Service (E&OS), Salim Al-Aydh, attended a Society for Organiza-tional Learning session with Peter Senge in Egypt. At that event, Al-Aydh experienced the World Café firsthand and saw the potential of Café dialogues to align people's aspira-tions with the company's strategic direction. Equally important, he saw the World Café as an extension of the type of dialogue and hospitality that was characteristic of the Arab culture itself. For hundreds of years, tribesmen had met in an open forum called a *majlis* to discuss the issues they confronted.

In a radical departure from business as usual, Salem Al-Aydh convened *Café '03*, a forum building on Saudi Arabia's long-standing tradition of dialogue. He introduced the Café idea as a creative approach for fostering the mutual contribution of over seven hun-dred members of his management team across the four major E&OS functional areas. The purpose of the gathering, he explained, was to "have conversations with each other about things that really matter," focused on the E&OS mission, values, and business plan.

The logistical challenges of designing *Café '03* seemed overwhelming. But when the going gets tough, the tough get innovative! When the creative E&OS design team of Dan Walters, Alfred Hanner, and Jim Davidson discovered that no local hotel could handle the large number of participants, they converted the cavernous Saudi Aramco aviation hangar into the largest Café on the Arabian Peninsula! They created new ways to meet the audiovisual and technical requirements in that unlikely setting, mounting numerous screens on the hangar walls so that all participants could see the speakers. They brought in hundreds of Arabian carpets to transform the hangar into an inviting, intimate Café, Middle Eastern style. The carpets also served to muffle the sound of seven hundred people in exuberant conversation.

Saudi Aramco Café

The more organized Café conversations were complemented by a social lunch that encouraged informal exchange. All Café participants, as well as guests from the aviation department, sat on the floor around a hundred large platters of lamb and rice for a traditional Arabian meal—a *kabsah*. We used the occasion to host a ceremony honoring the outstanding contributions of individuals and teams during the previous year. It was a true celebration of people's capacity to give their best—a day of "serious fun" for leaders at all levels.

In March 2004, we hosted our most ambitious Café to date—the *Shaybah Café*—at our remote Rub-al-Khali desert facility. We brought together over two hundred members of Saudi Aramco's senior leadership with CEOs and business leaders from across the Kingdom of Saudi Arabia to share knowledge, forge new relationships, and contribute to building the nation's business community as a learning network. After the Café, we welcomed all two hundred participants to gather under the stars in the red sand dunes of one the most awe-inspiring deserts of the world. The group's sharing under the night sky—the culmination of our earlier Café dialogues—was powerful and moving. It connected many people back to their desert heritage, and to their desire to contribute the essence of this rich heritage to future generations. I've discovered that the Café concept strikes a familiar chord, not only with Saudi Arabs but with the many other cultures that are represented in the company. Whether people are Egyptian, Turkish, Malaysian, American, or Korean, they all have cultural traditions of sitting down together in a social setting to discuss their hopes and dreams for the future.

Our Cafés, by drawing on local traditions of hospitality, have made it possible for people to build wider personal networks of business relationships across traditional boundaries. When you've had meaningful dialogue over time—you've shared ideas and spread the possibilities for new ways for people to contribute—change happens. The World Café is a simple, natural way to foster it. Maybe that's why I've seen Café conversations take root and grow and thrive at Saudi Aramco while many other programs have come and gone.

• • •

As Andrea discovered, creating a personal connection is a key element in creating hospitable space, as is the inclusion of art. Think of those elements that make a café or a living room inviting—the pictures on the wall, groups of plants, vases of flowers, and other homey touches. In this setting, Andrea added the extra personal element of having the artwork come from the participants' home countries. Not only were they able to bring something of their personal lives into this work setting, but the art gallery also honored the diversity of cultures in the Café.

Bo Gyllenpalm, the former CEO of Phonogram, a Philips subsidiary in Sweden, and himself a very experienced Café host, describes another innovative Café setting. It was an outdoor Dinner Café that David and I hosted under a tent on the island of Lidingö, outside Stockholm. We invited fifty of our Swedish friends, many of whom did not know each other, to be part of a World Café experience in which they moved to a different table for each course of the meal. At each turn we posed a different query to help people explore what they cared about and the questions at the heart of their lives and work. When I asked Bo, "What do you think helped the Dinner Café work well?" he smiled and said, "Well, the whole atmosphere. The surroundings were very beautiful. It was the garden, the water, and the very relaxed atmosphere. It created an immediate openness to what would happen there. It didn't force or push us into discussion, but I was surprised at how fast people were able to speak from their heart."

Bringing nature to the Café—or the Café to nature, as we did in this case—serves as a reminder that the Café itself is a natural process, reflecting nature's deepest self-organizing principles. To the degree that you, as a host, create a space that taps into this element, you invite participants to engage more easily in authentic conversations and enjoy creative ways of being with one another.

You can invite members to experiment with having a different conversation in a number of ways. For example, Colonial Pipeline Corporation created a more inviting environment for strategic

> Creating a personal connection is a key element in creating hospitable space

conversation by explicitly adopting the name "The Pipeline Pub" to signal a more informal tone for their Café dialogues. In another business setting, Tammy Sicard, an organizational learning consultant, used an Italian café theme for participants who were charged with crafting a global human resources strategy after a major corporate merger. For Tammy, focusing on fun and creativity in the Café was an essential part of both reducing the natural tensions created by a post-merger situation, and for opening the participants up to experimentation and innovation in developing their new HR strategy. "First, we had HR people from all over the world sit on a panel and talk about the challenges and questions unique to their area," she said. "Then we taught people how to do mind mapping (a visual recording process). After a break we had them walk into the Knowledge Café. It was set up like an Italian café—Italian opera music playing, Chianti, and red-and-white checkered tablecloths. The minute you walked in, it felt like a different place. People had both fun *and* rich discussions about topics they had a shared interest in. They were using their mind-mapping skills right on the butcher paper on the tables. People hooked right into it."

The integration of mind-mapping practices and other visual elements in the Café brings right-brain processing into the conversation and allows for the integration of different learning styles. It has often been our experience that one person at a table might not say a word during a Café, but then he or she will draw a picture that coalesces the whole conversation. We're continuing to discover ways to help the Café environment feel safe for people to bring their unique gifts and perspectives to the conversation in whatever way is most comfortable.

Part of the challenge of creating powerful conversations—especially ones about questions that really matter to people—is that there is often not enough trust to make those conversations safe for people to share their deepest beliefs and most courageous

> The integration of mind-mapping practices and other visual elements in the Café brings right-brain processing into the conversation

ideas. That was clearly the challenge facing Sharif Abdullah, director of the Commonway Institute in Portland, Oregon.

After being introduced to the World Café concept at a Fetzer Institute meeting focused on "Peace Building for the Twenty-First Century," Sharif decided to experiment with a Commons Café, bringing people of diverse backgrounds together to explore issues of race, class, ethnicity, values, and politics. A variety of local organizations were asked to send members of their constituencies. Sharif recalls, "Our goal was not simply to have members feel good about each other. We wanted people to shift their consciousness from thinking 'I am separate' to thinking 'we are one.'"

Balancing safety and adventure . . . is at the heart of good Café hosting

Sharif describes his choice of location as key to success. "We wanted to have a relatively light and very safe atmosphere. We didn't want anyone to feel, 'I'm going to get beat up physically, mentally, or emotionally if I go to this.' On the other hand, we wanted it to be an adventure. So we held it in a festival marketplace that had public café tables. The coffee vendor was one of the sponsors and there were other patrons all around us. One of the incentives from the sponsoring organizations was that participants got $5.00 worth of lattes and desserts for free."

Balancing safety and adventure, as Sharif discovered, is at the heart of good Café hosting. It seems that having small café-style tables (or small circle groups of not more than four or five members) is one aspect of achieving this balance. Lloyd Fell, a research scientist who attended an initial Conversing Café hosted by Alan Stewart to redesign a local cultural center in Australia, noticed a "tremendous wave of energy . . . right across the room. It was as if something had suddenly been unleashed by the invitation to speak freely in the more intimate setting of the café tables."

Stefan Wängerstedt, who has introduced World Café conversations to large banks and hospital systems in Sweden, provides a provocative image of the way in which the World Café creates a safe psychological space for the birth of new ideas. In sharing with me his first experience of Café hosting with executives at a major Swedish bank, Stefan described the Café as a "sort of pregnant place where you can explore all phases of the new life of ideas in your conversations. The World Café provides a safe place, nourishment, and all of the things that an unborn and newborn life needs. The tablecloth becomes a collective place where the birth of the ideas can come out in the center." Safety, adventure, playfulness, intimacy, and inclusion all contribute to creating a space that is alive, inviting, and open to new ways of seeing and connecting.

The Quality That Has No Name

As I re-read these reflections from both interdisciplinary researchers and from our learning conversations with Café hosts around the world, I am once again drawn to the ideas of Christopher Alexander, the famed architect. In his early work, *The Timeless Way of Building,* Alexander describes the deep, life-affirming patterns embedded in the human species that, when honored and expressed in physical form, allow what is natural and whole in us to emerge. In a beautiful passage, he speaks of the "quality that has no name"—the quality embodied in places and spaces that he describes as being comfortable, free, whole, and alive. "Places which have this quality, invite this quality to come to life in us. . . . It is a self-supporting, self-maintaining, generating quality. It is the quality of life. And we must seek it, for our own sakes, in our surroundings, simply in order that we can, ourselves, become alive" (1979, p. 53).

And so it is with intentional creation of hospitable space as part of the Café approach to catalyzing collaborative conversation, shared learning, and collective insight. Our varied experiences with the World Café across cultures affirm Christopher Alexander's fundamental insight. Perhaps it really is that simple and obvious after all. We are able to confront difficult questions, explore underlying assumptions, and create what we care about more readily in environments that evoke warmth, friendliness, authenticity, and real conversation than in environments that are less hospitable to the human spirit. Discovering creative ways to evoke the quality that has no name is both our greatest challenge and our greatest opportunity as Café hosts.

Think about times when you participated in a really great
conversation. What was it about the setting or the environment (physical or psychological) that contributed to
its success?

Consider a meeting or a conversation you have coming up.
Think about the place where it will occur. What are the
few small things that you can do to make the space more
comfortable and inviting? What can you do personally
to make people feel welcome?

Which of your colleagues do you think might find these
ideas relevant? How might you engage them in exploring
how to make your meeting and gathering spaces more
hospitable to the human spirit?

FIVE

PRINCIPLE 3
Explore Questions That Matter

Because questions are intrinsically related to action, they spark and direct attention, perception, energy, and effort, and so are at the heart of the evolving forms that our lives assume. . . . Creativity requires asking genuine questions, those to which an answer is not already known. Questions function as open-handed invitations to creativity, calling forth that which doesn't yet exist.

—Marilee Goldberg, *The Art of the Question*

What if the gold lies in
discovering the big questions?

A CAFÉ ON QUESTIONS

As Told By

Members of the World Café Community

In this imaginary Café, I include the perspectives of various World Café hosts who have contributed to our mutual learning about the power and potential of questions that matter—a defining feature of the World Café approach to dialogue. I also include the voices of colleagues who have both hosted Café dialogues and written about the "question of questions." As part of this synthesis, I've kept the spirit and essence of individual reflections while taking creative license by including ideas from other Café hosts who have contributed to our mutual discoveries. Listen in. The members of the conversation are just beginning to introduce themselves as they take their seats at the tables. . . .

Round 1: Beginning the Conversation

Juanita: Welcome to our Café on Questions. Everyone here has been part of other World Café conversations, but let me just share again how we'll be working together. We'll have three rounds of conversation. As your Café host, I'll let you know when each round is coming to a close. One person will stay at the table as a host to welcome guests who have been a part of other conversations. They'll be bringing seed ideas from their tables into the next round. The important thing is to capture the essence of what's been said in drawings, symbols, and words on your tablecloths. Continue to link and build ideas. Notice patterns and common themes as well as the aha's. Perhaps we could play with the Café question I've put on the flip chart here:

What are you learning about the use of questions for engaging collaborative learning and collective intelligence that might be of help to others?

Some of you know each other, but others don't, so it would be great if you could introduce yourselves at your tables before jumping in.

(A brief silence ensues, then the conversation at one of the tables begins. . . .)

David M.: Well, I'll start. I'm David Marsing. I worked as a senior executive with Intel for many years. I'm now developing new commercial as well as community ventures. I first encountered the World Café as part of the original Intellectual Capital Pioneers.

Verna: Hi, I'm Verna Allee. I wasn't at the first Café but was invited to a later session of the Intellectual Capital Pioneers. I had just finished writing a book called *The Knowledge*

Evolution: Expanding Organizational Intelligence. As you can imagine, the whole subject of questions fascinates me.

Toke: I'm Toke Møller. You can probably tell from my accent that I'm not from California. I'm Danish. My wife, Monica, and I have been convening seminars on the art of hosting in Europe, Canada, and the U.S. I'm interested in the World Café from the perspective of collective wisdom.

David I.: Welcome, Toke. I'm Juanita's partner, David Isaacs. Why don't I just start? I think questions open doors to collective discovery. The word question comes from "quest"—to be on a journey, to search for something important.

Toke: For me, a good question opens that search into the realm of new possibilities. For example, I was hosting a Café in a small community in Denmark about the future of their local school. We went around and around to find the right Café question. Sometimes it's harder to find a good question than to actually host the Café! The question we finally came up with was not "How could the school be better?" or "How can we fix the problems in the school?" but *"What could a good school also be?"* The question had no judgment about what was already happening, and it didn't require immediate action. That framing of the question created more of an open invitation to explore creative options for the future.

David I.: People often want to jump too quickly into action. But I've found that even beginning to explore the question allows people to deepen their collective understanding of each other's perspectives. People also begin to take responsibility for giving it their best thinking. That is a very important part of co-evolving effective action.

Toke: Right! Effective action often comes out of it if you are exploring a question that is really alive for people. The paradoxical thing is that action almost always does come out of a conversation that has life in it, but it doesn't have to be the primary stated goal.

David I.: So the question you talked about in the Education Café in Denmark was more like an invitation to bring more of people's creativity to the exploration, rather than a mandate to go out immediately and do something or fix something.

Toke: Yes, the question has to catch people where they are, meet them where there is the most interest and relevance, and then use that collective energy to create forward movement. Actionable knowledge flows naturally from that.

David M.: What kinds of questions do that?

Verna: I've thought a lot about what kinds of questions have the most life. To me, the most energizing questions are those that engage people's values, hopes, and ideals—questions that relate to something that's larger than themselves, to which they can connect and contribute. People don't have a lot of energy around questions that are about removing pain or fixing problems.

David I.: But that comes up, the pain.

Verna: Well, I don't mean that you can't address the pain. But you can set the context for the question to evoke collective possibility rather than pain. Here's an example. I recently worked with a large organization whose best people were walking out the door to work for a competitor. Most people would pose the question, "How can we keep from losing our best people?" That's an OK question to ask, but it's not an energizing question. It's about how to stop the pain. A better question might be, "How can we retain our best people?" That's a more positive framing, but it's still not a particularly energizing question. You need to find a question that will get people excited, energize them, and matter to them.

David M.: So what would be an example in the case you're describing?

Verna: I would work with key people who are going to be part of it to come up with a question that is really alive for them and holds an element of personal connection as well as collective possibility. For example, "What would this workplace be like if it were the kind of place I looked forward to getting up and coming to every morning?" Or, "What have been my best times here in this organization, the times when I've really looked forward to coming to work? What contributed to that?"—and then build your next question from there.

David I.: Framing problems as questions is an important shift. I did a Futuring Café with the leadership team at a global leather goods company. At the end, when I asked the participants what had the most value for them, almost all of them said that the single most powerful learning for them was in converting a challenge, issue, or problem into a question.

Verna: What changed for them when they did that?

David I.: There's always a subtle feeling of disempowerment in a problem. "We've got a problem. . . . Oh, no! Another problem!" There's a weariness and stuckness about it. Simply shifting the focus from problem to evocative inquiry helps people get unstuck and opens doors.

David M.: One way I like to look at a good question is that it is like a seed crystal. A good question starts a conversation that begins to take on a more complex, richer form. It grows in amazing and unpredictable ways. The conditions have to be right for this, of course, but the seed itself, the original question, is very important. The crystal won't grow without that seed, or it won't grow as beautifully or fully.

Verna: In addition to revealing new facets of a situation, I've found that a good question can simultaneously focus our minds in much the same way as meditation. A catalytic question magnetizes an intense quality of individual and collective attention, and we need to respect that.

Toke: I like how you give a powerful question such respect. In a Café conversation, the question seems to be an "attractor" for the collective intelligence and deeper wisdom of the group to reveal itself. It can bring more coherence. It's almost as if an invisible energy field forms around the question.

(There is a pause in the conversation.)

David I.: We've touched already on several attributes of a powerful question: it is a question that matters, it attracts and generates energy, it opens up possibilities, it invites deeper exploration, and so on. Any other ideas?

Toke: Well, I would add that a good question is simple. If the question is too complex, impersonal, or abstract you miss what's at the heart of it. A simple question can invite in a variety of voices, like the question, *"What could a good school also be?"* Even young children from the school were able to help take responsibility for that question. We could then take it to the next step and ask everyone, *"What do you want to say about the future of the school based on these ideas?"* The young people had great contributions, like creating their own Ten Commandments outlining the responsibilities of the parents, the students, and the teachers—which completely surprised the adults! It all came from that first simple question.

Verna: In my experience, a good question is one that creates a certain tension, a certain dissonance that pulls us forward in order to lessen the gap between our current knowledge and our new learning.

David I.: And it might not be just one question; it could be a series of related questions that build on each other over the life of the Café. But you have to watch what's evolving so either you or the group can try to find the next question that will take the inquiry forward and deeper.

(Juanita raises her hand quietly. Others see her doing this and they begin to raise their hands. The room becomes quiet as this round of conversation comes to a close.)

Juanita: So, let's take it to the next phase. Please move now to a new Café table and continue the conversation. One person should stay as the host to greet the guests who are coming from other conversations. Whoever is the host, could you make sure everyone does a quick introduction as you get started? Then show your new group what's on your tablecloth and let your guests know where your conversation has taken you so you can continue to link your thinking. And be sure to keep doodling on the tablecloths. In this second round, begin to listen even more deeply to see what patterns and connections are emerging.

David M.: I'll stay as host.

(Three others arrive and everyone shakes hands across the table as they get settled.)

David M.: Welcome. I'm David Marsing, the host at this table. I was a line guy at Intel and took World Café conversations into my operational work as a leader.

Barbara: I'm Barbara Waugh from Hewlett-Packard. For me, even though I've never conducted a formal Café learning event, the World Café pattern describes what I've done on my whole journey at HP: seeding conversations

Round 2: Moving Between Tables

with good questions, sending people out to cross-pollinate and connect ideas, and letting things grow on their own. It's been quite a ride.

Eric: Hi, everyone. I'm Eric Vogt. I coordinate the International Corporate Learning Association (InterClass) and was also a part of the early intellectual capital dialogues at Juanita and David's.

Susan: And I'm Susan Skjei. I've developed an executive leadership program for the Marpa Center for Business and Economics at Naropa University that combines reflective practices with leadership skills.

David M.: You can see our beautiful drawings and scribbles here on the tablecloth. . . .

(Laughing, he shows the group the drawings, ideas, and scribbles from the first round. The new guests begin to add their ideas.)

Eric: *(commenting on the drawings and notes)* It's amazing! Some of the same things came out at our table. The one example you have on the tablecloth of making the questions more open-ended while still being directly connected to what people care about touched on something we also explored in our group. Can I draw a little diagram here? *(He takes a green pen and draws a little diagram with the words "construction," "scope," and "assumptions," on the tablecloth.)* Now, this is a little rough, but here goes.

The *construction* part has to do with the actual architecture of the question: Is it constructed as an open question that's more than a yes/no or multiple choice? For example, the question "Should we move the company to Albuquerque or not?" evokes a yes/no response rather than a more open question like "What are all the things we need to weigh in considering if we should move to Albuquerque?"

A *scope* question might be what you were talking about earlier at this table in relation to problem-solving or fix-it questions. If you ask, "What's the one biggest problem in the school?" the question has a narrower scope than "What could a good school also be?"

The *assumptions* aspect of a question is even subtler. Understanding and working more intentionally with the beliefs and assumptions that underlie the question can make a real difference to the outcome of an inquiry. That's as far as we got. Maybe you can help.

Barbara: Eric, I really like that way of thinking about questions. It helps me see my own situation at HP in another light. I think I can add something to the part related to assumptions. Can I give you a real-life example of a key question at HP and how it evolved?

(Heads nod in encouragement around the table.)

I was helping to mobilize a visioning effort at HP Labs around the question, "How can we be the best industrial research lab in the world?" We started a whole global network of interconnected conversations around that question. As I look back on it, we were hosting a World Café, even though the dialogues weren't happening in the same room. One day Laurie, one of our engineers, came into my office and said, "What would really energize me would be to ask the question, 'How can we be the best industrial research lab *for* the world?'"

(Barbara puts the two alternative HP visioning questions under the part of Eric's diagram that says "assumptions.")

That one word profoundly shifted the assumptions that underpinned our inquiry—how we could become the best <u>for</u> the world as the deeper context for becoming the best <u>in</u> the world. This shift mobilized a huge amount of collective energy, not only at HP Labs but also throughout the whole company. It was no longer just the lab's question; it became the question many others at HP began to ask themselves. As I thought about it, being the best *in* the world was based the assumption of competition. Being the best *for* the world was based on the assumption of contribution.

(Barbara adds "competition" and "contribution" under her questions on the tablecloth.)

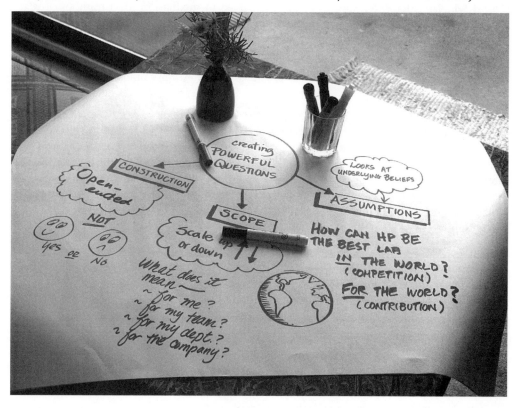

Once we got the core question, "How can we become the best for the world?" we could increase or decrease the *scope* depending on the situation. I call that scaling up or scaling down the question. For example, decreasing the scale would be, "What does 'HP for the World' mean for *me*? What does it mean in my life, in my own work?" Or we could scale it up: "What does 'HP for the World' mean for my work group? For my department? For HP as a company? And what might it mean for the world itself for HP to be *for* the world?"

(Susan scribbles "scale up/scale down" on the tablecloth.)

David M.: That's fantastic. Maybe we should be asking the "for the world" question more intentionally in all corporations!

Susan: You know, David Isaacs shared with me that he sometimes finds it works well not even to have prepared a question in advance. He often likes to ask a Café group: "What core question, if explored, could make the most difference to the situation we're considering?" or "What do we *not* know, that if we did know, could transform this situation for the better?" That way, they can use their own knowledge to generate the questions.

David M.: Isn't that interesting? I've been involved in meditation for a number of years. Intentionally engaging people's "not knowing" is actually what is called "beginner's mind" in meditation. In the Eastern tradition, it is considered the start of all wisdom.

(The room is buzzing with energy. People are leaning forward, intent, focused. Juanita quietly puts up her hand again, and as people notice, they begin to raise their hands. The room quiets down.)

Juanita: Now for the third round. Please return to wherever you started—your home table. Spend a few minutes sharing how the conversation has evolved and ask yourselves, "What remains at the edge of our 'not knowing' here? What deeper questions do we still have regarding how to use questions effectively for engaging collaborative learning and collective intelligence?" Get a sense of the two or three questions that, together, you think are really important. Put each question separately on the large hexagonal stickies that are on each table. When this round ends, we'll open up into a "conversation of the whole" to see what emerges in the middle.

(People return to their original tables and begin to share the common themes and insights that have emerged from their multiple conversations. They begin to frame the few deeper questions they collectively feel need to be a part of the continuing exploration. Juanita then moves into the middle of the room. The graphic recorder, Gretchen Pisano, is in front of the room, working on a large wall mural that serves as the tablecloth for the whole.)

Juanita: Let's hear from one table. Then, if another has a question that is connected to the first, speak up and we'll see what emerges. If others don't know who you are, please just say your first name and maybe a couple of brief words about yourself.

(People from a number of the tables begin to speak up.)

Paul: I'm Paul Borawski, executive director of the American Society for Quality. At my table we're still ringing with a question that relates to what David Marsing, sitting over there next to Verna, said about questions being the beginning of wisdom. I'm wondering: *"How do we shape rich questions that evoke a deep and thoughtful response versus what I would call 'flat' questions—ones that don't have that ring that evokes deep curiosity and creativity?"*

Monica: I'm Monica Nissén from Denmark. Toke Møller and I have been focusing our work on the art of hosting over the last few years. Our table had a related question that I think gets to the heart of how to help Café conversations yield their greatest insights: *"How can we make the question simple enough so that it really penetrates—gets through into the real heart of the matter? How little is enough?"*

Carlos: That's a great question. I'm Carlos Mota and I've been using Cafés in Mexico for scenarios and strategic planning. Once a friend told me about a time she was being interviewed. The interviewer said, "We're just going to ask you one question: What is the question we *should* be asking?" With that in mind, I'm wondering: *"Is it realistic to think that we as Café hosts can discover and frame questions that really get to the essence of what matters—or can only the people themselves who are closest to it do that job? If it's the people themselves, then what does that mean for who we involve in planning for our Cafés?"*

Bo: It's beautiful that you say that. I'm Bo Gyllenpalm from Sweden. I teach at the Fielding Graduate Institute, and I think our question is connected to yours. At our table we asked: *"What are the ways we can begin to discover what questions are at the heart of things, even before the Café begins?"* Perhaps it might mean including a request in the invitation for people to send in their own burning questions related to the Café topic ahead of time. Then you can post these all around the room for people to see as they come into the Café, or begin with a key question you've discovered in advance from the people themselves that seems really powerful and relevant.

Ken: I'm Ken Homer. I've helped to create the World Café Web site and am working with the development of the World Café community globally. Can we touch on a different area?

(Heads nod around the room, and he continues.)

At our table we raised a larger-scale question. We were thinking about Barbara's example of how a small shift in the question enabled it to travel even more broadly throughout the company. We're wondering: *"How do you discover the questions that will really 'travel well,' either throughout an individual Café gathering or, as importantly, beyond any one situation into a large-scale change effort like what happened at HP?"* For example, what are the powerful questions that can connect us as a community of Café hosts all around the world?

Juanita: That's a great one to reflect on together. I'm sure we haven't gotten all of the key questions out, even in this whole-group conversation. So, as we go out for the break, I'd love for you to put up all the questions you've written on your hexagonal stickies on the large mural here at the front—on our Wall of Inquiry. Maybe as you come back from break you can take a gallery tour and informally begin to group the questions that seem to relate to each other. After the break, we'll take a few minutes to see what might be the really big questions that we're holding together, which might take our understanding together to a deeper level. Thanks to all for being a part of this!

(Mellow jazz plays in the background. Many in the group continue sharing in small clusters around the room once they have gotten their coffee. Little by little they meander over to the Wall of Inquiry—individually and in groups. By the time the twenty-minute break is over, folks have played around with the hexagons until several clusters emerge that reflect their own collective sense of the patterns of meaning among the questions. Even though they were not asked to do so, people have gotten larger hexagons from Gretchen and put one "big question" over each cluster that captures the core idea of that cluster. As they come back from the break, the group does not sit down, but gathers around the Wall of Inquiry to see what they have created together.

Nancy Margulies, one of the early Café innovators, who was rather quiet during earlier Café rounds, takes the lead in helping the group refine and clarify the big questions. After another ten minutes, it seems that folks have finished. They have added several other key questions that came up in the context of bringing this circle of exploration to a resting point. There is a peaceful silence as people take in their collective insights.)

. . .

Perspectives and Observations

I first learned about the relevance of paying disciplined attention to questions that matter from Mike Szymanczyk, the current chairman and CEO of Philip Morris USA. Mike is a brilliant systemic thinker and an innovative architect of large-scale organizational change. He and other company leaders are creating multiple opportunities for collaborative dialogue and engagement with both internal and external stakeholders as they address the challenges of realigning with societal expectations and reinventing the future of their company. Mike and I have worked together for almost two decades on strategic change initiatives in several different corporations. Over time, I began to notice that he consistently came up with surprising business and organizational insights. Was Mike just smarter than other people? Was it that he had more highly developed intuitive capacities? Or did he simply have some secret access to the Goddess of Strategy? (My favorite explanation!)

I asked Mike if we could sit down with him to learn how he developed strategic insight. Mike's reflections during that session transformed my thinking about the role and power of questions in co-evolving the future. His perspectives have greatly influenced the way the World Café has come to place disciplined attention on discovering and exploring questions that matter as one of its defining features. Mike mused:

For me, developing strategy is like panning for gold. The gold lies in discovering the "big questions"—the really strategic questions that can pull people's energy and learning forward toward the future. But how can you find the gold? First, you have to care about finding it and you have to be curious. With that in mind, you head toward the general territory where you think the gold may be located, armed with your best tools, your experience, and your instincts.

You scan the horizon and contours of the land—the real-life situation you live in. In my case that's our business, organizational, and social landscape. You begin to notice the details of the terrain all around you, because, for all you know, the gold might be right at your feet. You take note of the interesting formations as you travel, knowing that you may be breaking new ground or making the path as you go. You begin to turn over rocks to see what shows up and to see if there are even small flecks of gold (issues and questions) that might point you to the places where the gold nuggets (the big questions) might be found. As you look at your particular situation, you scan the horizon looking for trends or other external signals. The purpose is to see where your curiosity and imagination lead you in order to identify the big questions that your situation analysis reveals.

I should emphasize that I mean questions, *not* problems—*questions stated in a way that ends with a question mark, not with a period or an exclamation point. Questions like, "How does A relate to C, and what deeper question does that suggest?" or "If X were at play here, what question would we be asking?" "Given Y, how can we . . . ?" or "What's the real question, the fundamental question here?" Framing your issues as questions rather than problems is the hardest part, because we're so used to thinking in terms of problems. But something fundamental changes when people begin to ask questions together. The questions create more of a learning conversation than the normal stale debate about problems.*

Based in large measure on Mike's insights about the importance of discovering big questions, I began to focus on exploring questions that matter as a key element in our early work with strategic dialogue (Bennett and Brown, 1995). As we deepened our experience with Café learning, Café hosts around the world began to realize how central the emphasis on catalytic questions for collaborative knowledge creation was going to be.

Why Questions Count

Consider the possibility that everything we know today about our world emerged because people were curious. They formulated a question or series of questions about something that sparked their interest or deeply concerned them, which led them to learn something new. Many Nobel laureates located their *eureka!* moment of discovery in the instant when the right question finally revealed itself—even if it took them considerable time to come up with the final answer. For example, Einstein's theory of relativity resulted from a question that he had wondered about as a teenager: "What would the universe look like if I were riding on a beam of light?" When asked what accounted for his success, another Nobel prize winner, physicist Arno Penzia, replied: "I went for the jugular question" (Vogt and others, 2003, p. 1).

> Genuine questions— ones for which we don't already have answers— are open invitations to innovation

Genuine questions—ones for which we don't already have answers—are open invitations to innovation, calling forth ideas and insights that don't yet exist. For every step into the future, someone or some group had to wonder what the possibilities might be for changing or improving the current situation—if only to ask themselves: *"What would happen if we thought about this differently? What questions are we not asking, that if we did ask, might make our situation better?"*

The importance of carefully crafted questions for breakthrough thinking and effective action is slowly starting to reach greater public awareness (Adams, 2004; Allee, 1997; Goldberg, 1997; Leeds, 2000; Strachan, 2001). For example, in addressing the results of more than a decade of research and practice in the area of Appreciative Inquiry, David Cooperrider and Diana Whitney state unequivocally that "the most important insight we have learned with AI to date is that human systems grow toward what they persistently ask questions about" (2000, p. 70). Laura Chasin, a founder of the Public Conversations Project, which fosters constructive conversations around divisive public issues, reminds us that questions have an unsung power. They carry the capacity to intensify conflict—"How can we get even?"—or deepen mutual understanding—"How did we each come to the perspective we hold?" Laura encourages us, particularly in these uncertain times, to help co-evolve the future by having "conversations focused on the right questions—the most constructive and catalytic questions we can ask" (2001, pp. 1–3). If asking good questions is so critical, how can we, as conversation hosts, become more skillful in shaping questions that matter?

The Art and Architecture of Powerful Questions

Although we've met only once, Fran Peavey, a pioneer in the use of strategic questioning for social change, has greatly influenced my thinking about how to construct powerful questions. Fran observes that "questions can be like a lever you use to pry open the stuck lid on a paint can. . . . If we have just a short lever, we can only just crack open the lid on the can. But if we have a longer lever, or a more dynamic question, we can open that can up much wider and really stir things up" (1994, p. 91). For example, in a community development effort to clean up the Ganges River in India, a "short-lever" question—one that will elicit a narrow yes/no response—might be, "Have you thought about cleaning up the pollution in the river?" "Longer-lever" questions might include these: "What do you see when you look at the river? How do you feel about the condition of the river? How do you explain the situation with the river to your children?" (1994, p. 105). These more open questions encourage a more thoughtful response that opens the door to further exploration and positive change.

Fran could have been sitting in any of our own learning conversations about the World Café when she said, "One of the basic assumptions of the strategic questioning process is that knowledge resides and is alive in all people. . . . The point here is to ask questions in such a way that it lets the ideas and energy come from the individual or the system itself" (1994, p. 100).

The art of framing strategic questions that call forth our innate wisdom has important implications for focusing intention, attention, and energy, as well as for increasing our collective ability to generate insights that help shape the future.

By understanding what makes a powerful question, you can experiment with increasing the power of your questions and seeing what impact they have on the conversations you host. For example, in advance of an important conversation, spend a few minutes with a colleague and write down several questions that are relevant to the topic. Rate them in terms of their power. See if you can spot why certain questions are more compelling than others. Experiment with changing the construction and scope of the question, as Eric Vogt (Vogt, 1994; Vogt and others, 2003) suggested in the opening story for this chapter and as Barbara Waugh (2001) demonstrated in her HP for the World project. Examine the assumptions that may be embedded in your questions and check to see if they will help or hinder your exploration. Notice the impact of the questions you hear, read, or introduce into your own conversations. Just a few practice sessions will greatly enhance your ability to engage in conversational inquiry stimulated by dynamic questions.

Looking at questions that have worked for others is a useful way to stimulate your own creativity in framing powerful questions. In their *Encyclopedia of Positive Questions* (2002), Diana Whitney and David Cooperrider share hundreds of questions that have been used in their work with Appreciative Inquiry to elicit innovative ideas and new possibilities in both organizations and communities. In chapter 10, we've included a number of generic questions that World Café hosts have found helpful in a wide variety of Café and other dialogue settings to focus collective attention, connect ideas, and create forward movement. In organizations as well as communities, questions that matter can enliven a generative and focused field of inquiry characterized by what we call "coherence without control," as growing networks of people share their own responses to questions at the heart of their common inquiry. Exploring your organization's or community's big questions and seeding wider fields of conversation with strategic questions that attract energy and "travel well" lie at the heart of cultivating the knowledge we need to thrive today, as well as the wisdom we need to ensure a sustainable future.

Questions Travel Through Networks

Questions for Reflection

Consider an upcoming conversation you are hosting and ask yourself these questions:

What question, if explored thoroughly, could provide the breakthrough possibilities we are seeking?

Is the question relevant to the real life or real work of the people who will be exploring it?

Is this a genuine question—a question to which I/we really don't know the answer?

What work do I want this question to do? That is, what kind of conversation, meanings, and feelings do I imagine this question will evoke in those who will be exploring it?

What assumptions or beliefs are embedded in the way this question is constructed?

Is this question likely to generate hope, imagination, engagement, new thinking, and creative action, or is it likely to increase a focus on past problems and obstacles?

Does this question leave room for new and different questions to be raised as the initial question is explored?

Questions adapted from Sallyann Roth, Public Conversations Project, copyright © 1998.

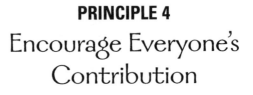

SIX

PRINCIPLE 4
Encourage Everyone's Contribution

The idea of contribution is especially instructive because it lies in the area that unites the "I" and the "we." We contribute because we are part of something larger than our own lives and efforts, but the form of our contribution is based on our uniqueness and our individuality.

—Carol Ochs, *Women and Spirituality*

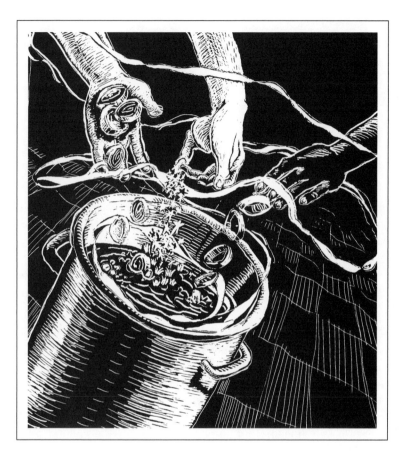

What if your contribution

is a key ingredient?

EVERY VOICE COUNTS: FOSTERING A CULTURE OF CONTRIBUTION: THE FINANCIAL PLANNING ASSOCIATION

As Told By

Janet McCallen, chief executive officer; Elizabeth Jetton, president, board of directors, 2004; Kim Porto, director, Career and Community Development; Sean Walters, group director, Community and Knowledge Management

> The primary aim of the Financial Planning Association (FPA) is to be the community that fosters the value of financial planning and advances the financial planning profession. This jointly told story, focusing on how Café conversations evoke mutual contribution, illuminates how the FPA has used Café conversations as a core process to engage a growing number of its twenty-eight thousand members in evolving its community and making a difference to its future.

As part of our effort to create a greater sense of community among our members, the FPA board decided to hold our first World Café—which we called a Knowledge Café—at our annual conference beginning September 12, 2001, and to make postconference Café follow-up available online. When news of the attacks on New York and Washington came, we quickly decided to postpone the conference, along with our planned Knowledge Café. But we took one additional step that proved pivotal: we invited the chapters into a community conversation about what was happening as a result of the attacks.

We set up a conference call at 4:30 P.M. Pacific time on September 11. Given the chaos of that day and the short notice for the call, we thought perhaps a dozen folks or so would participate. Imagine our surprise when 125 local chapter officers called in! They each wanted to reach out to help others as best they could. We immediately launched the online forum. Within a day, people who had never participated in an online dialogue were actively contributing to the conversation. A web of heartfelt relationships and authentic dialogue began to evolve that laid the foundation for building our FPA community in a way we could never have anticipated.

Over the following months, we began to engage our membership in face-to-face Café conversations focusing on their needs and the future of both the association and the financial planning profession. In the early Cafés, we learned a *lot* about how to ensure that the association's past culture did not derail the process of mutual contribution. For example, after several rounds of great conversation and idea generation at individual Café tables, we would bring the full group back together for synthesis and someone would invariably say to the association leaders, "So, what are *you* going to do about this for us?" We have learned to frame the Café in the beginning in such a way that the members understand that they themselves play a significant role in both raising issues and contributing to solutions. There are ways in which the association leadership can exert helpful influence, but we are less and less seen as the only ones responsible for "fixing" things.

We've now hosted dozens of Cafés at events ranging from our large annual convention of 4,000 participants to smaller gatherings for specific constituencies, such as our retreat for 275 advanced financial planners and our broker-dealer conference with over 500 financial product and service providers, as well as with our own board and staff. We've discovered from both our successes and our mistakes how important it is to clarify the purpose of each Café and spend adequate time designing the process to fit the desired outcomes. *Why is this group gathering? What do they want the attendees to experience? Is it a homogeneous group who will all be exploring the same question, or are there multiple stakeholders who need to explore a common theme but with different questions?* These are key questions to address in order to ensure that the Café process is successful and that each member's contribution can be put to good use. There are so many little details to attend to in order for the Café process to serve well. There are also lots of creative ways to innovate through using the basic Café principles. This is sometimes a surprise for new hosts. The process itself is very simple, but there's an art to it as well.

We've learned that you also need to be open to changing things if the Café isn't going as planned. A lot of our most interesting Café innovations have resulted from in-the-moment conversations beginning with, "Hmmm, that didn't work as we planned. What can we do to get back to the purpose we're here for?" One of the hard questions is asking ourselves, "Is this not working, or is it just uncomfortable?" Sometimes the uncomfortable is necessary to break through to new thinking and new knowledge. There are times when we come up against a personal fear or perceived limit and one of us will say, well, let's try this or try that. There are no hard-and-fast rules.

One of the most interesting things to observe as we host our FPA Knowledge Cafés is the way our members have responded to the Café format and our invitation to be active contributors. Newcomers sometimes arrive with hesitancy and skepticism. Yet in most Café gatherings, people thoroughly enjoy this way of working, even when they realize that, contrary to their initial expectations, there is no outside "expert." Instead, they are being asked to actively contribute their *own* expertise and knowledge for the betterment of the FPA community.

The World Café approach has had big payoffs in both networking and mutual contribution. For example, a Knowledge Café in Denver with seventy-five local FPA members focused on the future of the members' business by asking: "What do you need to take your business to the next level?" In the initial Café round, the members identified where they were in their careers. Over the course of the four Café rounds, as people moved between tables, the folks closer to retirement met newer planners looking for mentors and even possible candidates to whom they could pass on their businesses. At the end of the Café, the newer planners stood up and waved to the ones in the later stages of their careers and vice versa. Thanks to the World Café, they could now literally "see" each other and share the ways they might contribute to each other's success at each stage of their careers.

Through Café dialogues such as this one, we are putting more responsibility into the hands of our members. In the Café approach, they are responsible for offering the questions and ideas they feel are important to the future. They are the ones who create their own network of personal relationships in a Café. As a result, we are beginning to see a much higher level of member contribution and ownership. In fact, at a recent leadership conference with 250 chapter leaders, we provided participants with Café hosting materials and offered coaching support to help them begin to convene Café conversations themselves to foster active member contributions to the FPA community at the local level.

This overall process of engagement reflects the cultural shift we are engaged in at FPA. Our Café conversations have evolved from the members and staff simply giving input to the board into a much more collaborative focus on how everyone can actively contribute to the future of the organization and the profession. Board, staff, and membership are now more closely aligned around our best hopes for the future.

We think our next big frontier is deepening the notion of citizenship among our members. By definition, a citizen is a co-creator and a contributor—not just a passenger along for the ride. To be honest, we are not there yet. It's challenging for us as leaders to ask our constituencies to engage in truly meaningful conversation. Are we really willing to listen to them? How will they know they've been heard? Are we ready to share leadership and honor their contributions once we've encouraged them? Will our governance and decision-making approaches shift? These questions—and more—inevitably arise in this type of large-scale cultural evolution. The answers are not always easy or clear, but we're becoming more and more willing to engage with these questions as we see the fruits that this growing and evolving process is bringing—to us personally as leaders, and to our members.

· · ·

During my years with Cesar Chavez and the farmworkers' movement, I worked from the Pink House, a Spartan bungalow in a run-down, working-class neighborhood alongside Route 99 in Delano, California. The Pink House was always buzzing with activity. People streamed in and out—young and old, Mexicans, Filipinos, African Americans, and Anglos. There were farmworkers arriving straight from the fields. There were students, clergy, and well-dressed urban types. Everyone came offering what they could to help. A key emphasis in the movement was on asking, "What small thing can each of us contribute to the larger effort?"

That was a key word—*contribute.* There were ways for everyone to give, to volunteer, to be of service. I remember Cesar Chavez saying to me, "If you go to someone's home and they offer you their food, they're giving something of themselves. Once people give, then their heart is involved. Giving—making your contribution—is what brings community alive."

Years later, I was working on a corporate project where we were experimenting with what might be possible if we were to look at the organization as a community. As we shifted our thinking toward the idea of building community, we found that honoring and encouraging each person's unique contribution seemed more compelling than focusing on either participation or empowerment— concepts still dear to the hearts of many organizational change specialists.

> We found that honoring and encouraging each person's unique contribution seemed more compelling than focusing on either participation or empowerment

The distinction is subtle but important. Contribution has a different tone and feeling than individual participation. Important as it is, the focus on individual participation can lead to an overemphasis on the *I: I'm* voicing my opinions. *I'm* speaking up. *I'm* participating. In contrast, focusing on contribution creates a *relationship* between the *I* and the *we.* Employees in the corporate community began to ask themselves, "What is my unique contribution to *our* larger mission as a company?"

The Role of Contribution in Café Settings

There was something about our early Café conversations that had the same vitality and active sense of connection to the larger whole that I had experienced in the farmworkers' movement and in our efforts to build the corporation as a community. A conversation with Patric Carlson helped shed light on what that special quality might be. Patric is a former student with the Kaos Pilots, an innovative educational program in Denmark that has used Café learning extensively. "The orientation of the Café is toward contribution," he explained. "It starts with somebody giving something. The purpose of the Café is not to criticize, but to contribute. You can't blame anybody for giving. In the Café you don't have to perform, only contribute. And when you contribute, the knowledge grows."

> The purpose of the Café is not to criticize, but to contribute

In that moment, sitting with Patric at our kitchen table I realized, "Aha, contribution! *That's* what's happening when a Café conversation is really cooking." I began to think of Café conversations as being similar to potluck dinners. Contributing your unique dish is what makes a potluck so interesting, fun, and nourishing. It's always a surprise. If you simply come to partake of the potluck meal without bringing your unique contribution to the party, how can the party happen? In a Café conversation, each member bringing his or her personal contribution to the collective potluck of ideas and insights enriches the intelligence of the larger whole.

The philosopher John Dewey, in a poignant reflection more than fifty years ago, pointed to the same belief in the power and potential of collaborative contribution that we now intentionally foster in Café conversations. In a 1937 speech, "Democracy as a Way of Life," Dewey commented, "While what we call intelligence can be distributed in unequal amounts, it is the democratic faith that it is sufficiently general so that each individual has something to contribute, whose value can be assessed only as it enters into the final, pooled intelligence constituted by the contributions of all" (Singer and Ammerman 1960, p. 276).

As Café hosts, we've become increasingly intentional about encouraging everyone's contribution as a core design and operating principle—whether that be the contribution of ideas and insights or of concrete support related to critical operations. For example, World Café etiquette, often shared at the beginning of a Café dialogue (see chapter 10), focuses on inviting everyone's contribution rather than simply assuring each person a voice or asking that everyone participate.

Frances Baldwin, who has hosted Cafés among executive women, comments on the use of the language of contribution in Café dialogues. "There's something about the word *contribution* that's proactive," she says. "When you're offered the opportunity to actively contribute, it suggests having more responsibility and opportunity to make a difference than when you are simply asked to participate." A Café member in a dialogue hosted by Karen Speerstra at Christ Church, a small parish in Vermont, affirms Frances's insight. "At first, I admit I felt stuck," she said, "but then I began realizing I was one of four people responsible for how interesting this was going to be."

Along with Café etiquette, we've introduced other intentional structures that encourage everyone's contribution. Bronwyn Horvath of the Saudi Aramco oil company, who has hosted Café conversations with multicultural groups as large as seven hundred, emphasizes both the intimate size of the Café groups and the intentional use of small, café-style tables as supporting structures for mutual contribution. "Even your most introverted person usually feels comfortable speaking and contributing at those little tables of four," she observes. In addition, Café hosts often introduce a talking piece—a stone or other object—which slows down the conversation and provides an intentional space for each person to make his or her unique contribution to what is emerging in the center of the table. (See description in chapter 10.)

Café conversations also provide the opportunity for members who are more reflective, or who learn visually, to contribute through attentive listening, drawing on the tablecloths, or making a verbal offering later in the conversation. Laura Peck, reflecting on her use of the World Café to help redesign a California school program, observes, "There are people who listen, there are people who see patterns, and there are people who think in images. The Café honors and includes the diversity of how people process information and synthesize it. The way it's structured creates a field where you don't have to be the quickest talker in order to contribute. You can draw connections to other people's pictures, or you can create your own pictures and images. There's also a change in the dynamics of how you contribute with different people as you move between tables. . . . So because of the way the Café operates there are lots of different strengths that people get to bring."

In reflecting on his first Café experience, hosted by Meg Wheatley at the Institute of Noetic Sciences, Hans Kuendig was surprised to discover that "you're encouraged to contribute, but you're not pushed to contribute in a verbal way. Café conversations are respectful of the fact that any one of us might just be in the listener/observer mode. That's very exciting to me because someone who is sitting back and observing often helps others see the deeper patterns. Maybe that person will offer only one or two sentences, but that could be a very powerful contribution—they can see the forest for the trees." The World Café principle of encouraging everyone's contribution and the variety of media through which this is encouraged brings a broader range of learning styles to the table. When people can offer their diverse gifts in a welcoming and supportive environment around questions they care about, actionable knowledge is a natural outcome.

Susan Skjei, in discussing a Café she hosted at Naropa University for the development of Naropa's Marpa Center for Business and Economics, shares that "when people feel they can contribute in a way that creates new knowledge, that's when they get excited. They can feel that creative energy building. Then they go, 'Oh great, I have resources to bring to this because it's my baby too. Suddenly I can see that this thing we're creating together has a life and I want it to grow!'"

In addition to its capacity for fostering knowledge creation, an emphasis on contribution also fosters a sense of community. As people begin to contribute together, create together, and learn together, a feeling of connection—to each other and to a larger whole—begins to emerge. Sherry Immediato, managing director of the Society for Organizational Learning (SoL), points to this relationship between contribution, co-creativity, and community building. In Cafés hosted at SoL's annual meetings, she's noticed that "through their mutual contributions during the Café conversations, our members live the experience of truly co-creating together as a whole community."

> An emphasis on contribution also fosters a sense of community

Where inclusion and community are already an integral part of the cultural fabric, the World Café taps into that spirit of mutual contribution. Alexander Schieffer, who, with Barbara Nussbaum, hosted a Leadership Café at a university in South Africa, was surprised to see how readily African students adopted the World Café process. He points out that "because of how closely African principles of group participation and inclusion in decision making are linked to the World Café approach, the students did not regard the World Café as 'one of those Western tools.'"

The Culture of Connection

A fascinating article by sociologist Philip Slater in the *Utne Reader*, "Connected We Stand," offers some insight into the larger social implications of the World Café's focus on contribution (2003). Slater identifies two cultures that are now becoming more visible throughout the world: the *culture of division* and the *culture of connection*. These two cultures can be found in national, ethnic, and other traditional demarcations. They are part of both the traditional left and right.

He points out that the culture of division, wherever it is found, is based on creating and maintaining clear boundaries between people and ideas. The perception of difference and otherness infuses the divider culture, whatever its persuasion. In the divider culture, it is clear who is "we" and who is "them." The connector culture, in contrast, is characterized by a focus on linking people, perspectives, and worldviews. People in this culture focus on discovering the common ground and collective wisdom that can be accessed by moving beyond the political, social, economic, and organizational categories that so often narrow our field of vision and action. They thrive on diversity. He adds that the rise of the connector culture is based in part on what we are learning about the connectedness of all life from research in the new sciences and living systems (see Capra, 1996; Waldrop, 1992; Wheatley, 1992; Zohar and Marshall, 1994). Slater points out that the question of whether we choose to live our lives as part of the culture of division or the culture of connection "is the defining social issue today and probably for decades to come" (2003, p. 63).

We believe that enlivening the culture of connection is one of the unique contributions of the World Café to our common future. Café conversations intentionally encourage members to offer their diverse contributions while simultaneously increasing the density of connections among people and ideas as the conversations iterate and self-amplify between rounds. By intentionally engaging the network dynamics of living systems with a focus on questions that matter, Café dialogues enrich the web of personal relationships and foster the experience of community across traditional boundaries. As the sense of

Enlivening the Culture of Connection

connectedness and community grows, committed action for the common good is often a natural outcome.

Yvon Bastien, of Sanofi-Synthelabo, Canada, has used the Café process extensively in this pharmaceutical company. He sees the World Café as "an act of creation of a community—both among our employees themselves and in relation to the larger society. People realized that we don't work for ourselves alone, but also for our patients and our communities. Actively connecting with the larger society was an outcome of our Café conversations."

As more people have the opportunity to experience the mutual contribution, connectedness, community, and commitment that the World Café fosters, it is my deepest hope that many more of us—whatever our national identities or political persuasions—will value and embrace the culture of connection as one path to a life-affirming future for us all.

Questions for Reflection

Think of a gathering you are planning and then ask yourself these questions:

How many interesting and practical approaches can you imagine that would invite and enable each person to contribute his or her best thinking?

How might you help people evolve from thinking of themselves simply as meeting participants to thinking of themselves as active contributors to something larger than themselves?

How might you personally encourage everyone's contribution in the next conversational gathering that you are planning to attend or host?

SEVEN

PRINCIPLE 5
Cross-Pollinate and Connect
Diverse Perspectives

Whenever knowledge connects with knowledge, new combinations spontaneously take place. Ideas spark ideas, which synthesize with each other until more knowledge results. It is completely natural. . . . Sharing knowledge means bringing people into the conversation.

—Verna Allee, *The Knowledge Evolution*

What if intelligence emerges
as the system connects to itself in
diverse and creative ways?

THE PEACE CAFÉ: UNIVERSITY OF VICTORIA LAW SCHOOL

As Told By

Claudia Chender

In the period leading up to the war in Iraq, law school students from the University of Victoria, British Columbia, Canada, became involved in an online discussion forum debating the merits of the war. The postings quickly became sharp and divisive, but students had no other forum for discussing these issues in the school. Claudia Chender, law student, tells the story of how a group of students used a Café dialogue to connect diverse perspectives across traditional boundaries.

My first day of law school was September 8, 2001. September 11 fell during our orientation week. I was profoundly disappointed that although we're an innovative law school with a very diverse student population, there were few places to gather as a community to talk about what had happened. We heard whispers about it in the hallways, and a few of us who were more invested in the news made some hasty phone calls to learn what was going on. I remember standing outside of the campus pub, staring through the glass door at the TV screen, waiting for the pub to open. There was no opportunity for our law school community to get together and talk about it. No one who said, "If you feel like you want to go and find out what's going on, or take a moment, go ahead." Other gatherings and organizing were happening on campus, but at the law school, that day, nothing.

This need for community led a group of us to start a Human Rights Collective on campus. One of our key missions was to provide an alternative setting for learning conversations that would encompass as much diversity as possible, both of viewpoints and participants. I helped take on the responsibility for designing our monthly public forums.

In the summer of 2002, I attended a strategic conversation seminar at the Shambhala Institute for Authentic Leadership, where I experienced the World Café firsthand. When I returned to school, my classmates and I decided to give the Café format a shot in our public forums.

We hosted our first World Café to mark the first anniversary of September 11. People really appreciated Café conversations as a way to find their voice on this type of critical contemporary issue. We hosted several other Cafés that school year, and they were all very successful, but the one I really want to tell you about happened during the run-up to the war in Iraq in the spring of 2003.

We have an online forum at school that had been dormant, but suddenly in the period before the war began people started posting their perspectives about what was happening. Within ten days there were more than two hundred posts. Very quickly, many of the posts began to degenerate into insults, and an intense positionality became apparent. In the middle of all this, I posted an offer to host a Café dialogue so that we could diffuse the situation and meet each other face-to-face. Although the idea initially met with hesitation, it eventually took hold. With the backing of the Human Rights Collective and the help of the Student Union president, among many others, we hosted our largest Café ever.

It was scheduled for a Friday afternoon, and about one-quarter of the law school student body showed up—an amazing response! We had participants from twenty to sixty years of age, including a military officer, an international human rights activist, Middle Eastern students (some with family in Iraq), retired persons, and students with family members who were foreign correspondents in the region. In addition to a diverse cross section of the student body, a number of professors were in attendance, which was very unusual for a student gathering. Many of the people were clearly skeptical about the process. And most came with very entrenched opinions.

I was really nervous about what would happen, and the hosting team we brought together was crucial in providing mutual support. Leading up to the Café, we invited anyone who was interested to come together and help design the event, including the question we would pose and the agreements we would honor. In our other Cafés we'd used reading material to stimulate the participants' thinking in advance. This time, we decided to issue a general invitation to everyone who was coming to let us know if they felt inspired to share a very brief personal story about how the current specter of war was affecting them. Two professors (an immigration scholar and a constitutional expert), the human rights activist, and the military officer volunteered.

The military officer had gotten a lot of hostile responses to his postings in the online forum. He was actually the one who inspired the context we later set for the Café. He said in one of his online postings, "Look, regardless of all of our opinions on this, what we can agree on is that ultimately what we want is peace. We just have different views on how to get there." When I heard that I thought, "*Aha!* If we come at it from that point of view, it's not like 'You're a warmonger who just wants to wreck everything whereas I love peace and therefore I have some kind of moral high ground.'" It broke down the moral rightness and wrongness people had around their views, and opened up the space for dialogue.

When people arrived, we set the tone. First, I asked people to remember a time when they'd had a really good conversation—a conversation that made them think, or made them curious, or caused a good laugh or cry. I asked them to share it with a neighbor if they liked—and then to share with the whole table what had helped that good conversation happen. Then I said that I hoped that in this Café dialogue we could move beyond the normal adversarial law school way of talking. As the hosting team we asked the group if they would be willing to honor a few simple agreements—confidentiality, making sure there was space for each person to speak, and trying to listen with respect. Students who had participated in our earlier Cafés took responsibility for sharing these agreements and modeling them at their tables. I also described basic World Café etiquette. Doing these things all helped set different expectations for the conversation.

Before we began, someone spoke up and suggested that we take a moment of silence, because people's lives were at stake in this whole conflict. When we did that a real shift occurred in the whole room. The silence, and the small bell that we used to mark the transitions during the Café, lent the event a natural gentleness and pacing, giving people a chance to take a breath and listen more deeply.

The military officer was the first of the four volunteers to share his story. He shared how hurt he'd been when people attacked him in the online forum, and told of a friend who'd been a U.N. peacekeeper and seen people dying and not been able to stop it. He had faith that if the military, like the U.N. peacekeepers, were used properly in the service of stopping bloodshed and producing peace, there could be real hope. He had tears in his eyes. All the other presentations were like that—very personal and real. We just naturally took a moment of silence after each person spoke to really take in what they were saying, whether or not we agreed with them—simply to appreciate their contribution. By the end, many people in the room were also in tears. A big discovery for me was how powerful the sharing of personal stories can be for deepening the conversation.

We began the first of the three Café rounds by continuing the personal storytelling. We asked people to share their responses to the question, "How have you been personally affected by this war?" Afterward everyone had a chance to continue by reflecting on these questions: "Where does peace come into your questions around this conflict? What does peace look like? Where is the law in the process of peace?" In the second round we focused on this: "What societal and individual ideals are reflected in your roads to or visions of peace?" In the third round we brought it back home by asking, "What can you do in your life to work toward peace and to create further dialogue and understanding?"

There is something in the World Café process that makes being self-righteous and positional really false. Perhaps it's that there's no space for high horses and grandstanding when you're sitting talking together with four people at a small table with flowers and candles. Could that be it? Or maybe it's the moving between tables that keeps you from getting stuck. There's a chink in the armor, and then as you move to another table and connect with new people and ideas you realize that it's happening with everyone else, too. It's almost like a collective sigh of relief happens in that second round of conversation, when people realize that everyone in that room is actually having a genuine conversation, too.

There were, of course, some challenges. At some tables people would start to raise their voices or not allow others to get a word in edgewise. . . . I mean, it wasn't perfect. But one friend told me she felt that overall there was a genuine softness that came into the room—a feminine quality to the gathering that she really appreciated, especially in the context of a conversation about war.

When we did the large-group sharing at the end, I'd hoped to hear many great insights about the nature of peace. Instead, most of the conversation focused on acknowledging how disrespectful people had been toward each other in the Web forum and how good it was to have an opportunity to come together in this new way. Our student body president, Justin, even wrote me a letter and said we should use Café conversations for all of our major student issues.

I was genuinely inspired by what came out of that Café. It shifted my ideas about how you take action, particularly in polarized situations. I think that shifting the way you *are* with others is a powerful way of taking action. In the end, the legacy of the Café was that the diverse people in that conversation had a much deeper understanding of and respect for why others felt the way they did. That day, as we talked together in the World Café, people began to come alive to how we want to communicate and live in community together, especially when we have contact over time as we do in the law school. It felt to me like we were really modeling the kind of world I want to live in. That's action, isn't it?

· · ·

Perspectives & Observations

From our very earliest café experiences, World Café hosts have commented on the excitement and energy that spirals upward as people and ideas move from one round of Café conversation to the next, developing new connections and relationships. At times it feels as if the evolving rounds of conversation are sparking new synapses in the larger mind of the group as a whole. In addition, as Claudia's story illustrates, when members are charged with carrying not only their own but also others' key ideas into the next conversation, it seems to unfreeze fixed positions and create a more open and exploratory climate for the emergence of new insight. Emmett Miller, M.D., who hosted a Café for diverse community members in Nevada City, California, describes how this happens: "Usually in a group we get into our roles. We polarize or focus on our little corner of the whole topic or question. But in a Café conversation, when you move to the next table, even if you come in with your own 'position,' you can't get stuck there because you're asked to bring your whole table's key ideas about the question to the next conversation. You're saying, 'This is what came up at our table,' and discovering how another group makes sense of it. Then, together with others, you're taking it to the next level of thinking. You're having intimate conversations with a few people at a time, but as you move around the room you suddenly feel like you're having a common conversation with ten, or twenty, or thirty, or a hundred people—the whole room! There is a kind of magic in having this unexpected experience together."

The Way Life Works

It wasn't until I was introduced to Mitchell Waldrop's spellbinding book *Complexity: The Emerging Science at the Edge of Order and Chaos* (1992) that I began to consider more deeply the way the World Café process engages new levels of collaborative thinking and supports the development of unexpected insights, particularly in large-group settings. Waldrop brings scientific ideas to life as he describes the adventures of the multidisciplinary scientists at the Santa Fe Institute who did groundbreaking work in the field of complex adaptive systems.

Our best Café experiences seem to embody the discoveries about learning and change that have been illuminated by a number of the Santa Fe Institute researchers, as well as by authors from other fields who have been exploring the dynamics of living systems and their implications for human organizations and communities (Alexander, 1979; Allee, 2002; Capra, 1996, 2002; Hegelson, 1995; McMaster, 1995; Stacey, 2001; Wheatley and Kellner-Rogers, 1996).

John Holland, one of the Santa Fe Institute pioneers chronicled in Waldrop's intellectual adventure story, focuses his research on fundamental processes of learning and adaptation from cells to social systems. He emphasizes that optimum learning and development occur in systems in which there is a rich web of interactions, along with an environment of novelty where new opportunities and spaces of possibility can be explored. Holland's discoveries are complemented by Doyne Farmer's theory that surprising new possibilities in any system emerge not solely from the individual parts or nodes of the network but rather from the *connections* among them.

> Optimum learning and development occur in systems in which there is a rich web of interactions

In *The Embodied Mind* (1992), cognitive scientists Varela, Thompson, and Rosch point to the intriguing possibility that the dynamics of new learning and development in the brain involve the same type of relational networks as in other living systems, all of which exhibit self-organizing and emergent properties when there are simple components that have dynamic connections to each other. They add that when an "attractor" is present to focus attention, even a simple network has rich self-organizing capacities.

And, as we shared in chapter 1, Francisco Varela and Humberto Maturana made the key insight that in human systems we "bring forth" the worlds we experience through our "social coupling through language in the network of conversations" in which we participate as part of the ongoing flow of our lives (1992, p. 232).

Taken together, I found these diverse insights very intriguing. Might we be able to engage these discoveries about the way life works to enable groups in conversation to access greater mutual intelligence? Could the World Café process enable us to make the role of networks of conversation in co-evolving our future together more visible and actionable? By intentionally inviting diverse participants and encouraging each person's unique contribution, we bring more variety to the "ecology" of conversation. As participants then move from table to table, carrying seed ideas from one Café table to another, they link and connect their thoughts, ideas, and questions, mirroring Maturana and Varela's iterating networks of conversation.

The introduction of powerful questions seems to function as an attractor that focuses attention in the "synapses of the group mind," thus activating the conversational network's self-organizing capacity. The new connections simultaneously create a space of novelty, such as John Holland described, in which new opportunities and spaces of possibility can be explored with the opportunity to "bring forth a world" together.

In addition, the World Café intentionally connects the parts to the whole by combining the intimacy of a four- to five-person dialogue with the cross-pollination of ideas that occurs through radiating rounds of conversation. By encouraging people to carry forward the essential or most exciting ideas from their earlier

A Living Network

Question as Attractor

Diverse Perspectives

Cross-Pollination

Emergence

conversations, the essence of the whole tends to become more visible as key ideas and insights travel rapidly through the conversational web. Café participants have described this experience as a "resonance of thought," "lighting up the system in the room," or "an accelerated evolutionary development of ideas."

The Emergence of Wholeness

We're intrigued by the lines of inquiry that the new sciences are revealing and the questions they raise for the theory and practice of dialogue. World Café conversations hold the promise of providing one intentional way not only to engage the fascinating network dynamics of emergence but also to access—in their best moments—the unique relationship between the individual and the collective that enables a special type of mutual intelligence to emerge, the type of intelligence that the physicist David Bohm saw as the great promise of dialogue for our common future. Bohm described the type of awareness and holistic intelligence

In each conversation, individual contributions are focused on questions that matter.

People build on one another's ideas—everyone contributes from their own perspective to create new understanding.

As people make new connections, sparks of insight begin to emerge that no one would have alone.

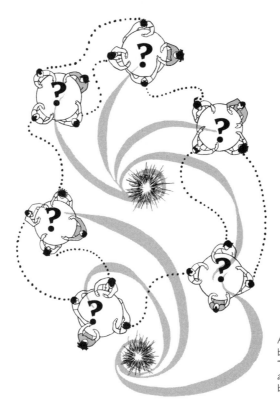

The whole continues to evolve into greater coherence—the discovery of collective intelligence.

As people share insights between tables, the "magic in the middle" and a sense of the whole become more accessible.

that emerges in authentic dialogue as occurring not only at the individual but simultaneously at the collective level. "It's a harmony of the individual and the collective," he said, "in which the whole constantly moves toward coherence" (1996, p. 27).

Our colleague, Tom Atlee (2003), describes the type of creative integration and higher-order thinking that occurs when diverse perspectives are engaged in dialogue as "co-intelligence." Co-intelligence is an apt description of the magic that World Café hosts and participants often describe when they reflect on their most productive Café dialogues. Mark Gerzon, president of the Mediators Foundation, provides a poignant example of "the magic." While hosting a very challenging dialogue between Israeli Arabs and Jews, he recalls that "at the crucial midpoint, when the group seemed at an impasse, I suggested that we shift into a World Café process over dinner. The question was: 'What story can you tell that will help the others at your table understand your perspective on the conflict in Israel between Jews and Palestinians?' A mathematics whiz who was participating in the meeting developed an innovative method for ensuring that everyone rotated to 100 percent different partners. The stories were incredibly powerful, and the experience of consecutive storytelling with different partners across the various fault lines fertilized the hard soil. The next morning, when the breakthrough happened, I knew in my heart that the fertilizing process of Café storytelling among all of the members was a key factor in making that breakthrough possible."

Kenoli Oleari, a community development specialist, describes the moment he had a similar experience in a large-group Café conversation. "Something clicked for me about the World Café," he says. "I developed a visceral sense of what could come from the 'voice in the center of the room.' As the conversations wove themselves through the Café, shifting between various configurations of people and chemistries of interaction, I could feel how a sense of the whole—of something more than the assembled individuals—could grow. I was a bit awestruck by this epiphany."

Carolyn Baldwin, the former assistant area superintendent of schools in Polk County, Florida, adds that the *(continued on p. 117)*

SUDDENLY, IT CRYSTALLIZED: THE FIELDING GRADUATE INSTITUTE

As Told By

Bo Gyllenpalm and Barclay Hudson

Bo Gyllenpalm, Ph.D., and Barclay Hudson, Ph.D., are founding core faculty members of the online master's program in organizational management and organizational development at the Fielding Graduate Institute. This is the story of the unexpected discovery, through a World Café dialogue, of a core strategic insight that shaped the future of their program.

We had been struggling for more than two years to explain how our program was different from other online programs, but we just couldn't find it. To help further our thinking, we invited our faculty counterparts at Golden Gate University, which offers online programs through both its traditional departments and its own "cybercampus," to participate in a joint World Café conversation focusing on the question: "What can we learn from each other regarding online delivery of courses?"

When our Golden Gate colleagues left, we continued with our own Reflection Café. During several Café rotations, we moved among tables, connecting our ideas about what was stimulated for us by listening to each other and to the perspectives of the Golden Gate participants in the earlier Café. Suddenly, toward the end of our large-group conversation, a core idea crystallized as if from nowhere: a clear vision of the unique contribution Fielding offers both in program purpose and design. Although it was one person who spoke it out, she voiced our collective understanding of the deep intellectual purpose that brought us together in the first place.

The idea was simple, but for us, profound. Maybe that's how insight is. It was the idea of "metalearning." Suddenly, we all saw our mutual commitment to what lies *behind and above* the online skills and professional content learning: the personal and collective self-awareness and critical thinking skills that carry over well beyond curricula and formal schooling to lifelong learning and life values. We are now using specific criteria related to metalearning in designing our curriculum and in sharing our program's unique identity with students and other institutions. The unexpected collective "surprise" that emerged that day from our faculty Café was a turning point in our strategic direction for the future.

• • •

networked structure of the World Café enables the group "to have multiple eyes focused from different parts of a system on the same set of questions. Those eyes are literally moving around the questions with all their perspectives." "The wholeness," she explains, "comes from being able to see the system from many different angles." Connecting people and perspectives around core questions in ways that make seeing the whole more likely is what World Café learning is all about.

Designing for Emergence

The World Café process is not simply an interesting vehicle for the random emergence of collective intelligence. Rather, it embodies a simple but intentional architecture of engagement—creating the conditions for the arrival of serendipitous discoveries, new patterns of meaning, and the "voice in the center of the room"—especially in groups that are larger than most traditional dialogue circles.

But how does this actually work? Our conversations with physicist Fritjof Capra have shed light on this question. He points out that there's a natural tension between designed structures, like formal organizational charts, and emergent structures, like the informal ways work actually gets done in most organizations. Designed structures have predetermined specifications; emergent structures often self-organize in ways that cannot be predicted. World Café conversations simultaneously engage both the intentional process of design and the natural process of emergence in order to encourage coherence without control.

All seven of the Café design principles work together as a design for emergence in order to increase the likelihood (but never the certainty) of enlivening a generative and focused field of inquiry, where the magic of collective understanding and insight can be revealed. *However, it is the creative cross-pollination of people and ideas* combined *with the disciplined use of questions as attractors that is perhaps the World Café's defining contribution to dialogic learning and collective intelligence.* David Marsing, former senior executive at Intel, points out that carefully framed questions operate as attractors around which the web of cross-pollinating ideas evolves to create coherent patterns of meaning.

In reflecting on how he believes this works, Marsing says, "You have the question sitting on the table as a starting point, but as people move in the rounds of dialogue, each person orients to the question in a different way. The connections grow fast with each rotation. You can imagine a three-dimensional network forming, both in depth and breadth, around the original question. I would call it the development of a higher fusion of thinking. It's more directional than random evolution. It is more like co-emergence."

Fritjof Capra adds that when a breakthrough or emergence to a new state of understanding occurs in this type of networked exchange, it "involves an experience of creativity that often feels like magic" (2002, p. 117). In fact, Danish World Café pioneer Finn Voldtofte describes the experience of new insight that emerges in the midst of many Café dialogues as "the magic in the middle."

Café Variations: Mixing People and Ideas Creatively

The variety of ways to increase the richness and intensity of interactions in a World Café conversation in order to reveal unexpected patterns of meaning is limited only by the goals of the gathering and your imagination as host. This is a domain where the art of hosting is especially important, and where your creativity as a host can make the difference between an interesting conversation and the magic of experiencing collective intelligence in action.

The most prominent and consistent World Café pattern for connecting people and ideas is for participants physically to move in iterative rounds of conversation that are usually twenty to thirty minutes in length, although rounds have gone significantly longer depending on the intention of the gathering, the time you have available, and the kind of information you are generating around the questions being explored. A round of conversation usually includes one host staying with his or her table to welcome guests and to offer them the highlights of their Café table's earlier conversation while the remaining members travel as "ambassadors of meaning" to other tables to share and gather collective insights. Sometimes one host stays for all rounds, particularly when you need the host to serve as a "content steward" for data that may be used in later action planning, or when you want members to travel during a second round and then return to their home table to deepen their exploration. At other times the host changes after the second round so that each host can also experience being a traveler. This can be especially useful when the goal is building a web of new relationships and fostering a sense of community.

Another possibility, developed by our colleague Finn Voldtofte, is for the host to stay at the table at the end of the first round, while the three or four others at the table "travel for the listening," each going to a new table for brief ten-minute learning visits. Their job is to collect one or two gems or seed ideas from the stories shared with them by the hosts of other conversations, and bring these key ideas back for consideration during the final round of synthesis at their home table.

Cross-Pollinating Ideas

Charles Savage, who first introduced us to the idea of cross-pollinating ideas as a part of the World Café pattern, uses a learning visit variation that he calls "dynamic teaming and knowledge networking" to help people develop new project ideas. After an initial round of conversation in tables of four, two members from Table 1, for example, will move to Table 2 and Table 3 while two will remain at Table 1 to share with their two new visitors the project ideas they've developed. The job of the visitors is to help enhance these ideas and offer additional creative possibilities. For the third round, people return to their home table, sharing the ways their original thinking has been enriched by their learning visits and considering the linkages between their ideas and those of other teams.

Another common variation can be used when there are multiple threads of inquiry on a common theme. In this scenario, each table tackles a separate, but related, question. For example, a Strategy Café that Verna Allee hosted for a computer firm in Australia had six overarching strategy questions. She divided the tables throughout the room into sectors, with tables in each sector addressing one of the big questions. Table hosts stayed as the "question stewards," while others in the group rotated to tables in other sectors to learn about and make contributions to additional parts of the strategy puzzle that interested them. They then returned to their home table to share the relevance of what they'd learned to the question they began with. Finally, all table stewards came together to share their tables' collective discoveries in relation to the strategy as a whole.

This approach can also be used when people generate their own questions on the topic being explored. In the first round, each table generates its own core question that is then posted on the table. In subsequent rounds, while one question steward stays, the other people move to other tables to explore the questions raised by their colleagues. These question stewards are not facilitators in the traditional sense but simply hosts, who welcome arriving members and share the essence of the evolving conversation as they understand it so all can continue to contribute their perspectives to what's emerging.

Marimba Giam, a Café host in Singapore, has experimented with creative ways to cross-pollinate ideas with teachers and others in a variety of settings. She shares this: "One might think that people would be confused with the movement, and the number of connections involved. On the contrary, as people move from table to table sharing the ideas that really struck them, the common themes or key insights that have practical applications tend to emerge naturally."

Peter Senge of MIT adds that he believes the commonality and patterns of meaning that can emerge in a World Café conversation by intentionally cross-pollinating perspectives and moving people between rounds of conversation is "not the commonality of homogeneity. In fact, it's virtually the opposite. The commonality emerges from internalizing a richer and richer diversity and then recognizing this richer and richer web that connects."

Sometimes it's not the people but the ideas that move. For example, at an Institute of Noetic Sciences conference, the room was too crowded to have Café tables or to have people rotate between groups. People sat in small conversational clusters. In that instance, each participant was given a card on which to write what he or she considered to be an essential idea or key insight from the first round of conversation. Each person then stood and faced outward from their cluster and exchanged the cards as an idea gift with a person from another group. Each small group continued by reading the ideas they'd received as gifts from members of other clusters, using the new connections these suggested for their ongoing dialogue. Members can also use cards or large sticky notes to synthesize core questions or key insights from the table as a whole, which can be sent forward from one table or conversation cluster to another to seed the inquiry as the conversation progresses.

We're continuing to discover new ways to connect diverse perspectives as Café hosts around the world experiment with myriad variations. The examples abound. A Café on the future of the Danish Constitution was hosted with participants in canoes on a lake. On a learning journey that explored Mexico's social development, members moved periodically between minivans at rest stops, sharing their emerging perspectives as they continued to travel. One innovative host had members move between Café groups located at nature's "tables," each of which was a large redwood tree. Another used different colored mugs to facilitate the mixing and moving of people from different functional areas in a single business unit. The colored mugs enabled a "max-mix" for creative exchange, and at the same time, allowed people from the same area to find each other easily during the action planning phases of the Café dialogue. Experiments like these are described regularly at the World Café Web site. We'd welcome your experiences as well.

Questions for Reflection

Take a moment to reflect on a time when diverse perspectives helped shed new light on a challenging situation. What were the conditions that enabled that diversity of thought to make its contribution?

Consider an upcoming meeting on an issue or concern that you care about. What diverse perspectives and voices could contribute to a more creative exploration of that question? How can you help those perspectives be included?

What are the various ways you might encourage greater cross-pollination of ideas during the meeting in order to gain greater collective insight?

EIGHT

PRINCIPLE 6

Listen Together for Patterns, Insights, and Deeper Questions

We listened, and through that listening a dynamic of its own developed. The end result . . . was a group spirit and group coherence stronger than any I have ever known, yet it was a "dance with many dancers," a group of individuals who had found an emergent reality drawing our differences into a meaningful whole.

—Danah Zohar and Ian Marshall, *The Quantum Society*

What if listening together
reveals a deeper intelligence?

WHAT'S IN THE MIDDLE OF THE TABLE?
SCANDINAVIAN SUSTAINABILITY FORUM

As Told By
Christina Carlmark

Christina Carlmark, former vice president of environmental affairs at the Swedish telecom corporation, Telia, presently serves as the marketing director at the merged Swedish/Finnish telecom, TeliaSonora. This is the story of a unique multi-stakeholder Café on the role of the infocom industry in creating sustainable futures—one that nurtured the capacity for listening together in new ways.

In my previous position as vice president of environmental affairs at the largest telecommunications company in Scandinavia, I had the opportunity to explore the role of the information technology and communication (infocom) sector in creating a sustainable future. The position was newly created, and I was happy to take on this challenge since I have been passionate about environmental and sustainability questions for most of my life.

Information and communication services play a key role in everyday life. For example, videoconferencing and other virtual meeting tools enable people to work together across long distances without requiring travel and the use of nonrenewable fuels. I felt that we could better harness the power of this sector to benefit the environment if we were able to create open dialogue in a global community of key stakeholders, so I decided to sponsor a strategic dialogue on the topic using a World Café approach.

In the first phase, we brought together global thought leaders who had an interest in infocom and a sustainable future. We invited out-of-the-box thinkers, environmentalists, scientists, academics, futurists, infocom specialists, young people, politicians, and corporate representatives. Their job at what we called the Focus Search Café was to help discover the areas of inquiry that would be critical for key stakeholders to explore in the next four to eight years. At this Café, the thought leaders came to a consensus that a key issue was to understand how the infocom services industry might help or hinder the development of a more sustainable future in relation to transportation. For example, trucking companies, by investing in computerized ordering and dispatching systems, can save huge amounts of mileage.

An internal/external research group then embarked on a five-month period of discovery on the critical questions related to the topic of infocom and transportation. Their synthesis, which they called the "World Insighters Report," posed key dilemmas and decision points for the next phase of the conversation. We called this second phase the Roundtable Dialogue, and we decided to hold it too in a Café format.

We took a big risk in the Roundtable Café. We really didn't know what would happen! We invited influential people from important cross-sector groups with very divergent perspectives: senior leaders from major transportation companies including DHL, UPS, and the Swedish railroads; CEOs from companies that use their transport services; key players from infocom companies who are developing transportation technologies; a member of the European Parliament; a key leader from Greenpeace; and the head of the traffic division of a large Swedish city.

As you can imagine, these are not people who often, if ever, sit down to think together. If they do, it may be in a heated negotiation, *not* a Café dialogue! These power players are used to meetings that are conducted as very formal discussions, usually around big conference tables, with structured agendas and tight control to make sure that nothing goes wrong.

As a sponsor of this event, I was somewhat concerned about what would happen when the people came to the meeting. We needed a natural way for people to really listen to each other's viewpoints and not get polarized. The Café environment helped set the tone. When people came in the door, some were a bit surprised by the friendly atmosphere and the small tables, but they joined in, got seated, and actually seemed curious to see what would happen next.

Then came our next innovation. Right in the beginning, after making introductions, we had a young, newly married woman in her twenties share her thoughts with the group. She talked about wanting to raise a family. She said she hoped that this group, who had the power to change the direction we were headed, could find ideas together that could help— not only for today but for future generations, including their own children and grandchildren. There was a very pensive atmosphere in the room when she finished sharing her story.

We then did something even more daring, but that worked amazingly well. We didn't do any teaching about dialogue. Instead, we simply introduced a "dialogue stone" as a way to encourage better listening and avoid arguments and defensive positions. We brought in beautiful stones that were thousands of years old from a pebble beach on an island not far from the outskirts of Stockholm. They symbolized our land and the history of the natural world. We placed one stone in the middle of each table, along with a small vase of fresh flowers and colored pens.

We then shared the basic idea behind the dialogue stones. We said that usually in meetings like this the discussion speeds up so fast that people have a hard time listening because they want to make sure their own ideas get heard. This is especially true when the participants come from very different camps. We asked the group to experiment with the dialogue stone as a practical tool for listening together and finding what was in the middle of the table. Only the person holding the stone would speak. As long as he or she held the stone, others would simply listen without interrupting. This would allow the individual who was holding the stone to stop and take a breath while thinking about what she really wanted to say instead of having to keep babbling so someone else wouldn't cut in while she finished her thought.

We also asked people to imagine themselves asking their inner judge to step aside and take a rest period, just for a little while, from determining whether someone else was right or wrong. The goal at this stage was just to listen together to see how everyone viewed the topic and what contribution each perspective could bring. We encouraged people to speak in the first person, for themselves, and not with their formal organizational hat on—another departure from traditional meetings. We also asked the members if they would be willing to hold off presenting solutions, because this initial phase was just meant to find the deeper themes and questions and not the answers.

After this short introduction, participants began the first round of the Café. Each member took the stone and shared the key insights, thoughts, or deeper questions that were triggered for them by the World Insighters Report. The task of the other three participants at each Café table was simply to listen, but in a special way. We asked them to keep track of the ideas that emerged, and to draw in the middle of the tablecloth any interesting connections they could see among the ideas. When all had shared their first ideas and thoughts, the stone was placed back in the middle of the table. Anyone could then pick up the stone and add any comments or thoughts that had bubbled up while they were listening to their colleagues.

Using the dialogue stones made a *big* difference, even though some people, of course, still had the urge to just jump in with their own solutions. We found out, however, that people basically already know how to listen well when they are really interested in what's going on. We just helped slow things down and focus their attention on what to listen for. Instead of standing opposite each other they were, in a way, standing next to each other, all looking and listening in the same direction—the center.

In the second Café round, we added something new. We asked everyone to begin *listening together as a group* for the deeper assumptions and patterns of meaning underlying their varied perspectives and write them on the tablecloth as well. People were still using the discipline of the dialogue stone. We encouraged them to ask questions to help each other clarify the different as well as common assumptions or mindsets.

We changed tables again and started the third round of Café dialogue, continuing to see what was being revealed in the center of each table. By this time people were really into it. Each time we asked them to listen together for the next deeper layer of understanding they actually seemed to become even more interested in each other's ideas and in the issues. That was a big surprise to me.

When the third round was over, we opened the conversation to the whole group to pool their collective knowledge and insights. We had hired a professional graphics specialist to create a large wall mural of people's reflections—which was like having a big tablecloth right in front of the whole group. We could see the themes, the assumptions, the connections between ideas, and the *aha's* coming out on the mural right in front of us. There was a special energy in the room that afternoon—very different than when everyone first entered with their individual mindsets. The participants were excited at this stage because they'd found something together that wasn't there when they started, or maybe it was there all the time but they just had not had common ways to see it together before.

When we had the checkout at the end, people said that this was the first time they had sat down with others who might be considered competitors—or even opponents—and had been able to arrive at a better understanding of each other's deeper beliefs. They found that they had more in common than they had originally thought and realized that none of them alone had the power to push the others into accepting their own solutions.

I believe this way of having strategic conversations may make it easier to get coordinated action, but it's not in the same way we think about it most of the time, with voting and long lists of action steps. Much of the time nothing comes out of those lists anyway. Instead, with the special Café way of talking and listening together, people become interested in going back into their own situations with their new understandings to make positive things happen, in large part because of the new personal relationships they've built with each other. People with very different perspectives and experience begin to see one another's common humanity. And that's a good outcome, whatever final decisions get implemented.

• • •

There's a word I love in Spanish—*el meollo* (pronounced el may-oy-yo). *El meollo* means the essential nature or fundamental substance of a thing. It also means understanding. As World Café hosts, we're searching for ways to access the human capacity to discover *el meollo*—not alone, but through weaving connected strands of meaning throughout the entire conversation, even when that includes dozens or hundreds of people. Listening together for patterns, insights, and deeper questions—both at an individual Café table and between tables as the conversations radiate outward—enables us to develop this collective capacity to sense the heart of the matter.

Listening *To,* Listening *With,* and Listening *For*

It was Anne Dosher, the elder, mentor, and "guardian of the soul" of the World Café, who first introduced us to the special kind of collaborative listening that has become a hallmark of World Café conversations. A former member of the core faculty and the board of trustees of the California School of Professional Psychology,

Getting to the
Heart of the Matter

Anne has spent a lifetime thinking about how we can discover innovative solutions to complex issues in communities and other collective settings.

In one of our many conversations during the early days of the World Café, Anne spoke to us about the importance of what she calls "gathered attention"—the capacity both at the individual and the collective level to engage in the type of listening that enables new patterns of meaning and innovative possibilities to be called forth in conversational exchange. Anne drew upon insights from the late theologian and author Nelle Morton (1985), who spoke of the special quality of listening to another person with one's full attention as being a creative force that can evoke ideas that actually didn't exist until the other was "heard into speech."

But gathered attention doesn't stop here. At the collective level, it moves beyond listening to other people speaking, and simultaneously engages our ability to listen with each other for connections and patterns of meaning as well as listen for new insights or deeper questions that emerge *in the space between* different perspectives. In fact, the word *intelligence* originally comes from the Latin *inter* and *legere,* which means "to gather understanding in between." That's what we mean in Café settings when we talk about the magic in the middle. Gathered attention involves a more holistic type of listening, one that pays attention to the intelligence or deeper meaning that is moving among us *collectively.* It focuses on the cluster of related meanings that emerge both within and between conversations, thus focusing the attention of the group in a different way.

Hans Kuendig, in describing his first Café, tries to capture what this type of listening feels like in real time: "You're in this exciting round of conversation, and you're hearing more and more of the threads coming out, and you're wanting to just jump in more, but everybody's also listening and thinking at the same time. Everyone helps to uncover the patterns. That's part of the energy that's created." In one of our seminars on strategic conversation, another Café member shared his own vivid description of

Listening Together

the interplay between the individual and the group that results from this type of shared listening. "It's not that it's common thinking or groupthink," he explained, "and it's not condensing. It's both individual and group learning in a larger context of collective relatedness of thought."

Relating to the Larger Whole

One of the dilemmas that most of us experience when coming to dialogue for the first time is the difficulty of moving away from our existing judgments and personal positions. Yet we've discovered that something quite unexpected happens in World Café conversations when we ask everyone in the room to become ambassadors of meaning—listening together and carrying forward the essential ideas or *aha* insights into progressive rounds of conversation. Rigid positions seem to drop away as people listen together in order to discover creative connections among the multiple perspectives that others contribute. That's when the "magic" often reveals itself in Café dialogues.

How does this work? Web site designer Amy Lenzo shares a beautiful image that came to her after a large World Café with several hundred people who were listening together for the deeper questions in their midst: "It was like making and refining clay pottery together. The pot wasn't being shaped by an individual's questions anymore. It became the group's questions that were being refined by the process of each individual speaking. Their essential form was being smoothed, refined, and made clearer by each other's words. The essence was being drawn out."

This type of gathered attention not only reveals the essence of the whole but can also reveal its broad expanse, as Claudia Chender, law student from British Columbia, points out. "There's something about the World Café that's hard to articulate," she explains. "It's like you come upon a landscape and you are standing on a hilltop with this wide vista spread out below you. You can't travel all of it, but you get a sense of and an appreciation for the whole." As Café hosts, we're continuing to discover new ways

> Rigid positions seem to drop away as people listen together in order to discover creative connections

to nurture that type of holistic appreciation. And what we have discovered is that using visual language may be one of the keys.

Visual Language, Visual Listening

In our conversation about hospitable space in chapter 4, I shared with you my excitement when we were first introduced to the discoveries of Michael Schrage, a visiting scholar at MIT's media lab, on the importance of informal environments for collaborative learning. However, just as important for understanding how Café conversations work is Schrage's reflection that shared visual spaces—from paper napkins in restaurants to computer whiteboards and other visual meeting tools—are critical elements for collaboration and co-creativity. According to Schrage, for real collaboration to flourish "the images, maps, and perceptions bouncing around in people's brains must be given a form that other people's images, maps, and perceptions can shape, alter, or otherwise add value to. . . . *It takes shared space to create shared understanding*" (1990, p. 99; italics in original).

Schrage's image of networks of shared spaces serving as a "conceptual and technical playground for the collaborators" clarified what World Café hosts have witnessed in Café conversations (1990, p. 156). The act of writing, drawing, and playing on the tablecloths at multiple Café tables seems be one creative example of the kind of lively network of shared spaces that Schrage is talking about. Could the simple process of intentionally engaging in shared listening, and then connecting the evolving ideas from multiple conversations visually on the Café tablecloths, be key factors in the kind of large-scale collaborative learning that we see in Café dialogues at their best?

I was intrigued and wanted to learn more. I invited Jennifer Hammond Landau and Susan Kelly, two pioneers in graphic recording who have participated in at least a hundred Cafés collectively, to share their experience of the relationship between shared space, visual language, and a group's capacity to listen together for collaborative insight. The conversation that follows is a synthesis of our musings together.

Juanita: I want us to explore the place where shared listening, collaborative learning, and innovation happen—where people begin to see in new ways, and where the connections and the knowledge base expand.

Jennifer: One thing occurs to me. It's important to listen for the connections without assuming that you know what they are. There's a fine line between the two. You can listen for connections and capture ideas in multiple ways and at different levels of scale—drawing on a cocktail napkin, on a Café tablecloth, on a billboard-sized wall, and electronically as well. What's important is that you're all looking at the same thing together and making the connections.

Juanita: What helps listening together to happen in the first place?

Susan: Color helps. Color actually connects people to a deeper reality. Black-and-white is abstract and linear is abstract. But the world exists in color, and it's not linear. So having color in the center of the table, whether it's the flowers or the colored pens, helps you come closer to your real world, together. And color opens up a wider range of expression.

Jennifer: What I've seen is that having the colored pens in the center gives a "visual voice" to those present—especially those who tend to be quieter in groups. The pens are a powerful reminder that "my voice can be seen and heard if I write on the tablecloth." Humans tend to think in symbols and images, so being able to see your own and others' scribbles and pictures can also help bring forth ideas that you're not even conscious of. That might be called visual listening.

Juanita: Maybe one of the interesting things about finding the magic in the middle has to do with people literally "noting" their voice by whatever scribbles, notes, or pictures they're putting on the tablecloth.

Making
Conversation
Visible

Susan: That relates directly to the size of the group at the Café tables. Once you get past four or five at a table, the ideas don't get placed into the center as easily. You might be doodling in your corner, but you're not talking and listening together with others focused on the ideas in the middle of the table.

Juanita: Let's imagine people have done whatever listening and connecting they can at their individual tables. Three new people have just arrived at my table. There are little diagrams in the center of the tablecloth, a few key words, and a bold colorful figure that somebody drew. As the host, I'm sharing what I understand from listening to the conversation during the first round and how that is reflected in the drawings on my tablecloth. Then what happens?

Susan: Everybody who comes to your table says, "It's amazing, because that's some of what we were talking about over there, and over there, and over there, too."

Jennifer: I always love that.

Susan: The conversation seems to build because all of the tables have been working with other pieces of the whole puzzle simultaneously. You begin to sense that you're part of a bigger whole—in real time. You see how it happens, how it works, how you deepen it by interchanging and listening to multiple perspectives around the same topic.

Jennifer: It's like concentric rings. The middle starts to expand, and paradoxically, at the same time, it gets more focused. People begin naming patterns and themes.

Susan: People get excited because things are getting illuminated, especially when they really care about the question or if they are interdependent in some way.

Juanita: What about people pressing their own agendas? Are there times when people have not contributed or not felt heard, and then they work their own individual agendas in the larger group?

Jennifer: That seems to happen less in Café settings than in other groups. By the time you get to the mural-size tablecloth or some other method through which the sense of the whole group is being reflected, most everyone has had multiple opportunities to be listened to and other people have built on or carried their ideas into other conversations. So they're not generally pressing their own individual agendas. That's quite rare.

Juanita: Now, let's imagine we're at the stage of hosting the conversation of the whole in a town meeting style. Instead of traditional report-backs, we're asking people to link and connect their ideas at the level of the whole room from their listening together in the earlier rounds.

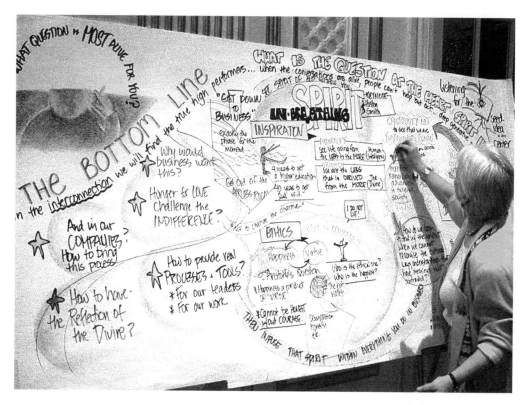

Jennifer: If innovation is going to happen in the whole group, this is the place where it sparks. Sometimes an image or symbol that appeared at one of the tables just pops out into the whole-group conversation and crystallizes the whole thing.

Susan: Then the group can acknowledge and bless their collective insight.

Juanita: That's a wonderful observation. Maybe through all this focused messiness and searching together—the visual listening that appears in the images, the symbols, and shared space of the table-cloths—people begin to sense what's really central, not only in terms of intellectual content but also discovering together the heart of what the community really cares about.

Jennifer: The magic is experiencing our own and other people's humanity around whatever the content is. That's what the World Café is about for me, and what having shared space and shared listening allows us to discover.

Reflection: A Different Type of Listening

Reflection is a core practice in Café conversations. The combination of gathered attention and collective reflection on what's at the heart of the matter—*el meollo*—is what enables the group to *listen to and for the whole* in order to sense patterns, themes, and deeper questions. Discovering the optimum balance between dynamic engagement and mutual reflection is one of our key learning edges as World Café hosts. Excitement builds as people move between tables, but depth can be lost if Café members aren't encouraged to slow down intentionally in order to reflect on their discoveries.

As the host, you can encourage more reflective listening and thoughtful consideration of ideas during the conversation by introducing a talking piece, like the dialogue stone that Christina Carlmark introduced to the Café participants in her opening story. In addition, many hosts use musical interludes or poetry related to the topic, coupled with individual journaling at appropriate times, to create a reflective tone. Samantha Tan of Singapore points out that the use of music and poetry has the unique capacity to "shift people into a different state . . . opening a space for true reflection." Using these approaches, or simply asking members to take a couple of minutes of quiet time to make notes on cards about what struck them in the conversation, all serve as powerful preludes to collective reflection on learnings, insights, and deeper questions, either toward the end of a round of conversation or prior to the large-group sharing of discoveries.

You may find that the simple act of encouraging moments of silent reflection—even without music or other introduction—can yield insights beyond your (or others') imagination. Silence provides an easily available yet seldom used opportunity to listen for and access the wisdom that often lies just beneath the surface of our mutual deliberations. I sometimes think of silence as a way to access a deep well in the center of the group. Silence is the pulley, similar to the rope in a well, that enables members to draw a deeper wisdom up from the common well of mutual exploration and experience. Jenni Dunn of Australia, who experienced her first

Ripples of Silence

World Café at a Systems Thinking Conference, found that the periodic moments of silent reflection "enabled something dramatically different to happen. It [the silence] assisted the group by helping us have the space to understand what was happening and not letting it rush away in the immediacy of conversation at the table."

As a host, you can evoke deeper insights by simply asking members to take a couple of minutes of silence to consider or make a few notes about what key insight, idea, or discovery they are taking from the conversation so far. Other reflection questions include these:

▸ *What did you most appreciate about this conversation?*

▸ *What's had real meaning for you from what you've heard? What surprised you? What challenged you?*

▸ *What's missing from the picture so far? What is it we're not seeing? What do we need more clarity about?*

▸ *If there was one thing that hasn't yet been explored but is necessary in order to reach a deeper level of understanding/clarity, what would that be?*

Additional reflection questions for focusing collective attention, finding deeper insight, and creating forward movement are included in chapter 10, "Guiding the Café Process." If you're hosting a conversation in a natural environment, you can also encourage people to spend some time alone outside to reflect on what has emerged in the conversation, prior to continuing their exploration.

We are discovering that thinking together in conversation requires spaces between the notes in order to hear the music of collective wisdom. As a conversation host, give yourself permission to experiment with multiple approaches to creating the space for reflection—for listening individually and collectively to the deeper currents beneath the surface. Time for refection is a gift that we too rarely give ourselves in the frenetic life of most organizations and communities. Yet World Café and other dialogue hosts are finding that creating time for reflection is essential to accessing the often surprising strategic insights that lie at the heart of effective action.

Think of a time when you felt heard and listened to. What were the conditions that enabled that to happen?

Consider an upcoming conversation that you will be part of hosting. How might you support the group not only in listening to one another but also in listening with one another for patterns, insights, or deeper questions?

What questions for reflection might you offer to deepen mutual inquiry and discovery in an upcoming conversation that's important to you? How and when might these be introduced?

In what ways might visual listening approaches (that is, graphic recording, drawing or sketching ideas together, or other visual displays) improve the quality of an upcoming conversation that you are hosting?

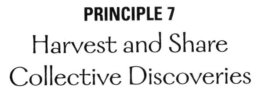

NINE

PRINCIPLE 7

Harvest and Share Collective Discoveries

There's another aspect to fostering mutual intelligence . . . what I call creating the "collective mindscreen." How can we help people sense the whole, together? Harvesting and sharing key ideas and insights is like putting up tent poles. It's what's in the circle revealed by putting up those poles, not any of the individual poles, where the meaning of the conversation as a whole lies.

—Finn Voldtofte, BDO ScanFutura

What if the harvest
provides nourishment for further
exploration and action?

HARVESTING AND PLANTING SEEDS OF CHANGE:
UNIVERSITY OF TEXAS AT SAN ANTONIO, EXECUTIVE MBA PROGRAM

As Told By
Robert H. Lengel

Bob Lengel, Ph.D., is the associate dean for executive education and director of the Center for Professional Excellence at the University of Texas, San Antonio (UTSA), College of Business. Through the center he has been a pioneer in introducing strategic conversation and World Café learning to organizational leaders as a way to foster creativity, synergy, and strategic innovation. This story, about a project done by a recent executive MBA (EMBA) class, demonstrates how insights from one Café can be harvested and used to seed future Cafés, creating an ongoing exploration that breaks down organizational barriers and initiates cultural change.

Convening productive conversations is a fundamental leadership skill in a knowledge economy. Because of this, the EMBA program at UTSA includes a focus on developing the capacities to host effective strategic conversations—conversations that catalyze deep learning and forward movement on issues of importance to leaders. We begin by teaching the basic structure and principles of World Café conversations and other dialogue approaches, as well as Appreciative Inquiry and strategic futuring. But to really understand their power to create change and move learning forward, you have to practice. The particular story I'd like to relate is about how one executive MBA class worked with the student affairs organization at UTSA as their practice field.

UTSA is one of the fastest-growing universities in the country. Over my twenty-year tenure, enrollment has grown from about five thousand students to twenty-five thousand. During this time we have also transformed from primarily an undergraduate school to a full-service research institution offering an expansive array of graduate programs. Under the inspired leadership of Dr. Rosalie Ambrosino, our student affairs organization has made significant progress in addressing student service issues related to our growth and changing academic mission.

Our EMBA class took on the challenge of helping Dr. Ambrosino and her organization support both graduate and undergraduate student services by designing and hosting a series of strategic conversations with cross sections of this four-hundred-person organization. The student affairs organization has six reporting units, so our class divided into six Café study teams, one team per unit. The initial objective was for each of the teams to do "temperature checks" in their unit by asking the following questions: "What is going on now in this organization? What are the key issues, challenges, concerns, and core questions?"

The study teams used a variety of World Café approaches. We wanted to give them that freedom so they could come back and compare Café approaches and talk about what they'd learned. I'll give you one example of an innovative approach used by one of the teams to harvest and share their Café discoveries.

The team wanted to uncover what they called "the state of the conversation" in their assigned unit. After opening the conversation with personal introductions in a large dialogue circle, the team invited the student affairs folks to join Café tables.

At each table the team gave participants four different piles of colored paper. They asked the members to first take the yellow paper and write one phrase or sentence per sheet that reflected what people were saying publicly during meetings in their unit. They collected the yellow sheets in a manner that preserved the anonymity of the author. Then they asked the group to take the blue paper and write on it what people were saying in the restroom after the meeting, or at lunch when they were with friends. What was that conversation like? The blue papers were then collected in a similar manner. On the pink sheets, participants

UTSA Monster Sticky Wall

were asked to write what they thought other people in the university were saying about student affairs. Finally, the green sheets captured the answers to the question, "What are you not saying that you wish you could?"

From these sheets, the Café team created a monster sticky wall with the colors clustered together from all the tables . . . all the yellows, greens, pinks, and blues. The idea was to harvest the group's collective thinking and make their ideas visible so people could see new connections. They asked the group to take a gallery walk and notice the common themes and unique perspectives that stood out.

Then the student affairs folks returned to their next round of Café conversations around this question: "What questions should we ask you in order to understand what all this is telling us about your organization?" Seeing all their previous thinking harvested and organized on the wall enabled the group to identify the most relevant questions for their situation in student affairs. It was a stimulating experience for the participants to have to think about their own questions as opposed to answers. The questions also triggered thoughtful storytelling about their current reality. And everyone had a lot of fun!

Once all six EMBA teams had finished their Temperature Check Cafés in the individual student affairs units, we came back together. Each team shared their Café design, the insights and questions they harvested, a synthesis of their findings about their unit, and their reflections about their own experience. To pull it all together, we held a fairly long Integration Café and had a graphic recorder there to harvest their collective learnings. From the Integration Café, the students discovered, after much deliberation, that what was needed next was not more bits and pieces of information from the individual units. Rather, in order to illuminate the larger picture it was going to be important to work in the space *between* the units.

So, in the second semester, we introduced the concept of the Future Search conference. Future Search is a structured step-by-step approach that brings diverse stakeholders throughout a system together to understand their past and present, seek common ground, search for innovative strategies, and build mutual commitment to their shared future (Weisbord and Janoff, 2000). We got permission to take two days with about sixty people from student affairs who had been carefully selected to represent the diversity of voices from all of the individual organizational units. Our goal here was to have a *whole-system* conversation, as opposed to a *parts* conversation. The Future Search conference made it possible to have the organization talk together and see their conversation of the whole made visible on the walls in the form of graphics and stickies, which we could then harvest and use for the next steps.

I think when people can see graphically what they hold in common, they can begin to connect the dots. What emerged from the Future Search event was a common sense of what they, as a whole, wanted student affairs to be in the future. One could say that they discovered their "commons sense." The student affairs group generated six initiative thrusts—areas where they wanted to act together—and we agreed to develop the four highest priority ones in subsequent Action Cafés. These Action Cafés would involve members from all of student affairs, not just the people who attended the two-day Future Search event.

As you can see, World Café conversations and Future Search are very compatible modes of working. So the next step was to figure out how to share the insights from the Future Search conference in a way that enabled those who hadn't been there to actively participate in the upcoming Action Cafés. Fortunately, to take on this challenge the EMBA class had assigned its most creative and technologically savvy class members to a special Future Search documentation team. This team had carefully planned in advance how to harvest the discoveries from the Future Search conference so the highlights could be shared with others who hadn't been there. In addition to graphic illustrations, the documentation team made audio and video recordings of all open conversations and kept journals capturing their impressions. From this material, the team developed a creative, multimedia synthesis in the form of a DVD that other EMBA teams could use as they delivered two follow-up briefings that were open to all of student affairs. At the conclusion of each briefing, we posted sign-up sheets, inviting anyone who was interested to participate in one or more of the upcoming student affairs Action Cafés.

For the Action Cafés, the class divided into four Café teams, one for each major initiative that had been chosen from the original six. We wanted this work to be sustainable, so each team worked in close partnership with someone from student affairs. This gave the people in student affairs the design and implementation experience to continue the Cafés on their own once our project was finished. At the end of the project we gave them written reports from the initial Temperature Check Cafés and the Action Cafés, as well as a final DVD containing audio, video, and other content harvested and synthesized from the entire process.

We've found that although the raw data like tablecloths and wall graphics are extremely useful for members who have participated in Café dialogues, they are rarely in a form that can easily engage focused conversations in other parts of an organization. This is a real challenge in Cafés as well as other types of strategic dialogue. But when the outputs are intentionally blended into a coherent story, then this story can travel and engage others. For example, the DVD stories produced for student affairs have been widely shared across the university and have stimulated conversations about key questions with groups far removed from the original participants.

I would say that we're learning two key things about harvesting and sharing collective discoveries from our Café experiences. First, intentionally harvesting the insights *is* important. This is one essential way that everyone who participates can contribute to weaving together the bits and pieces of their emerging collective intelligence into a coherent whole. This is true whether you are doing an individual World Café event or seeing Café conversations as part of a broader process of engagement, as we did with student affairs.

Second, effective strategic conversations—conversations that can move learning forward in a large system—are made up of a repeating cycle of planting seeds, harvesting the fruits, refining the new seeds, and replanting them in new soil. I believe that the role of the leader is to tend the garden of strategic conversations and make sure that this type of planting and harvesting happens throughout their unit or their organization. At the Center for Professional Excellence, we've found that Café conversations provide key ingredients that leaders can use for tending the soil, sharing food for thought, and discovering common ground.

. . .

One of the most exciting personal experiences I've had of seeing a group harvest and share its own collective knowledge occurred in a rustic lodge high in the mountains above Denver, Colorado. I was with the advanced technologies R&D group of a major global communications corporation. They had gathered in this remote place to spend three days in a knowledge exchange. The goal? One of the scientists put it this way: "None of us knows what all of us knows. But we need to know enough to be able to represent the whole of our R&D expertise to any client we are working with in the system."

The three days we spent together were a real turning point for my own learning about how to make collective intelligence visible at increasing levels of scale. We did a number of Café cycles over the first two days in which the scientists learned about client needs, shared knowledge about the variety of projects they were working on, and explored future opportunities for leveraging their collective expertise.

On the last day, the group found ladders and scaffolding and created a *huge* matrix on the wall, with boxes for client groups across the top and their various areas of R&D down the side. They began to fill in each of the matrix boxes with easel-size sheets that summarized the understandings they had gleaned from the previous days' Café conversations. I could see new connections emerging and evolving as they built the cells of the matrix, helping each other fill in the gaps. It was like watching a conscious, living organism evolve and grow.

I was deeply moved as I bore witness to the unfolding of their effort to make their own collective knowledge visible. Through their personal storytelling and multiple Café conversations, these scientists, engineers, and wizards in fiber optics had been able to co-evolve a mutual understanding of their shared professional worlds. They had demonstrated this understanding by literally constructing and displaying it together in shared visual space. There was a long silence as the sixty members took in the whole picture. Their heartfelt appreciation for each other and for their common work was palpable as people acknowledged the wisdom and experience they had assembled.

Café Variations: Documenting and Displaying Collective Knowledge

World Café hosts around the globe are discovering many innovative ways to make visible the essence of their learnings from Café dialogues. In these efforts, we're building on the pioneering work of Bob Horn (1998), Michael Schrage (1990), David Sibbet (2003), and others who have recognized that spoken conversation is often ephemeral. The absence of a verbal or visual memory means that creative ideas, images, and insights that are generated in conversations are often distorted or lost. Therefore, harvesting and sharing discoveries in multiple mediums that can both create and reveal people's individual and collective insights is an important part of being able to think and act together, especially in large-group settings.

As we saw in Bob Lengel's story and in my own experience with the R&D scientists, depending on your purpose and desired outcomes there are many ways to harvest and share discoveries as they unfold in World Café dialogues. Finn Voldtofte and his colleagues in Denmark have perhaps the most experience using different alternatives for harvesting and sharing discoveries. He shared with us some of the approaches he has tried. Here's a synthesis of his reflections:

We've done many things, of course. You can display the tablecloths and have people gather around those. It works particularly well if people from different tables give each other tours of their tablecloths. Then, later, the group can explore what's in the center of the conversation as a whole.

If there are a lot of tables, we may have each table turn in a large card or sticky note with one key idea that expresses the essence of what was important from their conversations. If the group size is smaller, each member can contribute a card with the idea he or she feels is most essential. Then we can post these on a wall or cluster related cards and make a gallery tour from that. Other times we do a quick computer turnaround and publish a newspaper right on the spot, so participants can read the headlines and build on them for further conversation or action planning. We've even used video to create news stories about what people have learned.

At times, we have people find a partner and just walk around the room talking about what they learned that day, or what idea had the most life for them. Then they link up with two others and then the four link with four more. With each linking up you have to get briefer and more focused on the deeper themes. Very quickly you can get a sense of what everybody is hearing, especially if everyone is listening for the collective wisdom in the larger group.

Another option is to have each Café table create an exhibition. You tell people, "In one hour you will have the opening show for the exhibition. We'll serve drinks and everyone can come to the gallery and see what each Café table or group of tables created in terms of the essence of what's been explored, what people learned, and possible action steps" (or whatever you want as output). After they have each created their own exhibition, people can take a tour of the other contributions in the gallery—but they can also add their insights and put actual comments on each other's contributions. It's like growing a living picture of the whole.

You can never actually capture the whole of what has occurred in a Café dialogue because each individual makes his or her own sense of it. However, by inviting multiple perspectives on the essence of what's been discovered, the group, together, can point toward the deeper knowledge of what's most important.

Our colleague Ken Homer, who is fostering the development of the World Café community globally, shares another harvesting approach he's found useful in a wide variety of situations. At the University of California, Santa Cruz, he and campus ombudsman Laurie McCann co-hosted a World Café for the IT services division to coordinate efforts to consolidate the operations of twenty-four different departments into a single entity. The final Café round asked members: *What is the most important question each of you has which, if explored, would allow you to move forward with your role in the project?*

As Ken recounts the day, "The final question generated several dozen areas for exploration. To make the collective wisdom in the room visible to the group as a whole we gave everyone four self-adhesive dots. One had an *X* on it and the rest were plain. The instructions were to place the dot with the X on the one question they most needed to explore before moving forward and use the remaining dots to identify the next most important ones. What emerged was a clear visual map of both the conversations needing the most attention and the order in which they needed to be engaged to move forward."

At Saudi Aramco, Dan Walters used art and symbols in a futuring session with company doctors, encouraging them to leave an empty oval in the middle of their Café tablecloths. At the end of their conversations, Dan asked each Café group to draw a simple picture or image in the oval to express their best hopes for the future. These core images became important data for setting priorities and determining future direction.

In Poland, the American Society for Quality was hosting a Café at a conference on quality sponsored by the United Nations, a situation where formality and hierarchy had often affected the free sharing of ideas. In this case, Paul Borawski, the executive director of ASQ, used keypad polling technology to harvest insights and stimulate further exploration. "We'd pose a Café question . . . for example, 'What do you think will be the future of quality in Poland?' While the groups were in their Café dialogues I put up several options along a continuum—such as 'It's strong,' 'It's at risk,' and so on. Then, based on their sense of the discussion at their Café tables, we asked people to respond to the questions and we posted the aggregated results of the anonymous poll for the whole group to see. The moment they saw the varied results it completely opened the conversation in the large group. People asked questions, listened to insights from others, and got the benefit of seeing how their answer fit with the sense of the majority of people in the room."

Discovering creative ways to synthesize discoveries and display Café insights in order to help participants notice the deeper connections between the parts and the whole is a learning edge in our work. We believe this is an important arena to consider for all of us who host conversations that matter, whether or not they take place in a Café format. *(continued on p. 149)*

CONNECTING THE PARTS AND THE WHOLE: THE FINANCIAL PLANNING ASSOCIATION

As Told By

Kim Porto and Sean Walters

Kim Porto and Sean Walters of the Financial Planning Association have discovered an extremely useful approach for harvesting and sharing individual and collective discoveries. It's one that can be effective in a wide variety of situations.

One of the more challenging aspects of the World Café is the whole-group synthesis and conversation that occurs after the Café rounds. We stumbled onto what we feel is one of the best ways of keeping people's energy and contribution level high when we invented our own version of the Gallery Walks. Here's how we do it. We create a three- or four-round Café on a particular topic. In round one we ask tables to come up with their own overarching question, which, if answered, could make a difference to the situation under consideration. That question gets written on a large piece of heavy paper that is folded in half as an easily visible "tent card" and becomes the core question for the next two or three rounds of Café dialogue at that table.

One host stays throughout all rounds as the steward for his or her particular table question. At the end of round one the other three people travel to new tables, choosing tables with a new question that interests them. In each round, people write personal insights and thoughts about their table's question on large individual sticky notes that they keep with them as they move to subsequent rounds.

The table host/question steward continues to make notes or drawings related to that table's question on the Café tablecloth. During round two or three, the overall Café host or hosts walk around the room and write down the question that's on each table's tent card. We create a flip chart page for each one of these questions. If several of the table questions are the same, we put them on a single flip chart page, and if several are similar or related we post them near each other. By posting the questions around the room, everyone can begin to see the emerging outlines of the larger patterns of inquiry.

At the conclusion of the last round, rather than giving a formal break (which tends to disperse the energy of the group) we give folks ten minutes to place their individual sticky notes next to the questions posted on the flip charts around the room. This gives people the opportunity to add their insights, ideas, inspirations, and *what-if's* to the questions they were part of exploring as well as any of the others posted around the room. People get pretty excited as they look at each other's contributions. It starts a whole new round of little "buzz groups"—people in two's or three's commenting on the ideas they are seeing posted during the Gallery Walk.

We continue by hosting the whole-group conversation, focusing on key ideas or insights. We start with one table question from the flip charts that intuitively seems to have the most energy and interest, or where there were a number of tables with the same or related questions. We continue by asking people to look *among* the questions for themes and patterns, new opportunities for action, or areas that need further discussion. Sometimes we ask people to share what they still want to explore that didn't get addressed, in order to ensure that all voices are heard.

One of the aspects that we think makes this particular approach to whole-group synthesis so engaging and useful is that people have control over what they contribute. They are not relying on the table host to summarize what they said, nor are they relying on a scribe to capture their words. Each person gets the opportunity (and has the responsibility) to contribute exactly what is most meaningful to him or her, and put it exactly where he or she feels it best fits in the overall synthesis. It also creates a tangible record of the conversation, which can be used for follow-up, action planning, priority setting, and other tasks, ensuring that nothing important will be lost.

· · ·

Hosting the Whole-Group Conversation

The World Café is designed to foster *collective* knowledge-sharing and knowledge creation; no individual is as likely to make these discoveries alone. Yet paradoxically, emerging insights can only be voiced through individual expression. How then can members share collective insights without resorting to traditional report-outs that rarely reflect the liveliness or depth of the smaller group conversations?

The conversation of the whole—which comes at the end of a sequence of Café rounds—is a key element in the harvesting and sharing of collective discoveries. Designing and facilitating this conversation requires special artistry and care. The goal is to continue to nurture a spirit of authentic dialogue while creating the opportunity to evoke collective insight in the larger group.

The approach you choose for designing the whole-group conversation depends on the Café's purpose and the ways that sharing discoveries can be most useful to your desired outcomes. We've found it generally helpful to pose catalytic questions that can focus the whole-group synthesis. You'll find examples of such questions in chapter 10. In addition, to help people connect into the larger field of collective thought, you can have them imagine that the emerging conversation is a ball of yarn that is being passed from one person to the next as people around the room focus on the essence of the dialogue, share personal reflections, and bring closure to the conversation. Ask members to listen closely to each person's contribution, rising to share their reflection if they sense it is connected to the person's before them in some way. This helps to weave a web of connected thought throughout the room. When one thread is complete, invite others to offer a new thread into the weave of ideas.

We've found it generally helpful to pose catalytic questions that can focus the whole-group synthesis

At other times, you might begin by asking everyone to consider what's most essential from the previous conversations. Ask them to imagine themselves as a system thinking together— listening for deeper wisdom before beginning to share insights and discoveries. These two simple approaches tend to bring more coherence to the large-group exploration. People begin to sense themes, patterns, and key ideas unfolding in the larger group, while still being free to offer to offer divergent views that spark unexpected possibilities.

Using a graphic recorder can also make a big difference in helping the group gain a greater sense of the whole as it unfolds from people's individual comments. After taking a gallery tour of the tablecloths or using another approach to display key ideas, this visual specialist records people's reflections in words and pictures on large wall murals or rolling blackboards. This "tablecloth in the center of the room" enables members to see the larger picture. Using this type of visual recording reveals how key ideas connect with one another, and enables people to think more systemically. See "Resources and Connections" and "Illustration

Credits," at the back of the book, to learn how to contact specialists in visual language.

Whether you use a graphics professional or not, we've found that it's important for the host to allow a few minutes of silence for individual reflection and note-taking prior to opening the whole-group conversation. In addition, ask people to speak *personally* (and briefly) about what's at the center of the collective conversations of which they've been a part. This enables what Swedish Café host Bo Gyllenpalm calls a "shared understanding of individual meanings" to emerge, revealing key facets of the conversational web while not requiring agreement on a single shared meaning in order for multiple perspectives to be included in later priority setting or action planning. In addition, encouraging the contribution of key personal meanings enables not only "head knowledge" but also "heart wisdom" to be revealed. This simple shift sidesteps the traditional roles of group reporter or official representative that are so prevalent (and often deadly) in other modes of large-group report-backs.

Helping Insight Travel

Yvon Bastien poses an important and provocative question related to this exploration: *How does insight travel?* Bo Gyllenpalm has been especially innovative in considering interesting ways to help insight travel to those who are not part of the original dialogue. He tells one story of several large-scale strategy conversations with a major Swedish bank. The regional director told his local managers they would receive overhead copies of the colorful murals created throughout their Café sessions. "Then something very interesting occurred that we hadn't anticipated," Bo says. "The local managers told us that after traditional strategy meetings they usually receive pre-formatted PowerPoint slides with bullet points from the formal strategy presentations. They were required to show them to their employees. These are often seen as obligatory presentations, with little engagement and enthusiasm." Bo smiled as he added, "But when they received the colorful overheads with the murals from their own

How does insight travel?

knowledge harvesting, they simply couldn't make a dry presentation like before. They had to tell a story! When local managers used the storytelling approach to share what had happened at the meeting, people became immediately engaged in a lively dialogue about what the different images and key words meant and what the implications were for their own work."

Storybooks, visual reports, CDs, or DVDs that share the core questions, flow of conversation, and outcomes from a Café dialogue can also be used as conversational "memory joggers" for follow-up and implementation planning. In addition, these creative syntheses of key insights can also be used to spread the word and engender larger networks of conversation. Although these approaches to helping insight travel rarely convey the full excitement and discoveries of the original Café dialogue, they can be used effectively as process tools to stimulate new rounds of conversation and action—whether in a Café format or not.

Our Learning Edges

Discovering the best ways to reveal and utilize the collective insights and stories that emerge in a World Café dialogue has unearthed a deeper set of challenges and questions we're still in the process of exploring. For example, Western learning and educational approaches have been shaped by an *individualistic* mindset. In both the United States and abroad, we're just beginning to employ what Michael Schrage (1990) calls "convivial tools"—as simple as Café tablecloths and graphic recording or as sophisticated as groupware and other collaborative technology tools—that enable us to make *collective* knowledge visible.

It's essential to discover innovative ways to link individual and collective intelligence in order to foster more holistic and systemic understandings of critical issues in our organizations and communities. On this subject, Finn Voldtofte has raised provocative questions for leaders to consider: *"How does a collective actually learn to think together? Are there different principles underlying the development of collective insight versus the development of individual insight alone?"*

Other Café hosts have built on this inquiry by asking: *"What approaches can we use to make collective insight both visible and actionable at increasing levels of scale?"* It does appear that to be effective we need to consider alternatives to the linear reporting modalities—the analytical reports and PowerPoint presentations that we're all too familiar with in traditional organizational and community settings. We're discovering that innovative methodologies like interactive graphics and other forms of visual language, theater, poetry, artistic expression, and interactive technology tools can play powerful roles in enhancing our capacities for thinking together about complex issues.

We're making great progress in learning how best to access, harvest, and share insights and stories from World Café conversations, with their focus on evoking collaborative versus solely individual intelligence. We are excited by the creative experiments that are happening around the world and the unique contribution the World Café is making to this inquiry. We'd love to learn from your experiences as you begin to experiment with hosting conversations that matter in your own organizations and communities as well.

Questions for Reflection

What are some of the most effective or innovative ways you've seen to enhance collective learning and discovery by making collective knowledge more visible to the group as a whole?

From your perspective and experience, how does insight travel and spread most effectively? What practical role can harvesting and sharing collective discoveries play in enhancing mutual intelligence and carrying key discoveries forward?

Consider an upcoming gathering or conversation you will be a part of. What creative ways for harvesting, documenting, and sharing discoveries can be most useful for (a) the group at the event and (b) carrying the insights forward to other constituencies?

TEN

Guiding the Café Process: The Art of Hosting

Hosting is an attitude as much as an activity.

—Carlos Mota Margain, World Café host

What if hosting means

welcoming all that arrives?

WORKING ON BEHALF OF THEIR SISTERS: AFRICAN WOMEN WITH DISABILITIES

As Told By

Marianne "Mille" Böjer

Mille Böjer is one of the founders of the Pioneers of Change, a global learning community of committed changemakers in their mid-twenties to early thirties. These young leaders are bringing leading-edge organizational, community, and leadership development processes to over seventy countries where the network has members. The art of hosting lies at the heart of what makes the World Café process successful. This is the story of Mille's discoveries about herself as a host in a unique Café situation in South Africa.

"I'm in!"

That was my excited response when I heard that thirty-five to forty women from across Africa were coming to my town, Johannesburg, to inspire each other, give each other ideas and tools for their work, and set up a new African network of women with disabilities focused on reproductive health and HIV/AIDS. I got the news from my colleague Marianne Knuth that the Danish Council of Associations of Disabled People was seeking a World Café host in South Africa to facilitate the meeting. The group was not interested in creating a new formal organization or international institution. Instead, they wanted to create a network that could work through their existing organizations and would get its energy from the group's clarity of purpose, creative ideas, and strong personal relationships.

Soon I was corresponding with Lena Nielsen in Denmark and Kirsten Nielsen in Uganda, the two Danish partners involved in the project, as well as representatives from their South African counterpart, Disabled People of South Africa (DPSA), to design the program. As I learned more, it became apparent that this group would present unique challenges in adapting the Café process to their particular needs. The group would be composed entirely of women with disabilities. A good number were blind or visually impaired, an equally high number were physically disabled (dependent on crutches or wheelchairs), and two were deaf.

I'd never in my life worked in this kind of situation! I e-mailed Lena and asked if she was sure they wanted to use the World Café for this gathering. Café conversations involve a lot of moving around and I usually hang things all around the room as the meeting progresses to visualize the group's journey as it unfolds. Would all this be possible with this group?

Although Lena hadn't experienced the World Café herself, she knew the members wanted to use a process that "put the participants' ideas in the center" and this was what she had heard was powerful about the World Café. Although still a bit nervous, I started getting excited by the challenge. I was also inspired by the possibilities of what I might learn personally about hosting and being creative in figuring out how to apply the World

Café principles in this unique situation. Sure enough, as the weeklong workshop unfolded, it turned out to be one of the most profound experiences of my life.

Since this gathering would be our first time together as a network of women with disabilities, we agreed at the outset to try as much as possible to practice network approaches in how we organized and hosted the meeting. For example, although participants had prepared a number of presentations, these were used to stimulate more interactive conversations in multiple small groups. We also invited each woman to share a question that mattered to her during her personal introduction, so the participants' own web of concerns could be at the center of the meeting.

Each afternoon we held a World Café around the topic of the day. We explored the strengths and weaknesses of various disabilities movements in the participants' countries, explored their unique African context, and came up with the vision for their network. One day was devoted to country reports. But instead of listening to fifteen presentations in a plenary session, we discussed them at small Café tables and drew out the common trends, patterns, and questions that cut across them all.

The women embraced the Café process. I noticed that their disabilities gave us all a reason for physical contact, which helped build relationships. I was constantly touching the women—touching the blind to let them know I was there, touching the physically disabled to aid their mobility. For the deaf, we had to work a bit more slowly so that the translators could keep up. And to accommodate everyone's pace of movement, we took longer to move between tables.

As the Café host, whenever someone would enter the room, I would acknowledge her presence and have her introduce herself so those who were blind could all know who was there and could hear where the newcomer was located in the room. I looked each person in the eye. I learned their names from day one. When I wrote something or drew something on the wall, I would describe what was there. I described the room setup every time it changed, and let them know if they should expect to come back to a room that was arranged differently.

After three days of sharing their struggles and learning about the alarming reality of reproductive health among African women with disabilities, we moved into visioning the future of their network and designing its structure—the purpose and principles, roles and relationships, and communication flows. Since we had been working with a networked process in the Café conversations throughout the week, it was easier for them to envision the kind of organization that could bring the fundamental network idea to life on a larger scale, while not losing the personal bonds and connectedness that the World Café had helped to establish.

It was very gratifying to spend five days with real, sincere women—disabled women working on behalf of their sisters who are also disabled. The feeling was so different from typical conferences, such as the one I had facilitated the month before, where the more the participants talked *about* poverty, the further away the actual poor seemed. Here, the more the women shared their personal stories and experiences within the weave of the conversations, the more present others who shared their situation seemed to be. Although I haven't seen many of the Café members recently, they are still in my heart, and from e-mail contacts I know the network continues.

My main lessons from this experience as a Café host were at the level of my "being," in contrast to specific tools. It seems that hosting is really about being yourself rather than just playing a formal role. The participants had a sense of humor and I had the feeling that they were being themselves. As I felt that, it created a space for me, as the host, to be more of myself, which I think encouraged them to be more of themselves. In a way, I was helping to host a mutual hosting!

I also learned how to be attentive in ways I hadn't experienced before. The World Café process creates a web of connections among the participants that generates collective wisdom. But beyond that, I discovered that the host can also play a key role in connecting people at many levels as the meeting unfolds. This can make a big difference in the group's ability to get in touch with its own wisdom.

One way this happens is through constant inclusion. I paid close attention to everyone's needs because they were so explicit, watching to see if somebody was outside the process or somehow not included, and then inviting her in and encouraging her contribution. This an important job for the host, even in more conventional situations.

I also think that it helps when the host introduces the Café with a lot of confidence. It can be challenging when people aren't familiar with what's going to happen and they start questioning the framework and assumptions, so you need to be clear when you introduce the principles and the process. It's also important that the host be available for people in a spirit of service. Don't assume that it's easy and that the conversations are all going to flow immediately, but move around and check to see if your help is needed.

It might seem as if the hosting practices I learned at this meeting are not directly applicable to a typical group of people who don't have disabilities. But at a deeper level I believe they apply just as much—it's about us as hosts having the courage and attention to practice them.

. . .

I've often wondered what it is about the World Café process and principles that enables those who have even a modicum of leadership, facilitation, or group skills to be successful in hosting Café-style dialogues, often with very large groups. We're discovering from our "research in action" over the last decade that creatively employing the seven World Café design principles, coupled with introducing Café etiquette and assumptions as the dialogue begins (see the following section, "Hosting a World Café"), tends to foster the enabling conditions for collaborative conversation while mitigating many of the dysfunctional behaviors often found in group settings.

However, it is important to emphasize that the "magic" of Café conversations at their best doesn't always occur. Determining that a World Café conversation is the appropriate mode for your group (see the following section, "Decide If a World Café Gathering Is Appropriate for Your Situation"), planning enough time for the conversation, and working with the seven Café design principles *as an integrated set* makes accessing collective intelligence more likely.

Hosting great conversations—whether Café dialogues or not—is an art that requires personal awareness and attention. Toke Møller, who has introduced hundreds of people to the art of hosting both in his native Denmark and internationally, observes that "you cannot host a Café or any deep learning space without being fully present yourself. It's about real-life practice, not theory. Sooner or later, something will happen that will take you past your limits of understanding and create a new possibility. But entering into that new space requires going beyond your fear and coming into a calm place where you, as the host, can see what you need to do in the present moment."

Finn Voldtofte, another Danish World Café pioneer, points out, "As the host, I'm putting my own attention on the wholeness that is emerging in the spaces in between all the participants. I'm always seeking creative ways for the members to make visible what's emerging in the middle of their own table and what's emerging as their conversations connect and weave together."

Toke adds that hosting involves an understanding of the multiple systems embedded in World Café conversations. "The system of knowledge-sharing, the system of working with the questions, the system of relationships—all need to unfold so that they can come alive. When you can be open with great curiosity to how things are actually unfolding, you gain access to your best contribution. Good hosting is a privilege, not a job. It's very important leadership work."

Jan Hein Nielsen, a friend and colleague of Toke's, echoes these ideas but also stresses the importance of trust: "The host must trust herself and her capacity to open up space for everyone to give their best. She needs to trust that the participants have the capability and willingness to enter a learning field together. The participants also need to trust that they will be hosted in such a way that learning can enter, that action can enter, that anything that they really want to happen can enter the room. If trust is not on the menu, hosting cannot take place. It will be something else, but it will not be hosting."

As a host, one invites people into a creative space—a space of "not knowing." It must be open, but not intrusive, so that people feel comfortable and able to unfold their best thinking. As Monica Nissén, another Danish colleague, describes it, "If the field of discovery is open, emergence can happen and you need to be prepared to be surprised. You cannot know exactly what will come out of it. You are sometimes standing on the edge right there with everyone else."

What does a host do that makes me feel welcome?

Most of us are not aware of how a good host cultivates the open field that Monica describes unless we stop to ask ourselves, *What does a host do that makes me feel welcome?* And that question is perhaps the doorway to discovering the essence of Café hosting. When we speak of hosting, we're not referring to traditional facilitation or leading. Instead, by engaging the Café principles you are creating the conditions within which members can self-organize to host each other at their individual tables around questions they care about.

As a conversation host, ask yourself: *What can I do to make whomever I am with feel physically comfortable, emotionally safe, and intellectually challenged? How can I support members in discovering a deeper understanding and appreciation—for each other and for the questions we're exploring? How can I engage the Café participants themselves in hosting each other and in discovering the magic in the middle of their conversations?* Whatever answers you get and however they reveal themselves, begin to experiment with putting them into practice. Leave aside the techniques that don't work and refine the ones that seem most effective. Above all, keep asking yourself the questions and integrate your answers into your hosting practice. You'll soon discover the way of hosting that is most natural for you.

The remainder of this chapter is designed to be used, with acknowledgment, as a World Café hosting guide independently of the rest of the book. This hosting guide is not a recipe. It simply provides the initial ingredients to cook up creative conversations, based on your unique needs and situation. You will find many other practical examples and tips in other chapters of this book as well as on the World Café Web site.

The World Café Hosting Guide

Advance Preparation: Convening a World Café

When you convene and host a Café conversation, you can use your personal imagination and have great fun! Although the traditional setup of café-like tables and flowers creates a special ambiance, it is by no means the only way to go. We know of exciting World Café designs in which people have moved among conversation clusters in living rooms, rotated between large trees in a forest, or shifted places among several minivans on a learning journey. Whatever specific form you choose, engaging the seven Café principles *in combination* increases the likelihood of active engagement, authentic dialogue, and constructive possibilities for action. Use whatever space you have available, be creative with the setup and supplies, pay attention to the seven design principles, and use your imagination to help the World Café achieve your purpose. Be the best host you can, and then trust the process.

Decide If a World Café Gathering Is Appropriate for Your Situation

Designing with the World Café principles in mind (see p. 174) allows you to adapt and engage in conversations that matter in almost any circumstance. Cafés have been designed for sessions as short as ninety minutes as well as for conferences lasting several days. A Café can stand alone or serve as part of a larger meeting.

World Café conversations are especially useful for these purposes and in these circumstances:

- For sharing knowledge, stimulating innovative thinking, building community, and exploring possibilities around real-life issues and questions.

- For conducting an in-depth exploration of key challenges and opportunities.

- For engaging people who are meeting for the first time in authentic conversation.

- For deepening relationships and mutual ownership of outcomes in an existing group.

- For creating a meaningful interaction between a speaker and the audience.

- When the group is larger than twelve (we've hosted as many as twelve hundred) and you want each person to have the opportunity to contribute. The World Café is especially suitable for connecting the intimacy of small-group dialogue with the excitement and fun of larger-group participation and learning.

- When you have a minimum of one and a half hours for the Café (two hours is much better). Some Cafés have spanned several days or become part of a regular meeting infrastructure.

The World Café is not an optimal choice under these circumstances:

- You are driving toward an already determined solution or answer.

- You want to convey only one-way information.

- You are making detailed implementation plans and assignments.

- You have less than one and a half hours for the Café.

- You are working with a highly polarized, explosive situation. (Hosting a World Café in this setting requires highly skilled facilitation.)

- You have a group smaller than twelve. In that case, consider a traditional dialogue circle, council, or other approach to fostering authentic conversation.

Set the Context

Once you've determined that a Café conversation is appropriate for your circumstances, you'll need to clarify the context. This means paying attention to the three Ps: purpose, participants, and parameters.

- Determine clearly your *purpose* for bringing people together, along with the best possibilities or outcomes you can see emerging from your Café. Once you know your Café's purpose, name it in a way that reflects that purpose. For example: Leadership Café, Knowledge Café, Community Café, Discovery Café, Anniversary Café, and so on.

- Identify the *participants* who need to be included. Diversity of thought yields richer insights and discoveries.

- Take into account the *parameters* with which you are working (time, money, venue, and so on). See if you need to stretch the parameters in order to achieve your purpose.

Create Hospitable Space

Café hosts around the world emphasize the power and importance of creating a welcoming environment—one that feels comfortable, safe, and inviting for people to be themselves. In particular, consider how your invitation and your physical setup contribute to creating a welcoming atmosphere.

In your invitation, pose an initial question or theme that you believe is important to those you've invited. Choose a question that arouses curiosity and opens the way for more conversation. Craft your invitation to convey that members can expect to have fun, be engaged, and learn new things. When sending a written invitation, find ways to make it stand out from the usual e-mail or written correspondence by making it informal, creative, personal, and visually interesting.

Whether you are convening several dozen or several hundred people, your guests should notice immediately that this is no

Creating a Café Environment

ordinary meeting. Arrange the room to be as welcoming as possible. Have music playing when people arrive. Natural light and an outdoor view are always inviting. If your room doesn't have windows, bring in plants and greenery to enliven it. You can quickly transform a dull meeting room into a welcoming space by hanging pictures or posters on the walls. Hospitality and community thrive on food and refreshments; have snacks and beverages available throughout the gathering.

Please don't limit yourself with these suggestions. Look at the room setup and supplies list near the end of this chapter. Then *use your own imagination and creativity* to create a setting that participants will enjoy.

Explore Questions That Matter

Finding and framing relevant questions that open the way for great conversations is an area where careful thought and attention can produce profound results. Your Café may focus on exploring a single question, or you may develop several lines of inquiry to support an emergent discovery process through successive rounds of dialogue. In many cases, Café conversations are as much about discovering and exploring powerful questions as they are about finding immediate solutions. The question or questions you choose or that participants discover during a Café conversation are critical to its success. As Eric Vogt of the International Corporate Learning Association points out, a powerful question has these characteristics:

▶ It is simple and clear.

▶ It is thought-provoking.

▶ It generates energy.

▶ It focuses inquiry.

▶ It surfaces assumptions.

▶ It opens new possibilities.

Experienced Café hosts recommend posing open-ended questions—the kind that invite exploration. Good questions need not imply immediate action steps or problem solving. They invite inquiry and discovery rather than advocacy and advantage. We've included a list of generative questions near the end of this chapter (see p. 173) that can help you craft your own questions for exploration. You'll know you have a good question when it continues to surface new ideas and possibilities. Test questions before using them. Bounce them off trusted friends or colleagues who will be participating in the Café to see if they sustain interest and energy. If you are featuring a speaker, involve that person in helping to create questions that, if explored, could make a difference to the real-life concerns of those attending.

At the Event: Hosting a World Café

A World Café generally consists of three rounds of progressive conversation lasting approximately twenty to thirty minutes each, followed by a dialogue among the whole group. Rounds have gone longer, but people often feel rushed in less than a twenty-minute round. The number and length of rounds prior to the whole-group dialogue will depend on your focus and intent. Feel free to experiment.

The job of the overall Café host (or the hosting team at larger gatherings) begins with welcoming people as they arrive, directing them to the refreshments, inviting them to their seats, and answering any logistical questions before the first round starts. Once everyone is seated, explain the purpose and the logistics of the Café. Let people know that they will be moving from table to table and that the end of a round may come when they are in the middle of an intense conversation, just as happens in life. It is natural to feel some resistance to the interruption, but they can pick up the conversation again at the next table. Explain that when a round ends one person will remain behind as the host of that table, and the other people will travel to new tables to sit with a different mix of people.

The job of the individual table host is to engage in the conversation as a participant and steward, not as a formal facilitator. The added role of this person is to share the essence of the conversation for the guests who arrive for the next round. Everyone at the table is responsible for supporting the host in taking notes, summarizing key ideas, and if so moved, making drawings that reflect interesting thoughts and insights as they unfold. This "table recording" helps the host do the best job possible in conveying to new members the key ideas that have emerged. *Be sure to encourage people to write, draw, or doodle on the tablecloths in the midst of their conversations.* Often these tablecloth drawings will contain remarkable notes, and they help visual learners link ideas. Members who will be traveling to a new table should bring with them the key ideas, themes, and questions from their last round to seed their upcoming conversation.

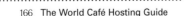

Before beginning the first round, it is helpful to introduce the Café assumptions and Café etiquette. You can display our graphics, shown here, on overheads, post them on easel sheets, or distribute them on cards at each table. Or use your own illustration style. Being clear about basic Café assumptions and Café etiquette orients members to underlying beliefs and personal behaviors that are useful in supporting constructive dialogue without being heavy-handed about "shoulds" and "shouldn'ts." Then allow time to answer any final questions prior to commencing the Café dialogue.

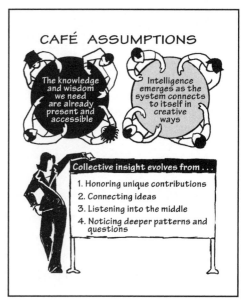

You are now ready to pose the question for the first round of conversation. Write the question—even if it's a question that asks people to discover their own question or questions—on flip charts or overheads and if necessary make extra copies to post around the room or distribute on cards to each table. Very often what people think they heard is different from what you thought you said. A visual reference can avoid a lot of confusion. Help clarify the question, if requested, but avoid providing answers or directing the conversation.

Encourage everyone to share their ideas and perspectives freely, and acknowledge that some people's special contribution may be their presence as attentive listeners. Some Café hosts prefer to ask people to identify the table host at the start of the round, while some opt for doing it at the end. Whichever one you choose, make sure that a host is chosen before people change tables.

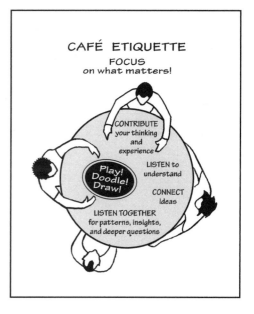

Upon completing each round of conversation, let people know in a gentle way that it's time to move for the next round. Many hosts use a raised hand that signals others in the room to fall silent and raise theirs as well, marking the end of a round. Encourage the departing travelers from each table to find new tables and different people to sit with. Ask hosts to welcome their new guests. Remind everyone that when they arrive at their new table, they should briefly introduce themselves before the table host shares the essence of the conversation from the previous round. Then the travelers add connections and ideas from the conversations at their previous tables. Ask everyone to listen carefully and build on each other's contributions. Let people know if there is a new question for this round, and make sure it is posted where it can easily be seen.

At times people will participate in the first round, go traveling for the second, and then return to their home table for a final round of synthesis. At other times, members will continue traveling for several rounds while the host stays as the ongoing steward of the evolving conversation and insights at their table. On occasion, people will simply travel for a very brief listening tour to hear what's being explored at other tables prior to returning to their home table to both connect common threads and introduce diverse perspectives. The variations depend on your purpose, as the many stories and examples throughout this book demonstrate.

Encourage Everyone's Contribution

One of the reasons for having only four or five people per table is to enable each voice to be heard. People who are hesitant to speak in a large group often offer rich and exciting insights in a more intimate Café setting. At most Café gatherings, once the question is posed people are encouraged simply to jump into the conversation and begin to explore ideas. Most of the time this works well.

However, we have found it often helpful to have a *talking object* on the tables to help ensure that no single participant takes over the group's airtime. Originally used by indigenous peoples, a talking object can be a stick, a stone, a marker, a saltshaker— almost any object that can be passed among the people at the table. Ask people to pick up the talking piece when they are ready to speak, and return it to the center of the table when they are done. The talking piece can also be passed around the circle, or the person who begins can offer it as a gift to whomever he chooses, though people have the opportunity to pass if they wish.

As the host, you can introduce the use of the talking piece as the Café begins or at any appropriate point in the process where you sense that deep listening and "slowing down the action" for more thoughtful engagement may be needed. There are two aspects to the talking object that encourage helpful member participation. Whoever is holding it is encouraged express his or her thoughts as clearly and briefly as possible. Whoever is not holding the talking piece is asked to listen with respect, appreciating the other's perspective as a part of the larger picture.

As host, you can assess what combination of free-flowing exchange and reflective listening to other members using the talking piece will work best. If you anticipate intense emotions or differences of opinion, it's often helpful to begin with a talking piece and then move to a more free-flowing dialogue.

Cross-Pollinate and Connect Diverse Perspectives

Moving among tables, talking with new people, contributing your thinking, and linking the essence of your discoveries to ever-widening circles of thought are hallmarks of the World Café. Patterns emerge, additional perspectives surface, and surprising

Conflicted Café? How to Deal with Differences and Tension

Ken Homer, World Café host and Webmaster

Cafés often surface differences of opinion and understanding; this is part of their ability to generate new insights. However, differences can foster either energy and excitement or anxiety and dissension. If you anticipate difficulties or discover that a conversation seems to be getting really stuck, then in an upcoming round you might encourage participants to use the following three statements as their dialogue unfolds.

‣ What I heard you say that I appreciated is . . .

‣ What I heard that challenged my thinking is . . .

‣ To better understand your perspective I'd like to ask you . . .

Using this simple discipline appropriately can make the difference between a conversation that is ineffective and divisive and one in which everyone takes advantage of the diversity of thought and opinion for their mutual learning.

combinations of insight and creativity reveal themselves in ways people had not previously imagined. The physical movement and cross-pollination of ideas in Café dialogues also reduces the common tendency of participants to "hang onto" their initial positions and opinions.

Sometimes it is not practical for people to move, but this does not mean people can't cross-pollinate ideas. As the Café host, you can ask all the participants to write one key insight, idea, or theme from their table conversation on a large index card. Each member then turns in a different direction and exchanges the card with a person at a nearby table, thus randomly cross-pollinating insights among table conversations. Members read aloud the "gifts" they've received to provide creative input for a deepening round of conversation.

Listen Together for Patterns, Insights, and Deeper Questions

Noticing patterns and connections lies at the heart of knowledge creation. Dynamic listening plays a key role in realizing such breakthrough discoveries. As the Café host, you can encourage the kinds of listening that will make insight, innovation, and action more likely to occur. At the start of the Café, ask members to enter the conversation with the goal of learning from each person at their table. Encourage people to view different perspectives and assumptions as gifts: even when they make us uncomfortable, they offer fertile ground for discovering new possibilities.

Breakthrough thinking occurs most often when people encourage one another to take their thinking further. Ask participants to give each other their full attention by linking and building on shared ideas rather than going off in random directions or personal tangents. Remind folks to listen together for the insights, patterns, or core questions that underlie the various emerging perspectives that no individual member of the group might access alone. Suggest that they watch for times when it might be helpful to pause between comments, allowing time for new ideas to surface. Finally, encourage each table to take some time to reflect during their inquiry together by asking, *What is at the center of our conversation?*

Harvest and Share Collective Discoveries

After several Café rounds, it is helpful to engage in a whole-group conversation. These town meeting–style conversations are not formal reports or analytical summaries, but a time for mutual reflection. Give people a few moments of silence to reflect on or jot down what they have learned in their travels, what has heart and meaning, or what is present now as a result of their conversations. Ask anyone in the room to share briefly a key idea, theme, or core question that holds real meaning for them personally. Encourage everyone to notice what discoveries from their own conversations link to this initial sharing.

Solicit additional ideas and insights, making sure to balance new discoveries with moments of silent reflection—for it is often in silence that a deeper intelligence, intuitive flash of new knowledge, or a new action possibility is revealed. Make sure key insights are recorded visually or gathered and posted, if possible. If you want to capture the specifics, ask everyone to contribute by writing a core idea or insight on stickies or index cards, which can then be posted and consolidated for action planning or other purposes.

Making Collective Knowledge Visible and Identifying Action Priorities

In most World Café gatherings, participants write or draw ideas on paper tablecloths, enabling other Café participants literally to "see" what they mean. Here are some additional ways ideas from the Café can be harvested and utilized in practical ways.

▶ *Have a graphic recorder* capture the whole-group conversation by drawing the group's ideas on flip charts or a wall mural. These colorful murals act like a big tablecloth for the whole group, enabling people to notice key insights and action opportunities.

▶ *Take a gallery tour* of the tablecloths. They can be hung on a wall so that members can see the group's ideas on a break as a prelude to posting key insights.

▶ *Post your insights.* Each participant can write one key insight on a large sticky note and place it on the wall so that everyone can review the ideas during a break. They can be used at the end of a Café for consolidating key themes or action items.

▶ *Create idea clusters.* Have volunteers group the insights into affinity clusters so that related ideas are visible. This can help a group plan its next steps.

▶ *Make a story.* Some Cafés create a newspaper or storybook to share the results of their work with larger audiences after the event. Or a graphic recorder will create a picture book, often with digital photos, along with text as documentation for future use.

Room Setup and Supplies

The room setup described here is an ideal situation. Your venue may not fit this model exactly. However, by using your imagination, you can improvise and design a World Café dialogue process, with or without café tables, that reflects your unique situation and embodies the seven basic operating principles. Be creative! For example, if tables aren't available, you can arrange chairs in small U-shaped clusters and ask people to form a circle when the conversation begins. Place index cards or pads of paper on the chairs along with felt-tipped pens for noting key ideas.

Room Setup

▶ *A room with natural light and view of outside foliage.* If this isn't possible, place plants or flowers around the room to give the Café a natural feeling.

▶ *Small round or square tables (approximately 36 to 42 inches in diameter) that can seat four or five.* Card tables work as well, although round tables tend to create more of a Café ambiance. Fewer than four at a table may not provide enough diversity of perspective, while more than five limits the amount of personal interaction.

▶ *A large enough room* so that people can move comfortably among tables and Café hosts can mingle without disturbing seated participants.

▶ *Tables spread in a slightly chaotic fashion, not in rows.* Create a random distribution around the room.

▶ *Checkered or other informal-colored tablecloths.* If none exist, then white tablecloths will work. Even just putting pieces of easel or flip chart paper on the table alone will work.

Supplies

▶ *Two pieces of white flip chart paper on each table* (similar to in cafés, where people often write on the tablecloths). Use more layers if you'll be removing and posting these sheets. Since people record ideas on the tablecloths, flip charts at individual tables are generally not needed.

▶ *Mural or flip chart paper* for harvesting and posting collective insights.

▶ *Flat wall space for mural paper or two large rolling whiteboards* for the work of a graphic recorder. Wall space is also useful for posting the sheets of paper from tables.

▶ *A mug or wineglass at each table filled with a variety of colored markers* (preferably water-based and nontoxic). You can use Crayola watercolor markers, Mr. Sketch, or other pointed felt-tipped pens or markers in darker colors such as red, green, blue, black, and purple.

▶ *One small vase with sprigs of fresh flowers on each table.* Flowers should be small so they don't obscure the view. Add a small candle as well, if the venue permits it.

▶ *One additional Café table* set up in the front of the room for the host's and presenters' materials.

▶ *A side table* for coffee, tea, water, and refreshments for participants.

▶ *Name tags and chairs* for all participants and presenters (with capacity to remove extra chairs).

Optional Equipment

▶ An overhead projector, screen, a table for overheads, and a digital camera.

▶ A sound system with good speakers that can play both tapes and CDs.

▶ CDs or tapes of mellow jazz or other upbeat music to play as people enter.

▶ Microphones with speakers for Café hosts. Two wireless lavalieres, if needed, and two handheld wireless mikes for town meeting–style sessions.

▶ Two to four flip charts with blank white paper.

▶ Two or more 4 ft. × 6 ft. or 4 ft. × 8 ft. rolling whiteboards or blackboards.

▶ A box containing basic supplies: stapler, paper clips, rubber bands, markers, masking tape, extra pens, pushpins, pencils, and sticky note pads.

▶ Colored 4 in. × 6 in. or 5 in. × 8 in. cards, in colors other than white, if possible—enough cards for each participant to have several for personal note-taking or sharing insights across tables during the gathering.

▶ Bright-colored 4 in. × 6 in. large sticky notes, divided into small packs of twenty-five sheets, one package for each table. You will need these if you are going to ask people to write ideas and post them.

Questions for All Seasons

Here are generative questions that we and other colleagues have found useful to stimulate new knowledge and creative thinking in a wide variety of situations around the world. Look at these questions to jump-start your own creative thinking about the most appropriate ones for your specific situation.

Questions for Focusing Collective Attention

▶ What question, if answered, could make the greatest difference to the future of the situation we're exploring here?

▶ What's important to you about this situation, and why do you care?

▶ What draws you/us to this inquiry?

▶ What's our intention here? What's the deeper purpose—the "big why"—that is worthy of our best effort?

▶ What opportunities can we see in this situation?

▶ What do we know so far/still need to learn about this situation?

▶ What are the dilemmas/opportunities in this situation?

▶ What assumptions do we need to test or challenge in thinking about this situation?

▶ What would someone who had a very different set of beliefs than we do say about this situation?

Questions for Connecting Ideas and Finding Deeper Insight

▶ What's taking shape here? What are we hearing underneath the variety of opinions being expressed? What is in the center of our listening?

▶ What's emerging that is new for you? What new connections are you making?

▶ What have you heard that had real meaning for you? What surprised you? What puzzled or challenged you? What question would you like to ask now?

▶ What is missing from the picture so far? What are we not seeing? Where do we need more clarity?

▶ What has been your major learning or insight so far?

▶ What's the next level of thinking we need to address?

▶ If there was one thing that hasn't yet been said but is needed in order to reach a deeper level of understanding/clarity, what would that be?

Questions That Create Forward Movement

▶ What would it take to create change on this issue?

▶ What could happen that would enable you/us to feel fully engaged and energized in this situation?

▶ What's possible here and who cares about it?

▶ What needs our immediate attention going forward?

▶ If our success was completely guaranteed, what bold steps might we choose?

▶ How can we support each other in taking the next steps? What unique contribution can we each make?

▶ What challenges might come our way, and how might we meet them?

▶ What conversation, if begun today, could ripple out in a way that created new possibilities for the future of [our situation . . .]?

▶ What seed might we plant together today that could make the most difference to the future of [our situation . . .]?

Principles for Hosting Conversations That Matter

The following set of seven integrated World Café design principles, *when used in combination*, can help to intentionally engage the power of conversation for business and social value.

Set the Context

Clarify the purpose and broad parameters within which the dialogue will unfold.

Create Hospitable Space

Assure the welcoming environment and psychological safety that nurtures personal comfort and mutual respect.

Harvest and Share Collective Discoveries

Make collective knowledge and insight visible and actionable.

Listen Together for Patterns, Insights, and Deeper Questions

Focus shared attention in ways that nurture coherence of thought without losing individual contribution.

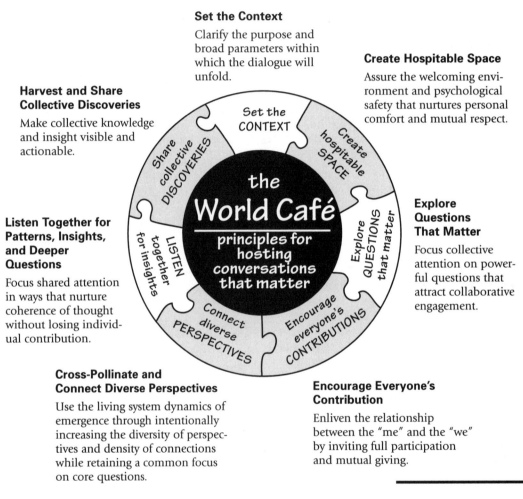

Explore Questions That Matter

Focus collective attention on powerful questions that attract collaborative engagement.

Cross-Pollinate and Connect Diverse Perspectives

Use the living system dynamics of emergence through intentionally increasing the diversity of perspectives and density of connections while retaining a common focus on core questions.

Encourage Everyone's Contribution

Enliven the relationship between the "me" and the "we" by inviting full participation and mutual giving.

Go Forth and Multiply

The World Café is a continuously evolving practice, refined by hosts taking the seven Café principles and utilizing them in innovative ways to create exciting breakthroughs in collaborative thinking and effective action. When dealing with choices or situations that are not covered in the hosting guide or in other parts of the book, use your own best experiences with groups and your intuition about appropriate paths forward to guide you. Conversational leadership is an art, not a science. Use your own creativity not only to design formal Café experiences but to enhance your conversational leadership in other aspects of your life and work where authentic dialogue makes a difference to positive outcomes. Try it. . . . You'll like it!

Questions for Reflection

What are some of the creative ways you might apply the World Café principles and process to an upcoming conversation that matters in your own life or work?

Consider an upcoming meeting or conversation that you are hosting or helping to host. What are some of the specific things you can do to create a welcoming environment, set the context, and frame key questions for the conversation in a way that opens the possibility for greater collaboration, learning, and discovery?

If you are going to host your conversation as a World Café dialogue, what logistical considerations, personal preparation, or other support do you need to feel comfortable guiding the process?

What challenges might you encounter and how can you deal with them?

What difference might your becoming more skilled in the art of hosting make to situations you care about in your life, your work, or your community?

ELEVEN

Conversational Leadership: Cultivating Collective Intelligence

A life-affirming leader is one who knows how to rely on and use the intelligence that exists everywhere in the community, the company, the school, or the organization. A leader these days needs to be a host—one who convenes people, who convenes diversity, who convenes all viewpoints in creative processes where our intelligence can come forth.

—Margaret Wheatley, The Berkana Institute

What if conversational leadership
is like tending a field?

In this chapter, we include four short stories that reveal varied ways that the World Café process and principles can serve conversational leaders in creating valued outcomes. These stories help to highlight key conversational leadership skills and organizational infrastructures for cultivating collective intelligence in twenty-first-century organizations and communities.

STORY

FOSTERING CONVERSATIONAL LEADERSHIP IN EDUCATION: POLK COUNTY SCHOOLS

As Told By
Carolyn Baldwin

Carolyn Baldwin is a former area superintendent in Florida's Polk County public schools. Over a five-year period, she and her colleagues used Café conversations and dialogue circles to engage the knowledge and experience of the district's 138 school principals and five thousand teachers in order to improve school performance among the county's eighty-four thousand elementary and secondary school children. Carolyn coined the term "conversational leadership" to describe their approach to large-scale change. This is the story of how it unfolded.

Dr. Ray Jorgensen, a respected organizational learning consultant, first introduced the concept of the World Café to our thirty-person Executive Leadership Team. Sue Miller Hurst, an early member of the MIT Dialogue Project, which did pioneering research in the dialogue field, later hosted a three-day program with all of our principals at which we experienced the power of dialogue circles. Over a period of several years, we developed learning conversations as a core leadership practice and way of working in our school system—first with the principals, then with the teachers and staff of individual schools. It was a demanding but exhilarating experience!

The first Café with our Executive Leadership Team was really wonderful. Sitting in circles talking to one another is *not* a format that has been used much in school bureaucracies, but we found that Café conversations provided a nonthreatening way for people to think together and explore ideas. The Executive Leadership Team met monthly, and over the period of our initial year we started each meeting with a Café dialogue. By the end of the school year we had experienced several Cafés and we became very familiar with the process. Café dialogues became our primary means for talking about significant issues and creating consensus as well as for building trusting relationships among our very diverse leadership team.

Based on this experience, the five area superintendents began to take this conversational way of leading back to our school principals. For example, early in our use of the World Café approach, the principals in my geographic area used Café conversations to develop a long-term plan and a key strategic initiative for improving student achievement. It worked! At that time, the state of Florida had started to "grade" schools. My particular geographic area had many Title 1 schools, meaning schools with a large percentage of low-income families. When we began we had no A schools, three B schools, some C schools, some D schools, and one F school. In the year after my principals began using the World Café to establish learning communities among their teachers, my area schools had no F-grade schools. All of the schools improved their grades by at least one category, and some by more than one. I don't think we'd have achieved these results without the key ideas and actions for improvement that came out of our Café dialogues.

Using the World Café as part of our conversational leadership approach created other unexpected outcomes. When I began using these conversational methods, the prevailing attitude was "I don't want to share my ideas because then other schools will know my secrets for success and my school might lose its competitive position." But through our Café conversations, the principals began to realize that they were more effective together as a team and as a system than they were alone. I knew that internal competitiveness had truly diminished when a representative from a local shopping mall came to one of our meetings to pitch a competition among our schools during a holiday sales drive—complete with financial incentives for the winning school. When the mall representative left, the principals said, "We don't want to do that this year because it undermines our whole philosophy. We're *not* just individual schools, we're a system of schools and members of the same team." And I thought to myself, "Wow, this is pretty powerful stuff!"

After that breakthrough moment, the principals began to have really deep conversations about the problems in their schools, and to use one another's wisdom to seek positive change. One of the principals had been at the same elementary school for twenty-nine years, and so he had a wealth of experience to share. During his tenure he had seen many initiatives come and go. Most of his contemporaries had either died or retired. During one of the Café conversations he said, "At first I thought this Café stuff was really stupid—this moving around the room having conversations and sitting in circles for dialogues. I thought, 'I'll just outlast it.' But you know what? I have really found friends again." He became one of the strongest advocates for conversational leadership.

Once the principals were comfortable with the Café and dialogue circle formats, they brought conversational leadership to their own schools. The teachers discovered that they didn't need a whole lot of training or new materials in order to have productive dialogue; they just needed the focused time to talk together and discover what they already knew about their kids and about what needed to be different. And what they did as a result made a real difference! For example, the kids improved their standardized test scores in both math and reading. There were consistent achievement gains each year of the five-year project. And discipline problems dramatically decreased in the area schools, as demonstrated by a reduction in school suspensions and disciplinary measures.

I think what really happens in Café conversations is that professional titles and other things that usually separate people fall away. The Café is almost like a time-out, where everyone can step back from themselves as actors in the system and reflect on it together. People begin to see that things can be improved and changed by the combined wisdom and perspectives of all the people who work there, whatever their formal roles. Through this process, we enhanced our capacity to co-create together. That's what I found most rewarding about my conversational leadership experience in the Polk County public schools.

· · ·

THE RESULTS ARE IN THE RELATIONSHIPS: HEWLETT-PACKARD

As Told By

Bob Veazie

Bob Veazie, a senior engineer with Hewlett-Packard, focuses on organizational performance. He has led system-wide shifts in safety and quality, and is now focusing his efforts on the customer experience. Here Bob talks about how he applied the World Café pattern and principles in his role as the conversational leader of a major safety improvement effort affecting fifty thousand employees over a four-year period.

The first time I experienced a World Café was at a program on living systems at the Berkana Institute. At the time, I was an HP manufacturing manager, leading about three hundred people. Something profound but disturbing happened to me during those Café conversations. I realized that the boxes on my organization chart might be more accurately depicted as webs of conversations. This realization carried with it the feeling that "managing" these conversations might not be the best way to achieve results. Each day we are engaged in conversations about different questions, just like those table conversations—and we move between the "tables" as we do our work in the company. Seeing the World Café in action hit me with laser beam clarity. *This is how life actually works!*

Sensing the power and potential for networks of conversations and the connections among them to produce real value was disconcerting to me as a leader. I began to wonder: *If our conversations and personal relationships are at the heart of our work, then how am I, as a leader, contributing to or taking energy away from this natural process? Are we using the intelligence of just a few people when we could gain the intelligence of hundreds or thousands by focusing on key questions and including people more intentionally?* These questions haunted me.

About a year and a half after that first Café, I became the safety leader for a small production area of Hewlett-Packard's inkjet operations in Corvallis, Oregon. The job quickly evolved to include HP's worldwide inkjet manufacturing business—about fifteen thousand employees at five sites around the world, including Ireland and Puerto Rico. Later, as I collaborated with the corporate-wide safety group, our approach expanded to other manufacturing sites and HP business units, a total of about fifty thousand people throughout the company.

When we started, there was a high accident rate. In Corvalis, for example, 6.2 per hundred members of our workforce were hurt every year. In Puerto Rico the percentage was 4.1 percent. In Ireland it was 2.5 to 3 percent. Those are big numbers! The first year I worked on safety, we used Du Pont's program called STOP, an approach where people give each other feedback about how well they are doing relative to a predetermined set of risks. Our test group loved it for the first couple of months, and then they began hating it because it was somebody else's list of risks—they had not generated their *own* ideas about what their own risks really were. In other words, we didn't start with a question that evoked people's own curiosity and creativity. We started with someone else's answer.

In my second year, we dropped Du Pont's program and put together a small group of full-time internal safety experts, called "safety change agents," who defined our own set of risks for the whole organization. Here's where we made our second mistake. I told myself that by doing the work internally I was congruent with the principles of the World Café, since one assumption of the World Café is that much of the wisdom lies with the people themselves. But in reality, we had created a small group that still functioned like outside experts or a management committee. We weren't being mindful of yet another a key principle of the World Café: the importance of encouraging everyone's contribution.

So we changed our approach. We began to ask ourselves, *What are the few key questions that would improve safety results if we were to ask them to people already in conversations about their daily work?* We didn't present those questions in the form of World Café events. In fact, we've never actually designed or hosted a formal World Café event. Instead, it dawned on us that what we needed to do was pose key safety questions to people in the already-existing but invisible "HP Café"—the current web of relationships—so they could integrate the questions into the conversations they were already having.

We began by meeting with people where they normally gathered—in staff meetings, in worker assemblies, and on the shop floor. We'd start by sharing their local facility's safety record with them. Then we'd show them the funnel diagram that Juanita had shared with us at that first World Café I attended. Thousands of people saw that funnel slide! It helped people visualize more clearly the powerful pattern of the World Café in action and opened the door to talking about how change actually happens in large systems (see next page). It also helped employees grasp that we were making a shift; rather than using predetermined training programs that focused only on solutions, we were trusting that their own conversations, relationships, and mutual intelligence were the way to deal with critical safety questions.

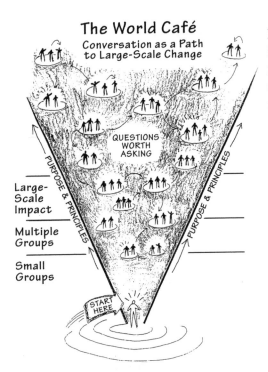

The World Café
Conversation as a Path to Large-Scale Change

QUESTIONS WORTH ASKING

PURPOSE & PRINCIPLES

PURPOSE & PRINCIPLES

Large-Scale Impact

Multiple Groups

Small Groups

START HERE

So, first we asked, "If you were to get hurt, how would that happen?" People began answering the question with risks that they identified from their own work situations. Then we'd ask the second question: "Do you want to manage these risks before people get hurt or after?" And of course they'd say, "Before." Then we'd ask the final question: "Great! What do you want to do about it?" At that point, we didn't have to facilitate anymore. We had invited them into in a meaningful conversation called "I don't want to get hurt at work." We'd talk together about methodologies— their own creative approaches for managing those risks. And finally we'd say, "Try out the answers you've come up with. Keep asking the questions, and revisit your answers as you learn more."

Throughout the whole development of the safety effort, I held a guiding image of the World Café as the deeper pattern for what was happening in the organization. Each of the employee meetings I attended was like a table in this large, ongoing Safety Café—this network of conversations. The tables all over the company were connected by the key questions, just as they are at an actual World Café event.

Our group of full-time safety folks became the nucleus of hosts. Four or five of us began "table hopping" between key sites around the world, some on multiple occasions. We began to share the stories of our travels with the employees at the different sites. We also brought people together from product lines across the company to learn with and from each other. As we were leading the safety effort we were simultaneously learning about how conversation as a core business process really works to enhance performance.

And talk about performance! For example, during our effort the recordable injury rate at our Corvallis, Oregon, site was dramatically reduced—from 6.2 to 1.2 per hundred. Puerto Rico went from 4.1 percent to .2 percent, among the world's best. The company as a whole was able to reduce the overall accident rate by approximately 33 percent. Today there isn't a week that goes by without a problem being discussed and people asking, "How can we approach this like we did with safety?"

Nonetheless, even with these impressive results, I still have a key question I'd love others' thoughts about. In the several years since the group of safety hosts and I were reassigned to other roles because we'd achieved such outstanding results, the safety rate has begun inching back up, particularly at the original Corvallis site. It's now about 2.5 per hundred—still an improvement of more than 50 percent from the original 6.2 per hundred, but not as out-standing as Puerto Rico, which remains a world leader at .2 percent years later.

What's different about the two sites? In Puerto Rico they continued their own internal system of hosting conversations on safety issues, whereas in Corvallis continuous hosting of safety conversations became less intensive. This leaves me wondering: *In a world that is always dynamic and changing, what kind and level of conversational leadership is needed to create long-term sustainable performance on any key issue of systemic importance,* whether it be safety, quality, new product development, or on a large scale, the sustainability of life on our fragile planet?

. . .

STORY

LIVING STRATEGY: DISCOVERING THE FUTURE, TOGETHER: AMERICAN SOCIETY FOR QUALITY

As Told By

Arian Ward, with Paul Borawski and Ken Case

Who are we?

Why are we here?

How can we make the biggest difference?

These seem to be universal questions that matter to us at the personal level. But what would it mean if these were also the questions that mattered most to an organization and its stake-holders? That's what we embarked on a journey to find out as we developed a "living strategy" approach to discovering ASQ's future. At the heart of our work was a commitment to creating a dynamic story of the shared aspirations, future direction, and strategic outcomes for ASQ and the community it supports. We wanted to create a process through which this story could con-tinuously evolve, through expanding the network of ongoing strategic conversations among all members of the community. We hoped that, over time, the story would become woven into the fabric of the organization through a continuous process of reflection and sense-making.

> An exciting experiment using World Café principles to design an inquiring system has been underway at the American Society for Quality (ASQ), led by Paul Borawski, executive director, and Ken Case, volunteer president. ASQ is the largest quality association in the world, with over 130,000 members in fifty countries on six continents. Arian Ward, of Community Frontiers, is a pioneer in engaging the World Café with membership associations and community groups.

What prompted this new way of thinking was a belief that continued success would not come simply from doing traditional planning better. As Paul Borawski, ASQ's executive director, explains, "I was personally looking for a planning approach that could help make the connection between the mindset and the 'heartset' of our board and members. I was seeking a way to unleash the spirit of our members around the deeper meaning of quality, not only in the workplace but in the larger society as well."

The first meeting that employed the World Café methodology—conducted with the board's Strategic Planning Committee—was definitely a risk! Unlike past sessions, this two-day meeting was not designed to produce a traditional one-page plan. Instead, the goal was to develop key strategic questions that called for further exploration. "I think if anybody who knew us had listened to what we planned to do with Cafés they would have laughed and said that it wouldn't work," Paul recalls. "But you should have seen the room come to life with the first set of Café questions! This session turned ASQ strategically inside out. The committee began to ask questions that they concluded weren't theirs to answer. Some needed to go to the full board; others needed the input of the full membership. The whole thing started to blossom into a realization that many more voices were needed to discover the answers to the key strategic questions raised at that initial session."

As a result of this and subsequent strategic dialogues, ASQ's strategic planning process has evolved into an ongoing inquiry spreading out from a small group of people (the Strategic Planning Committee), to a larger group (the board), to many other stakeholders. Members of the ASQ board and staff have now actively hosted Cafés on key strategic questions for ASQ members, former members, non-quality professionals who are using quality tools in their work, executives who need to leverage quality in their organizations, and people from the service sector where formal quality tools haven't traditionally been employed. Strategic questions and storytelling based on the outcomes from previous Cafés serve as the connectors for linking the evolving collective intelligence from these growing networks of conversation.

Supported by ASQ staff, who help coordinate Café events and organize the feedback and collective intelligence gathered from the Cafés, this approach also involves creating "sense and respond" opportunities throughout ASQ's far-flung membership. A growing number of members of the global quality community use Cafés and other forms of strategic dialogue to explore what's happening in their environment. They provide ongoing feedback to the association, which helps with collective sense-making in relation to emerging issues and opportunities.

Ken Case, the ASQ president, provides a rich image of this living process for creating an inquiring system: "It's an ongoing dialogue spreading in waves. We're trying to ask the right questions—which is really an art as well as a science. Our purpose is to cause people to dig deeply and to think together about who we are, what we are about, and what we want to be. Based on the key questions, you can see the ripples going out. And, if you notice, those ripples come back too: pearls of ideas suggested by our outer constituencies that get fed back to the board. That's the beautiful dynamic of this approach. We hear rich discussion going on that we haven't heard in any prior year of participation on the ASQ board."

ASQ's ripples-in-a-pond living strategy process uses Café dialogues to engage an expanding web of conversations around its most important questions. We're learning that true strategic leadership is about seeding these conversations with the right questions, hosting the ongoing dialogue, and helping the organization make sense of and take action in response to the insights and opportunities that emerge. It's not easy to change traditional ways. Paul Borawski shares that: "Our transformation is young and fragile, but it has begun. What's exciting is the knowledge that living systems thinking is transforming a community deeply rooted in mechanistic traditions." Through this approach we're slowly discovering ways to create engagement environments that work in concert with the organization as a living system to co-evolve our future in ways that are worthy of our best effort.

. . .

Perspectives & Observations

The first time I encountered Alan Webber in person was in January 1995, when I welcomed him at the door of our home for the strategic dialogue on intellectual capital, the evening before the World Café was born in our living room. But the former managing editor of the *Harvard Business Review* and soon to be co-founder of *Fast Company* magazine was no stranger to me. Unbeknownst to Alan, he was one of David's and my heroes.

Two years earlier, Alan had written an *HBR* article, "What's So New About the New Economy?" (1993, p. 28) where he posited— may I add, somewhat before his time—that in the new economy, where ideas and information are key currencies of exchange, conversation is the mother of invention. Contrary to popular opinion, he said, it's not having new technology platforms that create business value. Rather, Alan argued, it's flesh-and-blood people in conversation, learning from each other, sharing their knowledge and experience, who create the innovations and solutions that make or break the organization. Alan was unequivocal in his belief that "the most important work in the new economy is creating conversations". In today's world, he stressed, it becomes the leader's primary responsibility to facilitate the kind of collaborative environment, mutual trust, and authentic conversations that enable the organization to access the collective intelligence of its members. It was Alan's groundbreaking article that gave David and me the confidence to believe we were on the right track in our early musings about the centrality of conversation as a generative force in our lives and work.

How can we begin to cultivate both the organizational infrastructures and personal leadership capabilities that are needed to access and act on the wisdom that already exists in our organizations and communities?

While it was Alan who pointed to conversation as the lifeblood of the knowledge era, it was Florida educator and Café host Carolyn Baldwin who coined the term *conversational leadership* to describe the leader's intentional use of conversation as a core process to cultivate the collective intelligence needed to create business and social value. Yet even today, conversational leadership is not taught in most leadership development programs. How can we begin to cultivate both the organizational infrastructures and personal leadership capabilities that are needed to access and act on the wisdom that already exists in our organizations and communities? Although we're still at an early stage in our exploration of conversational leadership, here are some initial areas to consider based on the stories in this book and our own research-in-action. We'd welcome your thoughts and insights as well.

Engage Strategic Questions

Mastering the art and architecture of powerful questions that evoke knowledge-sharing, inspire strategic dialogue, and invite committed action is a critical personal leadership skill (Vogt and others, 2003). Strategic questions create forward movement and new possibilities for collective discovery. But they can also serve as the "glue" that holds together overlapping webs *(continued on p. 189)*

Designing Organizational Infrastructures for Dialogue: Philip Morris USA

As Told By

Mike Szymanczyk

I'm an architect at heart. If you want to use conversation as a core process, then you have to be intentional about designing the infrastructures that will evoke people's capacity for thinking together in new ways. It's one thing to have the personal leadership skills to host a great conversation. It's another to create an organizational architecture that channels how people collaborate to discover their mutual intelligence. I've found that ordinary people in a good infrastructure will create better results than their more brilliant counterparts operating in a poorly designed system.

> As the current chairman and CEO of Philip Morris USA, Mike Szymanczyk is leading his company through the challenges of realigning with society and reinventing its future. Collaborative dialogue around critical strategic questions lies at the heart of this evolution toward a more positive future. Here Mike talks of the conversational infrastructures being used to engage the organization's best thinking.

We've done a number of things over the years to create infrastructures for collaborative dialogue and engagement. Some of our choices might seem "outside the box," but we've found they've made a real difference. For example, very early on we invented a strategy process, the Game Plan, based on collaborative dialogue and inquiry that is used organization-wide. It focuses on discovering the big questions at the heart of shaping the future and on creating initiatives that respond to those critical strategic questions.

We also regularly utilize a variety of conversational architectures and creative meeting formats that foster collaborative thinking and innovative solutions. As part of our large-scale change effort we've introduced World Café conversations, dialogue circles, Open Space sessions, scenario planning, outdoor experiential learning, and even dramatic theater presentations to stimulate dialogue and breakthrough thinking around critical issues. We also use graphic recording and visual language as a key resource to help people think more systemically, connect ideas, and surface difficult concerns.

Introducing other infrastructures for learning, information sharing, and dialogue have enabled us to create organizational venues for thinking more deeply together about key strategic questions. For example, my regular full-day senior team meetings and three-times-per-year off-site senior team sessions, our mission goals conversations with cross-functional groups, and our town hall–style gatherings with employees all help surface the organization's collective intelligence around key questions.

Putting younger leaders with diverse perspectives into exploration teams that reach out to key stakeholders has also brought fresh thinking to important emerging issues.

Not long ago the company moved its headquarters from a skyscraper in New York City to a tree-filled campus in Richmond, Virginia. The design of the building encourages greater cross-fertilization of ideas and a more collaborative environment. Our senior team, who helped design the space, wanted places where people could gather informally to talk together, so we put a large coffee bar and café in our lobby area. People pass through the café area whenever they enter or leave the building. Throughout the day people will say, 'Let's meet downstairs for a coffee.'" We co-located groups that need to work closely together and created comfortable living rooms with whiteboards on each floor. There's also a library and special meeting room designed for Café conversations on the ground floor with plenty of wall space for graphic recording that groups can reserve for their "think meetings." We've created special meeting spaces with double-screen technology to support conversations at a distance in ways that allow us both to see our colleagues from different sites and to work with visual materials related to the questions or projects we're exploring. And most offices also have a view to the outdoors and natural light.

As you can imagine, all of this is a *big* change from New York—and it's already having a significant organizational payoff. People are now making more connections across functional boundaries, and we're seeing a greater diversity of perspectives and richness of thought on key projects. Hosting regular community gatherings with local stakeholders in our new building is also bringing in fresh points of view.

By intentionally designing these conversational infrastructures, we're able to engage both our own employees and key external stakeholders in thinking more creatively about what a tobacco manufacturer needs to do to meet society's expectations of a responsible corporation. I believe that engaging in collaborative dialogue, along with the other positive steps we are taking to reinvent our future, are slowly but surely enabling us to distinguish ourselves as a leader in our industry.

. . .

of conversations through which diverse resources can combine and recombine to create innovative solutions. As Bob Veazie discovered in his safety work at Hewlett-Packard: "It was the questions themselves, coupled with the invitation to explore them, that moved people from compliant behavior to committed performance. Managers would ask me, 'How can results come from just asking our people questions? I want answers, not questions!' But we found that results *do* come from the questions. The results lie in the personal relationships, the knowledge, and the mutual caring that gets strengthened in people's conversations together *about* the questions, along with the discovery of their *own* answers."

Especially in a volatile and uncertain business environment, another important leadership opportunity lies in creating conversational infrastructures—like the Philip Morris USA Game Plan process—that encourage members at all levels to discover their own key strategic questions. For example, when leaders are willing to ask, *What is the question that, if explored deeply, could give us a real breakthrough?* people's own collective wisdom often reveals a path less traveled that shows an innovative way forward.

Convene and Host Learning Conversations

A core aspect of the new work of leadership involves convening and hosting gatherings to engage productive dialogue around challenging questions. As educator Linda Lambert and her colleagues point out, "Leading the conversations is not a neutral role: it is a role of active involvement. . . . Leaders need to pose the questions and convene the conversations that invite others to become involved. . . . Developing meaningful dialogue is about creating conceptual fields that deepen or shift thinking" (Lambert and others, 1995, pp. 101, 105).

Authentic conversation that deepens a group's thinking and evokes collaborative intelligence is less likely to occur in a climate of fear, mistrust, and hierarchical control. When the human mind and heart are fully engaged in exploring questions that matter, new knowledge often begins to surface. To succeed, leaders need to strengthen their personal skills in hosting dialogue and other approaches that deepen mutual inquiry.

These capabilities include:

- Creating a climate of discovery
- Suspending premature judgment
- Exploring underlying assumptions and beliefs
- Listening for unexpected connections between ideas
- Encouraging the expression of a wide range of perspectives
- Articulating shared understandings

Other aspects of effective hosting are also key, including clarifying the larger context, ensuring a welcoming environment, encouraging everyone's contribution, and managing divergent viewpoints. Your personal authenticity, integrity, and values become increasingly central to establishing your credibility as a legitimate host and convener who can inspire trust and foster collaboration among diverse constituencies.

Invite Diverse Perspectives

How often do you hear a leader pose the question, *Whose voices need to be included in this conversation? Who's not here who should be?* Not often. Yet cultivating conversational leadership requires leaders to become active connectors—of diverse people and stimulating ideas.

> You can foster creative insights and new collegial networks by convening strategic conversations across traditional boundaries

Just as an individual World Café conversation can create a rich web of unexpected insights through the cross-pollination of ideas and the creation of new personal networks, as a conversational leader you can foster creative insights and new collegial networks by convening strategic conversations across traditional boundaries. As Gary Hamel of the London School of Economics points out, "Strategizing depends on creating a rich and complex web of conversations that cuts across previously isolated pockets of knowledge and creates new and unexpected combinations of insight" (1997, p. 9). This means engaging diverse voices inside the organization, including those of younger people who are often not considered "ready" to be part of the inner circle by senior leadership. It also means convening and hosting learning conversations with key outside constituencies, including customers, suppliers, nongovernmental organizations (NGOs), community members, and others who have a stake in your organization's future.

Support Appreciative Inquiry

Searching for innovative possibilities requires today's leaders to shift from focusing primarily on what is *not* working and how to fix it to discovering and appreciating what is working and how to leverage it. Appreciative Inquiry (AI), developed by David Cooperrider and his colleagues at Case Western University, is a powerful conversational process for valuing previously untapped sources of knowledge, vitality, and energy (Cooperrider and others, 2003; Whitney and Trosten-Bloom, 2003; Watkins and Mohr, 2001). AI stimulates lively conversations about what the organization does well and uncovers its hidden assets. By focusing on aspects of the desired future that are already being lived today, AI enables leaders to foster networks of conversation that can leverage emerging possibilities rather than simply fix past mistakes.

This approach to organizational change creates a generative field of mutual trust and excitement about new opportunities. While taking an AI stance is not a "normal" approach for leaders who are paid to solve problems, we are finding that this simple shift of lens lies at the heart of the kind of conversational leadership that can bring out the best in an organization or community.

Foster Shared Understanding

In today's complex environment, leaders are discovering that one of their unique contributions is to provide *conceptual leadership*—creating shared contexts and common frameworks in which groups can deepen or shift their thinking together. We make meaning of our experiences through the language we use, the stories we share, and the images we favor. For example, holding the image of your organization as a battlefield, where members carry out "preemptive strikes" and "decimate the

> We make meaning of our experiences through the language we use, the stories we share, and the images we favor

competition" evokes very different behavior than a shared under-standing of the organization as a dynamic web of conversations and personal relationships, part of a living system that includes key inter-nal and external stakeholders—at times even those you've tradition-ally thought of as "the competition." Conversational leaders also put time and attention into framing a common language and articulating compelling scenarios—stories of the future—that can shape collective purpose and provide direction for organizational conversations.

Fostering shared understanding means creating conversa-tional infrastructures that carve out the time for true listening, thoughtful reflection, and mutual sense-making. Thoughtful lis-tening and disciplined collective reflection provide the founda-tion for creating productive conversations and shared understanding about how the organization's results are actually created, and how they can be improved. As Dennis Sandow and Anne Murray Allen, who have both worked with HP's Bob Veazie, explain, "With multiple experiences of shared understanding, we begin to see the flow of knowledge and performance in social sys-tems, much as one begins to see the flow in a successful musical, theatrical, or sports performance" (2004, p. 9).

Honor Social Networks and Nurture Communities of Practice

Many of the most provocative questions and leading-edge prac-tices that are vital to a creating sustainable value are discovered by accident on the front lines, in the middle of the action, in the conversations of everyday life. But this wisdom is often lost. Most leaders rarely notice, honor, and utilize the learning and knowl-edge creation that is woven into the informal conversations, per-sonal networks, relationships, and practices that are already part of the organization's social fabric (Sandow and Allen, 2004).

Etienne Wenger's pioneering work on communities of prac-tice offers many directions to take to engage the wisdom residing in these informal knowledge networks (Wenger, 1998; Wenger and others, 2002). Thoughtful leaders will pay special attention to ensuring that new work processes or redesigned organizational structures do not inadvertently destroy the ongoing conversations and knowledge that are woven into these informal webs of relationships. You can also provide informal meeting space, intranet knowledge-sharing infrastructures, or knowledge stewards who help facilitate the development of active communities of practice and learning conversations among people with the special expertise needed to address long-term organizational needs.

Rethink Training and Development

Most training and development efforts have been founded on deeply embedded assumptions about learning as an individual endeavor, and on the separation of training activities from the practical realities of action on the front line. You may remember your own early education, where the adage was "Listen to the teacher and don't talk to your neighbor." In today's organizations and communities, where continuous learning and knowledge-sharing are important, conversational leaders are rethinking training and development. Recognizing the social nature of learning, they are reallocating resources away from traditional training programs to support the evolution of communities of practice, investing in experientially based collaborative learning through peer dialogue, and designing interactive technology infrastructures to support learning conversations rather than simply store data.

Support Collaborative Technologies

Intranet and groupware technologies are now making it possible for widely dispersed work groups to participate in learning conversations and team projects across time and space. As these tools become even more widely available, the notion of conversational leadership will expand to include supporting widespread online conversations through which members can contribute their own questions and best thinking to critical strategic issues and ongoing learning opportunities. For example, Buckman Laboratories has created a worldwide intranet, K'Netix, that enables its employees in more than one hundred countries around the world to engage in ongoing learning conversations about customer needs and solutions. Users can contribute to the conversation at any time, from any place, and in several different languages. The system updates the evolving "knowledge threads" as questions are explored and solutions discovered. Far-flung employees who would normally never have the chance to be a part of the conversations are often the ones who provide key insights and expertise. K'Netix has become the central nervous system for the company's knowledge-sharing conversations (Prahalad and Ramaswamy, 2004).

These types of conversational infrastructures, along with complementary approaches like graphic recording and visual mapping, create possibilities for individuals and groups to be in conversation in ways that were previously unimaginable. Leaders who recognize their strategic importance and support their use will be at a significant advantage.

Design Welcoming Places and Spaces

As we initially shared in chapter 4, famed architect Christopher Alexander points to the deep human yearning for both physical and psychological environments that embody the "quality that has no name"—a special quality of aliveness, wholeness, and comfort that people recognize whenever they experience it, even though it is hard to describe. Designing or selecting physical and social environments that are alive and comfortable as a context for thinking together has not been high on most executives' list of strategic priorities. However, as our last decade of experience with the World Café and Mike Szymanczyk's story in this chapter demonstrate, creating physical spaces that embody the quality that has no name is important for conversational leaders to consider in stimulating innovative thinking and cultivating collective intelligence.

Co-Evolve the Future

Our challenging times require thoughtful consideration of difficult economic, social, and environmental questions. Leaders who cultivate their personal conversational skills and at the same time are able to design and implement conversational infrastructures tailored to the unique needs of their own organization or community will be in increasing demand. Seeing the ways in which conversation can help an organization create its future—and utilizing processes, principles, tools, and technologies that support this evolution—is everyone's job. We each have the opportunity to exercise conversational leadership in our lives and work. This is one powerful way that organizations and communities can cultivate both the knowledge required to thrive today and the wisdom needed to ensure a sustainable future for our children and grandchildren.

Questions for Reflection

How well does your organization foster conversational leadership and engage conversation as a core process? What might you do to foster a greater appreciation of its possibilities in your own setting? Consider the following questions:

To what extent does your organization consider conversation to be the heart of "real work"? How often do the leaders and members attend to the principles and practices of good conversation as they engage with key stakeholders?

How much importance do you place on your role as convener or host for good conversations about questions that matter?

How much time do you and your colleagues spend discovering the right questions in relation to the time spent finding the right answers?

What enabling infrastructures, processes, or tools are being systematically used to support good conversations and knowledge sharing in your organization or community?

How often do your meetings and conferences include well-designed opportunities for collaborative dialogue, peer exchange, and interactive learning?

To what extent is your physical work space or office area designed to encourage the informal interaction that supports good conversation and effective learning?

How much of your training and development budget is devoted to supporting informal learning conversations and sharing effective practices across organizational boundaries?

TWELVE

The Call of Our Times:
Creating a Culture of Dialogue

*Conversation is at the heart of the new inquiry. It is
perhaps the core human capacity for dealing with the
tremendous challenges we face. To engage in great
civilization we need to ask questions that matter. We
cannot afford to spend our time on issues that can't hold
our attention, that don't touch our hearts. The culture
of conversation is a different culture, one that could make
a difference in the future of our world.*

—Institute for the Future, *In Good Company:
Innovation at the Intersection of Technology and Sustainability*

What if a conversation
begun today could ripple out and
create new possibilities?

WHAT DOES IT MEAN TO CARE? CREATING A LEARNING CULTURE THROUGH DIALOGUE: SINGAPORE

As Told By

Samantha Tan

Samantha Tan, a Research Fellow at Harvard University's Kennedy School of Government, is exploring leadership issues in education. After being away from Singapore for three years, she returned home to visit with family and to explore the ways the World Café is being used as part of the Singapore's mission to become a "learning nation." Samantha's story demonstrates one of the ways in which the World Café is contributing to evolving cultures of dialogue around the world.

No one thought Singapore would survive once it separated from Malaysia in 1965. We're a tiny island with no natural resources except for a deep harbor and the collective talents of our 4.2 million people. That's it. It's miracle that we survived, and a greater miracle that we are thriving. We have a good, strong government. And yet, our progress has taken its toll. The very drive, authority, and unwavering focus that got us through the most difficult times are tough to shift now that we want to become a learning nation that's entrepreneurial, innovative, and creative. Singaporean poet Koh Buck Song sums this sentiment up in his poem "The Fragrance of Lallang" when he says, "But so strong is exertion's scent, it conquers all whiff of wonderment."

As a people, we often rely on "someone higher up" to solve our problems. Having worked in the government, I often wondered, *How can we build learning bridges between those in power and the other voices in our society so that something new can emerge?* It's hard to make the transition from old ways to the new ways—even when people say they want to. I went to study abroad precisely to understand that, and to spend some time looking at the world from different eyes.

This question was still in my heart when I learned that the World Café had been introduced to Singapore by Daniel Kim, a co-founder of the MIT Sloan School's Organizational Learning Center, and his partner, Diane Cory. It's part of a larger effort to engage leaders from across the government and other key institutions in the principles and practices of learning organizations. When I told Juanita that I was going home for a month's visit, she asked if I'd like to explore how the World Café was being used in Singapore. The day before I left, Juanita e-mailed key people involved with Cafés to tell them that I was coming home and wanted to learn more about the World Café.

And do you know what? By the time I touched down in Singapore there were already eager responses in my inbox—from the People's Association, the Police Department, the InfoComm Development Authority, the Housing Development Board, the Ministry of Manpower, and people working with local schools. They all wanted to meet and talk about their experiences with the World Café. I was amazed! Sheila Damodaran, of the Organizational

Learning Unit in the Singapore police force, not only attended most of my one-on-one meetings but also offered to organize a community Café among Singaporean World Café hosts and others from the Learning Organization Practitioners' Network, which she co-chairs. I'd like to share several vignettes of what I found on my Café learning journey. These aren't the only ones, but they will give you an idea of what's going on across our country.

Creating Bridges Between Generations

Eric Wee, a lecturer at the Temasek Polytechnic, teaches systems thinking to a group of seventeen-year-olds. He has them work in teams to apply systems thinking archetypes to issues like teenage pregnancy and youth smoking. He then invites policymakers and program funders (for example, the National Youth Council, the Center for Fathering, and the Ministry of Health) to attend a Café with the students. Students, in teams of three, host Café tables on the various issues they've studied. Groups of adults move from table to table during each Café round. The students present their systems analysis of the issues—for example, why teenagers smoke. The adults ask questions and have very thoughtful conversations with the teenagers at the Café tables. In the past, students would typically be (a) less informed and more myopic about the issues, and (b) afraid of talking to adults. But in the Café conversations the students have equal footing with adults. When people come together at the end of the Café, what emerges as a common theme is that parents and children really *want* to talk together more. The representative from the Center for Fathering is so inspired that he decides on the spot to initiate Café conversations between parents and children on a larger scale.

Guns and Flowers

Senior and junior staff on the police force are sitting together in a Café conversation—people from three or four different ranks, wearing their uniforms and carrying their guns, talking together at those little tables with flower vases and checkered tablecloths. They are really listening and hearing each other's perspectives for the first time on how street officers are being affected, for example, by a new computerized tracking system that's been installed in police cars. After the Café, the senior officers say, "No matter how bright or smart our ideas are, we now realize we need ideas from the people at the ground level to make policies that actually work." And the juniors come to appreciate that the seniors aren't just authoritarian; they really *are* concerned about the welfare of the junior members. The police department decides to use the Café format for its annual corporate planning exercise, to create conversations that include more voices in the process.

Nourishing the Community Through Dialogue

The People's Association of Singapore, through the National Community Leadership Institute (NACLI), decides to merge the World Café with our local culture by creating P2P (People to People) conversations between government representatives and grassroots leaders using a creative adaptation of the World Café called the Knowledge Kopitiam. *Kopitiams* are the traditional Singaporean neighborhood coffee shops that serve local specialties. They are places that local

people have frequented since our early immigrant days to relax and talk informally about the issues of the day. NACLI launches its Knowledge Kopitiams by recreating a traditional kopitiam setting for its inaugural conversation, "Creating an Active Community in the New Economy." They call the kopitiam approach the "knowledge-traveling process." NACLI's magazine Kopitalk spreads the word about this "old/new" way of encouraging authentic conversation on key issues, and the kopitiam idea begins to spread. After experiencing the Knowledge Kopitiams at NACLI, Yaacob Ibrahim, then senior parliamentary secretary for the Ministry of Communications and Information Technology, comments, "Today we want to spark a revolution, not to overthrow the government, but to reinvent ourselves. . . . These people-to-people or P2P discussions are essential to our development as a cohesive and well-informed people. I am pleased that NACLI has captured the relevance of such dialogues to reinvent the way grassroots forums can be organized."

The Café Travels

The Knowledge Kopitiam concept begins to spread to other government and institutional settings. Members of the organizational learning community find they can host a Café without too much difficulty, tailoring it to address their own organization's important questions. The Ministry of Defense hosts Café dialogues to explore the question, "How can we expand our purpose from deterrence to nation building?" In line with one of its corporate objectives—to be a learning organization—the Housing Development Board introduces Café conversations in its orientation program for new officers in order to create time and space for real conversation about their hopes, aspirations, and concerns. Schools convene Café dialogues among a broad cross section of schoolteachers and administrators around the question, "Given the changing needs of our country, what does it mean to teach?" The InfoComm Development Authority and the Ministry of Manpower adopt the Knowledge Kopitiam to explore how internal departments can learn from each other and focus their collective efforts on nurturing a culture of creativity and innovation in Singapore.

What Does It Mean to Care?

For me, the most surprising Café discoveries came at the end of my visit, when Sheila Damodaran from the police department, along with Ivy Ooi and Anthony Lim from the Housing Development Board, convened a community gathering of World Café hosts and other members of the Learning Organization Practitioners' Network. I was amazed when close to seventy people showed up! We decided to put the question "What does it mean to care?" at the center of the Café.

Several things happened that afternoon that showed me how the World Café is contributing to a culture of dialogue in Singapore—responding to our yearning and caring as a people for having real conversations across the boundaries of the hierarchies that so often separate us. For example, there was a woman in the Café dressed very plainly who seemed out of place, although I knew she'd been invited. I'd describe her as a "tea lady"—a service person who is usually pretty invisible in our society. In the whole-group conversation at the end of the Café, she courageously stood up and said softly, but with much certainty, "You know, it's important to feel people care, because when people care, it makes life worth living." The room was struck silent by her piercing humanity. Her words spoke to a whole national issue—to our utilitarian mindset where people sometimes feel like widgets—and how debilitating and soul-destroying it is. I was moved. Everyone was moved. And in that room, I knew that policy decisions would shift because of her. That moment somehow changed me forever.

I think one of the surprising learnings for everyone doing Café work in Singapore is that Café conversations are a constructive bridge between levels and between the past and the future. It's a national issue because we want to promote entrepreneurship, creativity, and innovation, and we're struggling to learn how to create environments that redefine the authority relationship. Yet to do this, we are partnering with the authorities! It's a paradox.

We like structure in Singapore. We've found that the World Café provides a clear structure, but like cooks using a large mixing bowl, we can put in different ingredients and invent new dishes. I've also tried to understand why Café dialogues have worked so well in Singapore, an Asian culture with so many diverse ethnic groups. The Café provides an informal and relaxed environment that celebrates and harnesses difference yet also helps us see what connects us. Seeing this happen gave me an insight into the real meaning of empowerment—power generated from the ground up by seeing new connections and building peer-to-peer relationships across the boundaries that so often divide us.

Could the World Café represent a new form of activism—an activism of the spirit? It's not an activism *against* the authority structure, but *for* the world we want. It's a humanistic activism, because in the Café you are responding to a common question, but you are called to respond from wherever you sit in relation to the question. It is fundamentally a very respectful process—a form of *pro-activism* rather than *re-activism*. That's what I want to see in Singapore—people actively co-creating—helping each other through dialogue to be, as it were, in our dreams awake . . . collectively shaping our future.

I've become very proud of the work that is happening in Singapore, especially because of the quality of heart that I now see exists here. I experienced that feeling in the many Singaporeans I met with who contributed to my being able to tell this story. I fell in love again with my country. By seeing where and how Café conversations are spreading, I realized that in addition to our logical, rational, practical, and results-oriented mindset, our small nation also has passion, enthusiasm, and soul, and has a positive role to play in the direction that Asia and the world are moving. This idea of conversation—talking together, reaching mutual understanding, and making meaning together across hierarchies—that's the work that needs to be done. That's where the potential is. The World Café is bringing that in practical ways to our journey forward as a nation.

. . .

On the evening before beginning to write these reflections on creating a culture of dialogue, I participated in a Café gathering of Latino and Anglo parents, teachers, schoolchildren, and local residents in the tiny community of Point Reyes Station, California. It's located at the tip of Tomales Bay, an endangered pristine ecosystem just an hour and a half north of San Francisco. This rural area is the home to a diverse population—oyster fishermen, cattle ranchers, organic produce and dairy farmers, environmental activists, urban-techno refugees, artists and writers—along with farmhands, nursery workers, gardeners, and tradespeople, many of whom come originally from Mexico. Interest groups often spar with each other. Local issues, including education, have at times become heated and acrimonious.

David and I have lived in this area part-time for the last decade, and we will likely spend our later years here. David had been asked by a small group of moms at the local West Marin School to host a World Café dialogue on the question, "What are the elements of an ideal educational experience for young people in our community?" The gathering was, it seems, a first—a large bilingual, bicultural event in which all advertising and every aspect of the meeting itself would be conveyed in both Spanish and English. The whole community, whether parents or not, was invited to attend. And for the very first time, schoolchildren were included as equal partners in the conversation about the future of their own learning.

Over one hundred community members turned out for the gathering, a mass meeting for our small community. As the Café unfolded, David and I were deeply moved by the unexpected connections being made. At one table, a Latino farmworker parent sat beside a nine-year-old boy, his ponytailed dad, and a local contractor who had run for county supervisor. At another table was a teacher, a twelve-year-old girl, the coordinator of the neighborhood radio station, and an environmental activist. All were deeply engrossed in thinking together about how, as a community, they could create the best learning for young people.

In the whole-group conversation at the end of the Café, members from very different worlds discovered that their hopes and dreams for the youth of the community were not so different from each other after all. People discovered that underneath what had appeared as local controversy was a yearning for authentic connection, personal relationships, good ideas, and committed action on behalf of the common good. Someone said, "I think it's important that we form a Parent-Teachers Association (PTA)." Another popped up and asked, "Why couldn't it be Parent-Teacher-Student-Community Association?"—and the room broke out clapping with excitement at the thought of it.

You might ask, "Why were you so moved? What's the relevance of a single Café of a hundred people in a tiny northern California town for the 'big question' of creating a culture of dialogue in the larger world?" David and I believe that this small local story is an important reminder of the call of our times, the call to actively engage across the imagined boundaries that so often separate us in order to address the challenges facing our families, our organizations, our local communities, our national societies, and our global village.

The Call of Our Times

Let's face it. The challenges we face are widespread and complex. They threaten the very survival of our species and our fragile biosphere. These "wake-up calls" include environmental degradation and climate change, unemployment, poor education, urban violence, and other problems associated with the growing schism between rich and poor, both within and between nations. These systemic issues are exacerbated by a host of military conflagrations, the availability of weapons of mass destruction, and the excesses of global economic competition.

The challenges we face are widespread and complex

We live with a growing awareness that important spiritual, ethical, and ecological dimensions of life have been sorely neglected and are now threatening to engulf us with unanticipated consequences. Perhaps most sobering is the rapidly escalating tendency to separate "us" from "them," to create chasms rather than bridges in the face of differences in religious or political beliefs, cultural values, and personal lifestyles.

It is becoming painfully clear that none of us in this vulnerable and interconnected world can go it alone. No matter what the level of system—from our own families to our global community—we are being called to forge paths to the future that will enable us to use the dilemmas and diversity in our midst in order to generate more creative, holistic, and wiser responses to the challenges we face.

The question for our times is how to do this. Philosopher Jacob Needleman asks, *"How can we come together and think and hear each other in order to touch, or be touched, by the intelligence we need? . . .* We need each other to think well about these questions. And therefore, we come round again to the question of how to structure our work of thinking together" (1997, p. 4). Our response to Needleman's challenge is to remind ourselves and others that authentic conversation is our human way of thinking together. It has been since our earliest days, when our ancestors gathered around fires in council to resolve differences and discover ways to confront dangers to their survival.

Council was one of the earliest structures used to focus the work of thinking together in conversation. The World Café stories in this book offer another intentional conversational structure for thinking together—one based on simple design principles that can enhance our capacities to think more holistically, embrace diverse perspectives, and create actionable knowledge across traditional boundaries. Whether it be exploring the future of education in a tiny California town, engaging a multistakeholder sustainability forum in Sweden, deliberating questions of peace and war at a Canadian law school, reaching across the divide between Israeli Arabs and Jews, including patients and physicians

> Authentic conversation
> is our human way of
> thinking together

in a pharmaceutical company's strategy, improving school performance in Florida, reducing company safety risks at Hewlett-Packard, or bridging organizational hierarchies in Singapore, the World Café is serving as a useful conversational process and pattern for accessing and enlivening co-intelligent action.

An Era of Opportunity

Thankfully, as our need for thinking together effectively and connecting together personally becomes more acute, creative approaches to dialogue and engagement are burgeoning. Appreciative Inquiry (Cooperrider and others, 2003), Open Space (Owen, 1997), Future Search (Weisbord and Janoff, 2000), and circle practice (Baldwin, 1994), along with other approaches to shaping the future (Bunker and Alban, 1997; Holman and Devane, 1999), are making unique contributions. Innovative face-to-face and computer-assisted approaches to public deliberation and citizen engagement are on the rise (Atlee, 2003). Key initiatives like Conversation Cafés, Commons Cafés, Let's Talk America, From the Four Directions, Public Conversations Project, the Pioneers of Change, the National Coalition for Dialogue and Deliberation, and the Fetzer Institute's Collective Wisdom Initiative are highlighting dialogue processes that are showing great promise for accessing the collective wisdom that lies beyond traditional advocacy and argumentation—in the public sphere, in education, health, government, and in the corporate world. These exciting efforts are enabling many of us who have been adversarial activists in the past to experience a deeper intelligence that is grounded in our understanding of systems thinking and the interconnectedness of all life. Our discoveries are leading us to the recognition that there's no "them" out there. We're becoming what Tom Atlee, the founder of the Co-Intelligence Institute, calls "social process activists," who look beyond the adversarial stances that abound on both the right and the left. Process activism focuses on *how* we engage together around critical issues, not just *what* particular position we are advocating.

Social process activists seek to engage diverse perspectives as co-intelligent resources for the common good by employing a range of dialogue and deliberation approaches for discovering the greater wisdom of the whole. This type of proactive and interactive stance provides a clear contrast to our current culture of diatribe, which tends to demonize and demean the "other."

Another unexpected resource for creating an active culture of dialogue is also coming into play. The very communications technologies that have in many ways separated us from the rhythms of the natural world and from relationships with each other are, simultaneously, making our collective predicament visible in ways we could never have previously imagined. Mass media, assisted by the Internet and other Web-based technologies, now makes it possible for the whole world instantaneously to see young soldiers being killed and women or children being maimed in conflicts half a planet away.

As humans we have the unique capacity for reflective awareness—the capacity to step back together and ask, "Why is this happening? Is there a better way?" In fact, the word *consciousness* comes from *con-scire,* meaning "knowing together." Our capacity for knowing together is now being honed through the use of densely connected electronic networks that are catalyzing growing webs of connected conversations about what we want for our common future—not only in local communities and organizations but also in this global village that is our common place of origin. The World Café, as a similar pattern of networked conversations, is simply a smaller-scale version that we can use in order to engage our collective intelligence around the questions we most care about in order to shape our futures more intentionally.

As Peter Russell has pointed out, our "global brain" is awakening to its life-affirming potential (1995, 1998). Enabled by online connections, citizen action networks and nongovernmental organizations (NGOs) are springing up, helping millions of us reach out to each other, both locally and across the boundaries of geography, religion, class, and culture in our search for innovative paths forward. In the corporate world, customers who are talking with each other online about the quality of a company's ethics, products, and services are engendering a revolution in the ways corporations engage key stakeholders.

Perhaps Rick Levine and his co-authors of the best-seller *The Cluetrain Manifesto: The End of Business as Usual* summarized it best when they said: "The real point is that the Internet has made it possible for genuine human voices to be heard again. . . . There are millions of threads in this conversation, but at the beginning and end of each one is a human being. . . . It's not the end of the world. It's the beginning of a new one" (Levine and others, 2000, pp. xii, 32, 36, 37).

Across town, across sectors, and across the world, we now know that, in the words of Cesar Chavez and the farmworkers' movement of my youth, *"Sí, se puede!"*—"Yes, it can be done!"

A Time for Choices

However, as we look at today's challenges, the question remains: *Now that we know what is possible, how will we evolve a global culture in which people—including our national and international leaders—use dialogue and deliberation rather than vindictiveness and violence as the preferred way of dealing with differences and of living together as a human community?* The Chinese character for *crisis* means both danger and opportunity. We are living in such a moment, in which the future hangs in the balance. There is no certainty that just because we have the opportunity and the tools for constructive change we will choose to use them wisely.

> We can live in whatever world we bring about in our conversations

The work of biologist Humberto Maturana reminds us that "our human existence is one in which we can live in whatever world we bring about in our conversations, even if it is a world that finally destroys us as the kind of beings that we are" (Maturana and Verden-Zöller, n.d., p. 48). What if, as Maturana suggests, you knew that the meanings and choices you make each day in conversation with your spouse, your children, your friends, or your colleagues either contributed to the well-being of the larger whole or contributed to its demise? What if others began to see that, too? And what if you had access to simple tools, processes, and infrastructures that enabled you to host and convene life-affirming conversations around your own—or your organization's or your community's—most important questions?

As we shared earlier, architect and philosopher Christopher Alexander has deeply influenced our thinking about how large-scale change occurs in human societies. He points out that living systems, including human systems, are made up of wholes at every level of scale—from the individual, to the family, all the way to complex organizations, towns, cities, and societies. He suggests that life-enhancing improvements actually co-evolve not from grand plans or edicts from a central authority but from small acts of collaboration based on a repetition of life-affirming patterns—like the fundamental pattern of engaging in conversations that matter—at every level of scale. "Every act helps to repair some larger, older whole," Alexander explains, "but the repair not only patches it, it also modifies it, transforms it, sets it on the road to becoming something else, entirely new" (1979, p. 485). He shows how millions of these tiny transformations, carried out locally in any living system, can, over time, spread their effects to transform the character of the system as a whole.

Co-Evolving Our Futures

Perhaps it is as simple as that. . . . Exercising our ability to respond to the call of our times to foster more authentic and courageous conversations in whatever sphere of influence we have been given. . . . Knowing that growing numbers of people around the globe, in their own spheres of influence, are doing the same. . . . Sensing that, at a deeper level, all of these conversations and organizational innovations are already connected to a powerful life force that we as a species now have the opportunity to access intentionally on behalf of our common future.

An Invitation to Community

I invite you to engage in an act of faith. I ask you to imagine that we *do* have the power to make a difference through fostering conversation, community, and committed action in our lives and work. I deeply believe that when we help to change the collective conversation about a situation, we have the opportunity to influence the future of that situation, whatever it may be and at whatever level of scale it occurs. Creating the conditions from which life-affirming futures will emerge is not a spectator sport. It involves daily participation and practice, just like other activities we value.

In the Australian aboriginal culture there is a belief that there is one large song of life, and that each of us has our unique "songline" that contributes to the wholeness and beauty of that song. It is in a spirit of contributing our songline to this larger song of life that our work both with the World Café and with other forms of generative conversation finds its home.

There are many ways to participate. Experiment with Café conversations in your own life and work. Share your discoveries and questions with the World Café listserv where the World Café's community of inquiry and practice gathers to learn together. Visit the World Café Web site to hear the latest Café adventures and the emerging "Voices of the World Café." Take a look at "Resources and Connections" at the end of this book, as well as the bibliography, to discover many additional doorways to dialogue and deliberation. We hope you will experiment with those that seem most suited to the needs of your own situation and would love to hear from you about others that you think we should let people know about. By hosting, convening, and participating in courageous conversations about questions that matter, we can, together, contribute to creating a culture of dialogue and developing the collective wisdom needed to create a legacy of hope for future generations.

I would like to end these reflections with a poem written by our dear friend, colleague, and World Café creative partner, Nancy Margulies. She expresses the spirit that I, as your host, hope you will take with you from our journey together through these pages.

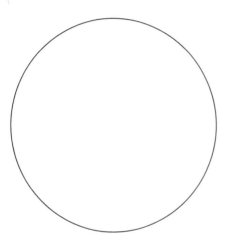

At the World Café . . .

At the World Café,
trusting the strength
that lives in the space between us,
filled with images and thoughts
that give meaning to our lives.

Experiencing
your words echoing in my thoughts,
as questions finding their answers.

Noticing
that it's always been this way,
Conversation enabling us to find meaning,
connecting across imagined boundaries.

I give the gift of listening.
Asking, I discover more than I knew.
Meaning emerges from our shared
sense of what is and what could be.

Becoming
a larger Self that knows its capacity.
Together, we create a future worth living.

What is one question or issue that you personally care deeply about in relation to your family, your work situation, your community, your church, or any other part of your life, that, if explored with others, could make a difference to the future of that situation?

Who else might you invite to engage with you in exploring that question?

How might you use the Café conversation principles (whether or not you use a Café format) to support the quality of that conversation?

What is the next step in your own learning about hosting and convening conversations that matter in your own spheres of influence?

EPILOGUE

How Can We Talk It Through?
By Anne W. Dosher

We are deeply grateful to Anne Dosher, Ph.D., now in her eighties, who has been a guide, mentor, and inspiration for the World Café and other related dialogue initiatives around the globe. One of the developers of the National Network for Youth, Anne received the California Woman-in-Government Award from the California legislative assembly in recognition of her many years of public service. She more recently became a co-founder of the Institute for Relational Development and elder of the Ashland Institute. Here Anne shares the story of the questions that have informed her own lifelong explorations in the field of dialogue and its promise for our common future.

At a World Café event in 2002, David Isaacs introduced me as the elder and "guardian of the soul" of the World Café. He asked why, toward the end of a long life, I was so engaged and committed to the World Café. Normally reticent, in that moment I found my memory spiraling back in time. Born on the northeast coast of England, of Viking and Welsh ancestry, I grew up as a granddaughter of the Empire and daughter of the Common-wealth. As a young girl in the years following the First World War, I puzzled and then grieved that the men came back so hurt—legs lost, difficulty breathing—and that so many were dead. *How could we have done this?* I wondered. *Why couldn't we have talked it through?*

Later, studying the armistice conditions ending the war, it became very clear that the lack of ongoing and authentic dialogue among nations created conditions for future conflict. I determined that, when I grew up, I would study ways in which these mistakes would not be repeated. But then, instead of peace, World War II came, and I spent almost five years in the Royal Air Force. The over-arching mission was simple: survive, defeat Nazism, end holocausts, and make the world safe for democracy. In the course of wartime, I lost friends, comrades, and home. One searing experience in Europe, in which I encountered ambulatory Jews being brought out of the camps, caused me to ask my commanding officer: *"Sir, how could we have done this?"* He snapped that, of course, *we* had not done this, *they* had. Yet I knew that somehow our human community as a whole had failed in the face of these atrocities.

I married an American soldier, and in 1946 my life in the United States began. I have served my adopted country as a com-munity psychologist for almost sixty years, including the develop-ment of services for youth and communities at risk. To that end, I've worked with local, state, and federal governments to develop equitable laws, sufficient funding, and innovative programs. As I sat with alienated youth in barrios and ghettoes, on beaches and reservations, the questions continued to haunt me: *How could we have done this? Why couldn't we have talked it through?*

In my contemplation and study of these questions, it became clear to me that every societal change process I knew of started with an informal conversation in which men and women—young or old—were witnessed and "heard into speech," sharing their dreams and hopes for making a difference around something they cared about. In being truly seen and heard, people were transformed and discovered their mutual commitment to act. That small group then went on to invite other groups into the conversation and the change became more and more real.

As a community psychologist, I used this understanding to design social networks for healing and transforming community and societal systems. I saw that these small circles of conversation were becoming the birthing place of a new human awareness. These networks of small circles of conversation springing up around the world were bringing forth an emerging collective consciousness that yearned for a more equitable and sustainable future for all people on this planet. After years of quietly living the insight about the relationship between dialogue circles and the evolution of larger-scale social movements, I encountered the World Café network. Immediately I recognized in Café conversations a clear metaphor for what life itself had taught me.

Since the day the Café was born in Juanita and David's living room, I have recognized its value and have been intimately involved in guiding its evolution. We make it a point to gather regularly with other World Café pioneers to share our experiments and learnings. The tragedy of September 11 occurred just before one of these gatherings was due to open in Sweden. In the wake of the collective grief, fear, and confusion, there was some question as to whether we should still go. Our Swedish colleague, Bo Gyllenpalm, decided it for us when he said, "Of course, you'll come. If you don't come, they win."

I remember feeling that we were meant to be there to harvest what the global pioneers of the World Café were discovering. Our vital question—*How can we talk it through?*—resonated even more profoundly and deeply under those circumstances. At our meeting in Sweden, I think the whole group felt the same sense of urgency to refine what we were all learning together so that our work could be a force for peace during these troubled times.

How can we talk it through? The question that has informed all of my life choices, now lies, I believe, at the heart of our capacity to survive as a species and to ensure that our home, this beautiful planet, survives. For me, it is the core question that informs all of our other questions. If we could converse and talk things out, we would find new ways of being together in the world. But instead, we separate, conflicts begin, and when worse comes to worse, we go to war. Then death comes in as a walking partner, instead of life.

I get so sad when I see how we adults cut off the conversations our children have with life—with grass, trees, birds, and their own imaginations. Engagement in the conversation of life is discouraged when in fact it is the most essential of our capacities, it is embracing a spirit of true conversation that connects us to all forms of life. We cannot have a true conversation when we're not open to the other, no matter what form the other takes. Often people don't know how to be open, to reach out to others. Authentic conversation without openness is not possible. I want to suggest to practitioners, to emerging leaders, and to our children, that life itself can be a conversation—with other people, with nature, and with all of life.

We have the opportunity to choose life, but to do so, conversation is essential

How can we talk it through? When we talk together, we have a choice between destructive diatribe and constructive dialogue. We can choose life and connection or separation and disintegration. We have the opportunity to choose life, but to do so, conversation is essential. Listening to each other and truly talking together—these are deep, sociospiritual actions. People think talking is not action. That's a mistake. Conversation is a profound action that helps us to expand our consciousness and connect together parts and people that are separated. I can't think of anything else that does that. It is one of our unique human paths to fulfillment and wholeness.

It is we, collectively, who can make the agreement as to how we will live together, and that only happens when we talk about it. We can't do it alone. We need to look at the dilemmas of our current situation and ask, *"How could we have done this?"* We need to look together at what has happened to humanity because we couldn't talk it through!

I have been part of many experiments in exploring the question: *How can we talk it through?* The promise of the World Café and other dialogue approaches is that we now know that we can experience a collective intelligence and wisdom in relation to complex questions. We can, by stepping in and becoming conscious participants in the conversations of our lives, increase the probability of the right choices being made—life-affirming choices. Life itself is asking us to become co-evolutionists—to be responsible for our common destiny—to reconnect with the natural world and with each other. I believe that making the choice to participate in this way is actually a sacred act. I define sacred as that which has value in and of itself and gives meaning to the whole.

The stories in this book flow into a great new story, inviting humanity to learn to speak honestly with one another, to listen truly to one another, and to listen intently *together* for what is emerging in our midst. The stories of the World Café invite us to search for questions that open gateways to co-create the future, to make visible new collective thoughts as they emerge, and to discover creative ways of living and being together. I invite you to find your place at a small Café table in the "world as Café," knowing that you are already connected and interdependent with this larger whole. I ask you to have the confidence that each wholehearted conversation you are part of can make a difference to our common future.

> It is we, collectively, who can make the agreement as to how we will live together, and that only happens when we talk about it

This is quite a long answer to the question David asked me in 2002, and yet I think you can see that, as elder and guardian of the soul of the World Café, I embrace this work as sacred and view life itself as a conversation. When I see the care and love of Café hosts setting out tables, placing the small flowers in the center, attending to the precision of questions that matter, and welcoming people at the doorway, I cherish the knowledge that our human souls and the soul of the world are being honored.

Now, with gratitude to our ancestors and blessings to all of life, I invite you to enter the gateway to the future, discovering your own best hopes along with honoring the needs of future generations, including the young and those not yet born. Welcome! Find a seat with people you haven't met. I invite you into conversations that serve life, and bless your efforts to discover how we can talk it through—together.

Discovering the Magic of Collective Creativity
By Peter M. Senge

All my life I have been drawn to the puzzle of collective creating. *How is it that sometimes, as if by magic, people create something together that has beauty, power, and life?* A sports team that suddenly moves to another plateau where the game is no longer the game but a vehicle for an aesthetic statement (and yet the game is still there). A symphony orchestra that disappears into the music. A dance troupe that ceases being individual dancers. An individual racer who joyously hugs her "opponents" at the end of a race, knowing that it was only from their collective striving that her performance was possible.

This question has drawn me and guided me, but it has worried me as well. Do the recurring examples of collective creating only happen in sporting events or in the performing arts? Is this why singing, dancing, drumming, running, and jumping have bound human cultures together for all our history? But these activities are less central in modern cultures, and as adults we are more likely to encounter them as spectators than as participants. Instead, our lives revolve around teaching, managing, engineering, parenting, doctoring, and coping with countless daily stresses. As one of many who has argued that collective creating can be cultivated in our daily working lives, I worry if the case has been overstated. While the possibility is undeniable, the practices for reliably realizing that possibility have remained elusive.

This is why the World Café has drawn me. Café conversations are the most reliable way I have yet encountered for all of us to tap into collective creating. The stories in this book provide ample illustration. They bring back many memories for me, from when Juanita and I first started experimenting with using World Cafés in countless different gatherings over the past decade—small and large, east and west, north and south.

Peter Senge is a senior lecturer at the Massachusetts Institute of Technology and the founding chair of the Society for Organizational Learning (SoL). Author of the widely acclaimed book *The Fifth Discipline*, which introduced dialogue as a key to organizational learning, Peter shares his decade of experience with the World Café and its contribution to collective creativity.

Throughout all of these experiences, I have been repeatedly struck by the ease of beginning a World Café–style dialogue—how readily people shift into heartfelt and engaging conversations. No formal instruction is needed to start, unlike most organizational development or group techniques. This suggests something important. The World Café is not a technique. It is an invitation into a way of being with one another that is already part of our nature.

I have been struck also by the power and impact of many World Café conversations. At the end of a three-day gathering of fourteen executives engaged in Café dialogues, Arie de Geus, one of the pioneers of organizational learning, said simply, "I am always amazed at what can arise from a collective learning process." As importantly, I have been struck by the elegance and simplicity of the whole process and consequently by its transferability. I can think of very few processes for thinking together that work equally well in executive retreats, annual corporate budget and planning meetings, one-thousand-person conferences, and community gatherings where strangers come together to consider the environment we create for our kids to grow.

The World Café is not only a reliable method for tapping into collective creating. It is also a powerful metaphor for transforming how we think about work in general and why organizations succeed or fail as vehicles for collective creating in particular. *What if we thought of teams of people working together—either formal or informal teams—as being like individual "table conversations" in a larger Café?* What if we thought about each such team interacting with other teams as being like what happens when team members rotate from one Café table to another, influencing and being influenced by each other through the web of conversations in which they are participating.

Following this line of imagination, it is not difficult to envision an organization as a living network of people and groups "in conversation." This is happening all around us, already. But it is

> The World Café is not a technique. It is an invitation into a way of being with one another that is already part of our nature

mostly happening much less powerfully than it might. Although interwoven conversations of people interacting are indeed occurring, these interactions do not necessarily carry the power and energy that they could. Indeed, this one distinction differentiates the vast number of mediocre organizations from the few great ones. It also suggests why organizations that are great for a while later fade. In short, *do the conversations that define the organization succeed or fail in generating creative energy?*

The answer to this question lies, I believe, less in the character or talents of the individuals involved than in the quality of the questions that sit at the heart of their conversations. A Café that fails to center on questions that have real heart and meaning becomes a mechanical process of people talking and moving and reporting back. It fails to generate energy and excitement for the same reason that most organizations fail to generate energy—the questions and issues with which people are engaging simply do not compel their commitment and imagination.

Having said that, it is curious how rarely this happens in actual Café conversations. Why? Could it be that, when left on their own in a conducive environment, people naturally gravitate toward questions that matter? That they naturally do not waste their time on things that are unimportant? Perhaps authentic conversation often fails to occur in organizations because we believe we lack the permission to focus on what truly matters to us, or because we are actually kept from doing so? Whatever the combination of internal and external forces, the nature of the problem is clear. Life is too short to waste time on anything but what is truly important—and we all know this.

The biologist Humberto Maturana, who has been a major influence on how many of us think about communication and human communities, says, "History follows the path of our desires." When I first heard Humberto say this, I was confused. It seemed to me that much of the history I have seen, including recent history, follows the path of no one's desire. Indeed, it seems to be dominated by unanticipated and undesired side effects of our actions—climate change that no one desires, growing stress between rich and poor that no one desires, growing insecurity that no one desires.

As I have pondered this statement I have come to realize that Humberto is inviting us into a stance of responsibility that we usually shirk. Although the consequence of our collective actions may not be what we seek, the motivations that give rise to these actions, and thus the consequences, are expressions of our desires. But these desires are too small. They are too self-centered. They arise in ways too disconnected from the desires of others. In short, the desires guiding history today are not the desires that can create a future big enough for all of us.

I believe the underlying purpose of the World Café is to let loose the true desires of the larger whole. Is it too big a stretch of our imaginations to envision a world engaged in conversations that have real heart and meaning for us all? Start hosting your own Café conversations and see for yourself.

Is it too big a stretch of our imaginations to envision a world engaged in conversations that have real heart and meaning for us all?

ACKNOWLEDGMENTS

It Takes a Village to Raise a Child

There is an ancient African proverb that tells us, "It takes a village to raise a child." Watching the World Café grow and evolve over more than a decade has been humbling and deeply rewarding for both David and me. We often sit with wonder and ask ourselves, "Who could have imagined . . . !" We feel honored and blessed by the love, competence, and commitment of all of those who have contributed to this work finding its expression across the globe. The World Café community of inquiry and practice is the true author of this book . . . we are but hosts to our mutual learning. The stories and reflections shared are simply illustrative of the many that could have found expression here. David and I offer our deepest gratitude to all those who have participated in and contributed to this journey and to this book— many more of you than we can adequately thank by name. Please know that you have all been part of the village that is raising this child.

Leif Edvinsson and the Intellectual Capital Pioneers: Without your presence, participation, and excitement, the World Café would never have come into being.

Charles Savage: Who first introduced us to the power of cross-pollinating people and ideas as part of the Café pattern language. The World Café would not have been born if you had somewhere else to go that day.

Bo and Margaret Gyllenpalm: Without whose discipline, patience, persistence, caring, sharing, partnership, and love there might have been no research into the dynamics of "conversations that matter" nor introduction of the World Café to Sweden.

Finn Voldtofte, Toke Møller, Monica Nissén, Uffe Elbaek, and the Danish Café hosts: True teachers of foundational Café theory and elegant Café design as well as believers in the "life net" and deeper wisdom through which the conversations are already connected.

Meg Wheatley, Myron Rogers, Fritjof Capra, and the Berkana Institute: For helping us learn about human systems as living systems. And Meg, for being a "kindred spirit" in seeing the power of conversation in helping us turn to one another.

Peter Senge: For being a great learning partner for over twenty years as many of these ideas were honed in the Executive Champions' Workshop and other organizational forums.

Society for Organizational Learning, Executive MBA Program at the University of Texas, San Antonio, and the Future of Work Network: For providing welcome homes for our World Café learning and experimentation with senior executives, multinational corporations, and organizational professionals from around the world.

LeAnne Grillo, Ginny Wiley, and Pegasus Communications: Who have been partners from the start in helping us create World Café experiences where we could discover what it might mean to support "a system thinking together."

Willis Harman, Wink Franklin, Tom Hurley, and the Institute of Noetic Sciences: For the Närings-Liv dialogues where so many of the threads of this work in relation to transformational learning were woven.

Tom Atlee: A true pioneer, with your other colleagues from the Co-Intelligence Institute, for fostering the idea of co-intelligence on behalf of a better world.

George Pør: For helping us understand how a collection of intelligences could become a collective intelligence.

Eric Vogt: Nuestro hermano, for helping us appreciate the art and architecture of powerful questions.

Christopher Alexander, Tom Johnson, Humberto Maturana, Michael Schrage, and Verna Allee: Your research has helped us view the power of conversation in new ways.

The MIT Dialogue Project: For stretching our thinking and research about dialogue beyond where we might ever have imagined.

Rita Cleary: You helped us see the deeper pattern of the World Café and how it might serve our mutual visions of a better world.

Joe Jaworski, Adam Kahane, Otto Scharmer, Dennis Sandow, Etienne Wenger, and the Fields Inquiry Group: For weaving additional threads into the tapestry of our understanding about social learning, fields, emerging futures, multisector dialogue, and profound institutional change.

Tom Callanan, Eric Nelson, and the Fetzer Institute: For supporting our hosting of the Inquiring Friends and the Fields Inquiry in the service of understanding the deeper sources of collective healing and societal renewal.

Bob Johansen, Kathi Vian, and the Institute for the Future: For the IT and Sustainability Working Group, which helped us understand the potential for the World Café in cyberspace.

Laura Chasin, Maggie Herzig, Sallyann Roth, and the Public Conversations Project: For your capacity to bring dialogue into public conversations on the tough questions and recognizing the World Café as a "kindred spirit."

Sara Cobb, Fred Steier, Will McWhinney, Barclay Hudson, and the Fielding Institute: For helping us experience what it means to become scholar-practitioners in a lively community of inquiry.

Barbara Waugh and Bob Veazie: For bringing the deeper principles of the World Café to life on behalf of large-scale systems change at Hewlett-Packard. Kindred spirits and brilliant organizers "for the world."

Mike Szymanczyk: For our collaborative learning journey at the leading edge of corporate life for almost two decades. Your focus on process tools, conversational infrastructures, strategic questioning, and the power of putting principles into practice is a true inspiration.

Ken Murphy, Mike Pfeil, Rob Driver, and Mark Becker: Who, with many other colleagues at Philip Morris USA, have helped put these ideas into action in the service of realigning the company with society and reinventing its future.

Yvon Bastien, David Marsing, Bob Lengel, Carolyn Baldwin, Wit Ostrenko, Jack Travis, and Joy Anderson: For being conversational leaders—bringing dialogue and reflection into organizational life, even when it wasn't easy.

Arian Ward, Beth Alexander, and the leadership of both the Financial Planning Association and the American Society for Quality: For seeing the creative ways in which the World Café could build association communities. And Arian and Beth, for being heartfelt stewards of the World Café and its global online presence.

Carlos Mota, Felipe Herzenborn, and Maria de los Angeles Cinta: For creating the World Café as a bridge to the soul of Mexico.

The Chenders, Susan Skjei, Susan Szpakowski, Bob Ziegler, and the Shambhala Institute: For welcoming the World Café to Canada and introducing it to support authentic leadership.

Alan Stewart and Jenni Dunn: For being conversationalists par excellence and for taking the World Café to Australia (and Alan, to Hong Kong!).

Roslie Capper: For our clam chowder conversations and for helping the Café meet the Húi in New Zealand.

Edna Pasher and Mark Gerzon: For bringing Café conversations to Israel in ways that may one day help the future of the Middle East.

Alexander Schieffer: For seeing the potential for the World Café in Germany and for your wonderful writing to help spread the word throughout Europe.

Martin Fischer and the Kings Fund: For introducing the World Café to England and showing its contribution in large health care systems.

Ulric Rudebeck, Eva Eklund-Nordin, Stefan Wängerstedt, Marjorie Parker, and Christina Carlmark: For bringing your unique talents to the World Café in Norway and Sweden.

Samantha Tan, Daniel Kim, Diane Cory, and the Singaporean Organizational Learning Community: Your fostering the reach of the World Café in Singapore has truly taught us the answer to the question, "What does it mean to care?"

Salim Al-Aydh, Bronwyn Horvath, Jim Davidson, and Dan Walters: Your creativity in bringing the World Café to Saudi Aramco and the nation of Saudi Arabia has shown us what true hospitality looks like in practice.

Mille Böjer, Sera Thompson, Marianne Knuth, Tim Merry, Bob Stilger, and the Pioneers of Change: For extending the reach of the World Café and other innovative processes for evoking collective intelligence to Africa and to the many countries where you operate on the leading edge of global change.

Bill Auerbach and Mitch Litrofsky of the Breakthrough Group, and Michael Jones: For creating "café theater" at its most inspirational and teaching us the importance of drama and music in fostering conversations that truly matter.

Betty Alexander, Gretchen Pisano, and David Sibbet: You, along with the visual practitioners network and those acknowledged in our Illustration Credits, have demonstrated the incredible power of visual thinking and of making conversation visible.

Vicki Robin and Sharif Abdullah: For birthing your innovative Conversation Cafés and Commons Cafés—all the while keeping alive our common vision of creating a "Café society."

Let's Talk America, the Utne Institute, and From the Four Directions: For showing how using diverse perspectives creatively can contribute to societal innovation and democratic futures.

Colleen Lannon and Karen Speerstra: For your thoughtful and skilled editorial support and sage advice all along the way. And Karen, for bringing the World Café to church.

Elaine Kremsreiter: For faithfully transcribing untold hours of learning conversations with Café hosts and participants.

Steve Piersanti, Jeevan Sivasubramaniam, Pat Anderson, and the entire Berrett-Koehler team: For nudging your "recalcitrant authors" along and nurturing this child's development far longer than any of us imagined. May she grow into a strong adult making a heartfelt contribution to a better world. And to Rick Wilson, Linda Jupiter, Sandra Beris, Laura Lind, Karen Marquardt, and James "Max" Maxwell,

Berrett-Koehler's production team, for holding our hands through the myriad details of "making it happen."

Marcia Jaffe and Hans Kuendig: For believing in the power of invitation and offering to spread the word.

Frances Baldwin, Sharon and Glenn Lehrer, Sandy and Emmett Miller, Brian and Betsy Hand, Nancy Margulies and Gary Warhaftig, the Swans, and the Delias: For always being there at critical turns on the path. And Nancy, for your beautiful concluding poem.

Cesar Chavez and John W. Gardner: For being great leaders and personal mentors who taught us the importance of community leadership to renew optimism in the face of challenge.

Trudi Blom: Woman warrior and adopted grandmother to Juanita. For thirty years of great conversations at the Na-Bolom Center in Chiapas, Mexico—a special place where diverse worlds meet at the dining room table.

Millie and Harold Cowan, and Marion Isaacs: Our parents, whom we're also proud to call our friends. For living the example of community, of spirit, and of "conversations that matter." And to our "Tío Felipe" whose life showed us what real inquiry means.

Anne Dosher: For being there since the beginning . . . as elder, mentor, and guardian of soul of the World Café. For holding the space for our entire World Café community of inquiry and practice on this journey of discovery.

Ken Homer: For furthering the global reach of the World Café Web site and community. Your unique multifaceted role since the early days has been a true gift to our lives and to the future of the World Café.

Jane Brunette: For being our colleague, friend, loyal teammate, counselor, insightful editor, and elegant designer. There is *no* way this could have happened without your professional skills and personal dedication far and above the call of duty.

And for all of the World Café hosts, participants, organizations, and communities around the world who are on this journey of discovery: Some of you speak directly on these pages as storytellers and contributors. Others are finding voice on our Web site and the World Café community of practice listserv. Many are being heard as conversations that matter spread over the globe and people everywhere lead the way.

ILLUSTRATION CREDITS

Visual language is an important part of the World Café. We are grateful to Sherrin Bennett, Susan Kelly, Jennifer Landau, and Nancy Margulies for contributing key conceptual illustrations, to James "Max" Maxwell, for his creative renderings throughout the book, to Kevin Woodson for his beautiful chapter openers, and to Laura Lind for her elegant book design. Here's how to be in touch with these artists as well as with other visual specialists. Their contributions appear on the pages listed.

Sherrin Bennett, Interactive Learning Systems: Sherrin maps the dynamics of complex adaptive systems. As a consultant to organizations, she helps people rise to meet a challenge with breakthrough thinking and innovative strategy. Using questions to clarify intent, appreciation to discover what works, and feedback to amplify improvements, her clients learn to co-create the future they want to see happen. Contact: sherrinbennett@earthlink.net. See pages 19, 37, 40, 48, 93, 104, 113, 114, 127, 128, 134, and 174.

Susan Kelly, Occasions by Design: Susan is an independent graphic artist, specializing in visual thinking and interactive group graphics as well as agenda, meeting space, and materials design. For the past twenty years Susan has worked nationally and internationally, creating stimulating environments that bring out the creativity in individuals and groups. Contact: Susankellylistens@mac.com. See pages 35 and 182.

Jennifer Hammond Landau: As one of the pioneers of graphic facilitation, Jennifer has provided visual process consulting and training to business, government, and community organizations since the early 1980s. Her specialty is "metaphor mapping," where information is presented and meetings facilitated with large, visual metaphors. Contact: jhlandau@earthlink.net. See pages 35 and 133.

Laura Lind, Laura Lind Design: An award-winning graphic designer, Laura has twenty years' experience. She has designed many books and other printed materials, specializing in well-crafted visual communications and reliable service. You can see more of her work at lauralinddesign.com.

Nancy Margulies, Mindscapes: Part of the World Café team since the early years, Nancy is an organizational consultant, creative artist, illustrator, and inventor of Mindscaping, an innovative form of graphic recording. Using her unique combination of visual and strategic dialogue skills, Nancy's clients have included Xerox, Hewlett-Packard, Meg Wheatley, and President Bill Clinton and his cabinet. Contact: nm@montara.com. See pages 5, 63, 80, 83, 119, and 208.

James "Max" Maxwell: Max served as sketch artist for NBC-TV and won an Emmy Award for his work in documentaries. Max writes, paints, sculpts, and illustrates books, magazines, and other publications. Contact: www.mcn.org/b/jamesmaxwell. See pages 4, 22–23, 49, 64, and 167. In addition, Max either rendered or enhanced for publication every image in the book.

Kevin Woodson, partner, Visual Ink, LLC: For the past fifteen years Kevin has been combining art, facilitation, and strategic thinking to create business illustrations with Fortune 500 companies, including Hewlett-Packard, Gap Inc., and Citigroup. Kevin uses his artistic gifts to tell the story of change, make the complex simple, and get people onboard and excited. Contact: www.visualink.biz. See pages 13, 27, 43, 61, 79, 95, 107, 123, 139, 155, 177, and 197.

Visual practitioners and graphic recorders: Visual practitioners can graphically record the whole of a conversation as it unfolds, enabling members to think more holistically and carry forward their insights more effectively because the "memory of the whole" is harvested and shared. You can find resources for graphic recording of World Café dialogues and other meetings at www.visualpractitioner.org, or by contacting inquiry@theworldcafe.com.

ADDITIONAL CREDITS

Page 11: Photo of people at a Café table used with permission of the Shambhala Institute.

Page 45: Artwork used with permission of FONAES.

Page 72: Photo of Cafe ́in airplane hanger used with permission of Saudi Aramco.

Page 85: Photo of Café tablecloth and markers used with permission of Sherrin Bennett.

Page 93: Questions for Reflection are adapted from "Questions and Ways of Being to Amplify Dialogic Possibilities: Stance and Focus of Attention." Unpublished manuscript. Public Conversations Project, Watertown, MA, www.publicconversations.org. Used with permission of Sallyann Roth.

Pages 131 and 133: Photo of Café tablecloth and photo of graphic recorder are both used with permission of Ken Homer.

Page 141: Photo of large stickie wall used with permission of Bob Lengel.

Page 164: Photo of Café setup used with permission of David Isaacs.

Page 195: Questions for Reflection are adapted from "Conversation as a Core Business Process" by David Isaacs and Juanita Brown, first published in *The Systems Thinker*, Vol. 7, No. 10 (Pegasus Communications, 1996).

Page 200: The Knowledge Kopitiam logo is used with permissionn of NACLI, Singapore.

Page 210: The poem, "At the World Cafe ́," by Nancy Margulies is used with permission of the author.

RESOURCES AND CONNECTIONS

THE WORLD CAFÉ

The World Café Web Site and Community of Practice

The World Café Web site (www.theworldcafe.com) is the best place to go for the latest information on the World Café, including articles, stories, and hosting resources, as well as for information on related dialogue initiatives. If you would like to learn how to participate in the growing online World Café community of inquiry and practice, visit the World Café Web site. There, World Café hosts are sharing their learnings and discoveries.

Materials for Purchase

Pegasus Communications distributes World Café materials, including resource guides, key articles from its newsletter *The Systems Thinker*, a pocket guide, my doctoral dissertation on the World Cafe, and other dialogue resources. You can find Pegasus Communications on the Web at http://www.pegasuscom.com.

Research and Internships

I conducted the first doctoral research on the World Café (Brown, 2001). We encourage other researchers and students to consider the World Café for their research and internship projects. Contact Dr. Fred Steier or Dr. Bo Gyllenpalm via e-mail at info@theworldcafe.com, if you'd like more information on this.

Nonprofit Foundation—Tax-Deductible Contributions

Proceeds from this book will be donated to the World Café Community Foundation, a nonprofit foundation whose mission is to develop and disseminate World Café and other innovative dialogue approaches for addressing key organizational and societal questions in the service of positive futures. You can contribute to this work by making a tax-deductible donation to the World Café Community Foundation, P.O. Box 783, Mill Valley, California 94941. For more information, send an e-mail to info@theworldcafe.com or call 415/339-8714.

RELATED RESOURCES

This section provides information on other forms of dialogue as well as on key dialogue initiatives that are also making wonderful contributions to this body of work. If you only have limited time, the first three Web sites listed here provide a treasure trove of information, leading you into the many-faceted field of dialogue, deliberation, and collective intelligence. Those listed after these first three highlight specific aspects of this emerging field. We'd love to hear about other sites that you have found useful. Please contact us at info@theworldcafe.com.

The Co-Intelligence Institute

http://www.co-intelligence.org
Tom Atlee has compiled one of the Web's richest and most informative collections on the people, processes, and Web sites that foster dialogue and deliberation, democracy, and action. Of particular interest are the pages on dialogue and the compilations of processes.

The Fetzer Institute

http://www.fetzer.org
http://www.collectivewisdominitiative.org
The Fetzer Institute is a private foundation that supports research, education, and service programs exploring the integral relationships among body, mind, and spirit. Its Collective Wisdom Initiative has been a leader in mapping the field of dialogue and collective intelligence.

The National Coalition for Dialogue and Deliberation (NCDD)

http://www.thataway.org/
NCDD is a broad coalition of organizations and individuals involved in dialogue, public deliberation, and civic engagement. It is one of the most extensive resources for those interested in learning about dialogue and deliberation methods, practitioners, events, perspectives, and processes.

America Speaks

http://www.americaspeaks.org
America Speaks is a national not-for-profit organization committed to fostering civic dialogue and engaging citizen voices in local, regional, and national governance.

The Appreciative Inquiry Commons

http://connection.cwru.edu/ai/
Appreciative Inquiry is an approach to positive change based on powerful questions and collaborative conversations about the best in people, their organizations, and the world around them.

The Berkana Institute

http://www.berkana.org
The Berkana Institute is a global charitable foundation founded by Margaret Wheatley and her colleagues. It supports life-affirming leadership around the world. Dialogue is a key component of the institute's work.

The Breakthrough Group

http://www.thebreakthroughgroup.net
The Breakthrough Group is a pioneer in engaging the art and the science of storytelling, including theater, simulation, and living case studies, to stimulate catalytic conversations and organizational learning. Breakthrough collaborates with the World Café to create innovative strategic dialogues in conferences and other organizational settings.

The Center for Nonviolent Communication (CNCV)

http://www.cnvc.org
CNCV is a global organization helping people connect compassionately with themselves and one another through Nonviolent Communication, a dialogue and feedback process created by Marshall B. Rosenberg, Ph.D.

The Center for Wise Democracy
http://www.tobe.net
The Center for Wise Democracy uses its unique Dynamic Facilitation process to help groups engage in dialogue and deliberation, especially through randomly selected Wisdom Councils of citizens through which the voice of "we the people" can be expressed in organizations and communities.

The Commonway Institute
http://www.commonway.org/cafes
The Commonway Institute hosts Commonway Cafés in varied venues, bringing people together across racial, political, and other traditional divides to encounter "the other" in ways that can transform our collective future. Commonway Cafés, Conversation Cafés, and the World Café have joined in a Café Collaborative, using common principles to nurture a culture of dialogue.

The Compassionate Listening Project
http://www.compassionatelistening.org
The Compassionate Listening Project, formerly Mid-East Citizen Diplomacy, is dedicated to empowering individuals to heal polarization and build bridges between people, communities, and nations in conflict through dialogue and heartfelt mutual listening.

Conversation Cafés
http://www.conversationcafe.org
Conversation Cafés are dialogues hosted in cafés and other public venues for meaningful conversations about our thoughts, feelings, and actions in these new times. Using a highly effective circle process, Conversation Cafés and the World Café have partnered in linking small-group and large-group dialogue approaches.

CoVision
http://www.covision.com
CoVision was one of the first organizations to introduce portable groupware systems designed to facilitate the engagement of large numbers of stakeholders in meetings involving collaborative thinking and planning. CoVision's "Council" technology enables large groups to engage in collaborative dialogue through supporting quick keypad feedback on the group's priorities and key ideas.

Fran Peavey and Crabgrass
http://www.crabgrass.org
Fran Peavey, founder of Crabgrass, an NGO working on social and environmental issues, is a pioneer in the art of strategic questioning, particularly in community settings. She and her colleagues offer periodic trainings in strategic questioning.

From the Four Directions
http://www.fromthefourdirections.org
From the Four Directions is a global leadership initiative of the Berkana Institute. It has hosted and convened conversation circles among leaders in more than thirty countries.

Global Renaissance Alliance (GRA)
http://www.renaissancealliance.org
Dedicated to furthering the work of peacemakers everywhere, the GRA has extensive conversational resources for convening Peace Circles.

The Heartland Institute
http://www.thoughtleadergathering.com
Using both circle and World Café dialogue processes, the Heartland Institute, a leader in the dialogue field, sponsors a series of Thought Leader Gatherings co-hosted by leading-edge thinkers.

The Institute of Noetic Sciences (IONS)
http://www.noetic.org
IONS is a global nonprofit organization with more than thirty-five thousand members. It conducts and sponsors research on the potentials and powers of consciousness. Its community groups have embraced both dialogue and the World Café process as effective learning and community group development models.

Interaction Associates (IA)
http://www.interactionassociates.com
IA is a pioneer in meeting and facilitation training for those who need basic group skills as a foundation for working with dialogue and other group processes.

The International Forum of Visual Practitioners
http://www.visualpractitioner.org/
Visual practitioners can graphically record the whole of a conversation as it unfolds, enabling members to think more holistically and carry forward their insights more effectively because the "memory of the whole" is harvested and shared. Those who work as visual practitioners include graphic recorders, conceptual illustrators, facilitators, artists, designers, and others.

Let's Talk America
http://www.letstalkamerica.org
The goal of Let's Talk America is to engage Americans from across the political spectrum in respectful, thoughtful dialogue around questions that matter to the future of our democracy. Online resources include conversational guides for small- and large-group gatherings.

The Mediators Foundation
http://www.mediatorsfoundation.org
The Mediators Foundation focuses on developing projects and leaders that use dialogue as a core process for creating bridges among conflicting constituencies.

New Stories
http://www.newstories.org
New Stories is an organization that supports healthy individuals and communities, linked globally through dialogue, to create new stories for our common future.

PeerSpirit
http://www.peerspirit.com
The core of PeerSpirit's work is "council," a powerful circle-based process that builds on the dialogue traditions of indigenous peoples.

Pioneers of Change
http://www.pioneersofchange.net
Pioneers of Change is an emerging, self-organizing, global learning community of committed young changemakers in their mid-twenties to early thirties from diverse cultural, social, and professional backgrounds. The network operates in over seventy countries and utilizes leading-edge dialogue and other group processes to support projects locally and globally.

Powerful Non-Defensive Communication
http://www.pndc.com
Powerful Non-Defensive Communication is an approach to interpersonal dialogue that replaces the traditional mode of communicating to win arguments with one that gives each person the ability to communicate effectively without engaging in a power struggle.

The Public Conversations Project (PCP)
http://www.publicconversations.org
PCP promotes constructive conversations among people who have differing values, worldviews, and perspectives about divisive public issues. It offers many online resources.

The Socrates Café
http://www.philosopher.org
The Socrates Café encourages and supports lively dialogue in cafés, schools, and other venues among people who are curious and perplexed about the big questions of our time.

Society for Organizational Learning (SoL)
http://www.solonline.org
Founded by Peter Senge and other researchers, practitioners, and consultants, this group has sponsored pioneering research on dialogue and is a leader in the field of organizational learning.

Speaking Circles
http://www.speakingcircles.com
Speaking Circles is a process for transforming the way people communicate, allowing them to more fully express their natural creativity, passion, and humor, personally and professionally.

The Study Circles Resource Center
http://www.studycircles.org
Based on the Scandinavian study circle approach, the Study Circles Resource Center is dedicated to finding ways for people to engage in citizen dialogue and problem-solving on critical social and political issues.

Wisdom Circles
http://www.wisdomcircle.org
A wisdom circle is a way for small groups of people to create a safe space for dialogue in which to be trusting, authentic, caring, and open to change.

World Café (Denmark)
http://www.worldcafe.dk
This site, hosted by Danish World Café pioneer, Finn Voldtofte, contains excellent information on Café hosting, conceptual pieces on dialogue and strategy, and leading edge thinking about "the magic in the middle."

BIBLIOGRAPHY

Adams, M. G. *Change Your Questions, Change Your Life.* San Francisco: Berrett-Koehler, 2004.

Alexander, C. *The Timeless Way of Building.* New York: Oxford University Press, 1979.

Allee, V. *The Knowledge Evolution: Expanding Organizational Intelligence.* Boston: Butterworth-Heinemann, 1997.

Allee, V. *The Future of Knowledge: Increasing Prosperity Through Value Networks.* Boston: Butterworth-Heinemann, 2002.

Anderson, H., and Goolishian, H. "Human Systems as Linguistic Systems." *Family Process,* 1988, 27, 371–393.

Atlee, T. *The Tao of Democracy.* Cranston, R.I.: The Writers' Collective, 2003.

Baldwin, C. *Calling the Circle: The First and Future Culture.* Newberg, Ore.: Swan Raven & Co., 1994.

Bennett, S., and Brown, J. "Mindshift: Strategic Dialogue for Breakthrough Thinking." In S. Chawla and J. Renesch (eds.), *Learning Organizations: Developing Cultures for Tomorrow's Workplace.* Portland, Ore.: Productivity Press, 1995, 167–183.

Bohm, D. *On Dialogue.* London: Brunner-Routledge, 1996.

Brown, J. *The World Café: Living Knowledge Through Conversations That Matter.* Mill Valley, Calif.: Whole Systems Associates, 2001.

Brown, J., and Isaacs, D. "Building Corporations as Communities: Merging the Best of Two Worlds." In K. Gozdz (ed.), *Community Building: Renewing Spirit and Learning in Business.* San Francisco: New Leaders Press, 1995, 69–83.

Bunker, B., and Alban, B., *Large Group Interventions: Engaging the Whole System for Rapid Change.* San Francisco: Jossey-Bass, 1997.

Capra, F. *The Web of Life: A New Scientific Understanding of Living Systems.* New York: Anchor Books/Doubleday, 1996.

Capra, F. *Hidden Connections: Integrating the Biological, Cognitive, and Social Dimensions of Life into a Science of Sustainability.* New York: Doubleday, 2001.

Chasin, L. "Searching for Wise Questions." Watertown, Mass.: Public Conversations Project, 2001. Available at: http://www.publicconversations.org.

Cooperrider, D., and Srivastva, S. "Appreciative Inquiry in Organizational Life." In R. W. Woodman and W. A. Pasmore (eds.), *Research in Organizational Change and Development* (Vol. 1). Greenwich, Conn.: JAI Press, 1987.

Cooperrider, D., and Whitney, D. "Exploring Appreciative Inquiry." *Perspectives: A Journal of the World Business Academy,* 2000, 14(2), 69–74.

Cooperrider, D., Whitney, D., and Stavros, J. *Appreciative Inquiry Handbook.* Bedford Heights, Ohio: Lakeshore Communications and San Francisco: Berrett-Koehler, 2003.

Goldberg, M. *The Art of the Question: A Guide to Short-Term Question-Centered Therapy.* New York: Wiley, 1997.

Greider, W. *Who Will Tell the People?* New York: Simon & Schuster, 1992.

Hamel, G. "The Search for Strategy." Unpublished, unabridged version of an article that appeared as "Killer Strategies That Make Shareholders Rich," *Fortune,* June 23, 1997. Original article available from: Strategos, 1110 Burlingame Avenue, Suite 211, Burlingame, Calif. 94010; 650/344-1999.

Hegelson, S. *The Web of Inclusion.* New York: Doubleday, 1995.

Heisenberg, W. *Physics and Beyond: Encounters and Conversations.* New York: Harper & Row, 1971.

Holman, P., and Devane, T. *The Change Handbook: Group Methods for Shaping the Future.* San Francisco: Berrett-Koehler, 1999.

Horn, B. *Visual Language: Global Communication for the 21st Century.* Bainbridge Island, Wash.: MacroVue Press, 1998.

Institute for the Future. *In Good Company: Innovation at the Intersection of Technology and Sustainability* (Outlook Project Report. SR-672d). Menlo Park, Calif.: Institute for the Future, 1999.

Johnson, E. *Contextual Teaching and Learning: What It Is and Why It Is Here to Stay.* Thousand Oaks, Calif.: Corwin Press/Sage Publications, 2001.

Johnson, H. T. *Relevance Lost: The Rise and Fall of Management Accounting.* Boston: Harvard Business School Press, 1991.

Johnson, H. T., and Bröms, A. *Profit Beyond Measure: Extraordinary Results Through Attention to Work and People.* New York: Free Press, 2000.

Kinsler, S. "Germany Ablaze: It's Candlelight, Not Firebombs." *New York Times,* Jan. 12, 1992.

Kofman, F., and Senge, P. "Communities of Commitment: The Heart of the Learning Organization." *Organizational Dynamics,* 1993, 22(2), 5–23.

Lakoff, G. *Metaphors We Live By.* Chicago: University of Chicago Press, 2003.

Lambert, L., Walker, D., Zimmerman, D., Cooper, J., Lambert, M.D., Gardner, M., and Slack, P.J.F. *The Constructivist Leader.* New York: Teachers College Press, 1995.

Leeds, D. *The Seven Powers of Questions.* New York: Perigee/Berkeley Publishing Group, 2000.

Levine, R., Locke, C., Searls, D., and Weinberger, D. *The Cluetrain Manifesto: The End of Business as Usual.* New York: Perseus/HarperCollins, 2000.

Maturana, H., and Bunnell, P. *Biosphere, Homosphere, and Robosphere: What Has That to Do with Business?* Unpublished paper based on June 1998 presentation to the Society for Organizational Learning, 1999. Available at: www.sol-ne.org/res/wp/maturana/.

Maturana, H., and Varela, G. *The Tree of Knowledge.* Boston: Shambhala Publications, 1987.

Maturana, H., and Verden-Zöller, G. "The Origins of Humanness in the Biology of Love." Unpublished manuscript, n.d. Available at: http://www.matriztica.org.

McMaster, M. *The Intelligence Advantage: Organizing for Complexity.* Isle of Man, U.K.: Knowledge Based Development Co., Ltd., 1995.

Morgan, G. *Images of Organization* (2nd ed.). Thousand Oaks, Calif.: Sage, 1997.

Morton, N. *The Journey Is Home.* Boston: Beacon Press, 1985.

Needleman, J. "Report to the Fetzer Institute." Unpublished paper, 1987. Available at: www.fetzer.org.

Ochs, C. *Women and Spirituality.* Lanham, Md.: Rowman and Littlefield, 1983.

Oldenburg, R. *The Great Good Place: Cafés, Coffee Shops, Community Centers, Beauty Parlors, General Stores, Bars, Hangouts, and How They Get You Through the Day.* New York: Paragon House, 1989.

Owen, H. *Open Space Technology: A User's Guide.* San Francisco: Berrett-Koehler, 1997.

Peavey, F. "Strategic Questioning: An Approach to Creating Personal and Social Change." In F. Peavy, *By Life's Grace: Musings on the Essence of Social Change.* Philadelphia: New Society Publishers, 1994, 86–111.

Prahalad, C. K., and Ramaswamy, V. *The Future of Competition.* Boston: Harvard Business School Press, 2004.

Roth, S. "Questions and Ways of Being to Amplify Dialogic Possibilities: Stance and Focus of Attention." Watertown, Mass.: Public Conversations Project, 1998. Available at: http://www.publicconversations.org.

Russell, P. *The Global Brain Awakens: Our Next Evolutionary Leap.* Palo Alto, Calif.: Global Brain Inc., 1995.

Russell, P. *Waking Up in Time: Finding Inner Peace in Times of Accelerating Change.* Novato, Calif.: Origin Press, 1998.

Sandow, D., and Allen, A. M. "The Nature of Social Collaboration." Portland, Ore.: Portland State University School of Business Administration, 2004. Available at: http://www.sba.pdx.edu/classes/Ba530/sec2/SocialColl.doc.

Sandra, J. *The Joy of Conversation: The Complete Guide to Salons.* Minneapolis: Utne Reader Books, 1997.

Schrage, M. *Shared Minds: New Technologies of Collaboration.* New York: Random House, 1990.

Seely Brown, J. *Seeing Differently: Insights on Innovation.* Boston: Harvard Business School Press, 1997.

Senge, P. *The Fifth Discipline.* New York: Doubleday/Currency, 1990.

Sibbet, D. *Principles of Facilitation: The Purpose and Potential of Leading Group Process.* San Francisco: Grove Consultants International, 2003.

Singer, M., and Ammerman, R. *Introductory Readings in Philosophy.* Dubuque, Iowa: William C. Brown, 1960.

Slater, P. "Connected We Stand." *The Utne Reader*, March-April 2003, 62–64.

Srivastva, S., and Cooperrider, D. *Appreciative Management and Leadership: The Power of Positive Thought and Action in Organizations*. San Francisco: Jossey-Bass, 1999.

Stacey, R. D. *Complex Responsive Processes in Organizations*. London: Routledge, 2001.

Strachan, D. *Questions That Work: A Resource for Facilitators*. Ottawa, Calif.: ST Press, 2001.

Toms, M. *A Time for Choices: Deep Dialogues for a Deep Democracy*. British Columbia, Canada: New Society Publishers, 2002.

Varela, F., and Maturana, H. *The Tree of Knowledge: The Biological Roots of Human Understanding*. Boston: Shambhala Publications, 1992.

Varela, F., Thompson, E., and Rosch, E. *The Embodied Mind: Cognitive Science and Human Experience*. Cambridge, Mass.: MIT Press, 1992.

Vogt, E. "The Art and Architecture of Powerful Questions." *Micromentor Corporate Learning Journal*, 1994. Available at: http://www.javeriana.edu.co/decisiones/Mapa_conceptual_basico.html.

Vogt, E. "Learning Out of Context." In S. Chawla and J. Renesch (eds.), *Learning Organizations: Developing Cultures for Tomorrow's Workplace*. Portland, Ore.: Productivity Press, 1995.

Vogt, E., Brown J., and Isaacs, D. *The Art of Powerful Questions: Catalyzing Insight, Innovation, and Action*. Waltham, Mass.: Pegasus Communications, 2003.

Waldrop, M. M. *Complexity: The Emerging Science at the Edge of Order and Chaos*. New York: Touchstone, 1992.

Watkins, J., and Mohr, B. *Appreciative Inquiry: Change at the Speed of Appreciation*. San Francisco: Jossey-Bass/Pfeiffer, 2001.

Waugh, B. *The Soul in the Computer: The Story of a Corporate Revolutionary*. Makawao, Hawaii: Inner Ocean Publishing, 2001.

Webber, A. "What's So New About the New Economy?" *Harvard Business Review*, January-February 1993, 24–42.

Weisbord, M., and Janoff, S. *Future Search: An Action Guide to Finding Common Ground in Organizations and Communities*. San Francisco: Berrett-Koehler, 2000.

Wenger, E. *Communities of Practice: Learning, Meaning, and Identity*. New York: Cambridge University Press, 1998.

Wenger, E., McDermott, R., and Snyder, W. *Cultivating Communities of Practice: A Guide to Managing Knowledge*. Boston: Harvard University Press, 2002.

Wheatley, M. *Leadership and the New Science*. San Francisco: Berrett-Koehler, 1992.

Wheatley, M., and Kellner-Rogers, M. *A Simpler Way*. San Francisco: Berrett-Koehler, 1996.

Whitney, D., and Cooperrider, D. *Encyclopedia of Positive Questions*. Euclid, Ohio: Lakeshore Communications, 2002.

Whitney, D., and Trosten-Bloom, A. *The Power of Appreciative Inquiry: A Practical Guide to Positive Change*. San Francisco: Berrett-Koehler, 2003.

Wittgenstein, L. *Philosophical Investigation*. Englewood Cliffs, N.J.: Prentice-Hall, 1999.

Zaleski, P. *Gifts of the Spirit: Living the Wisdom of the Great Religious Traditions*. New York: HarperCollins, 1997.

Zohar, D., and Marshall, I. *The Quantum Society: Mind, Physics, and a New Social Vision*. New York: William Morrow, 1994.

INDEX

ABOUT THE AUTHORS

Juanita Brown, Ph.D., with her partner, David Isaacs, is a co-originator of the World Café. She collaborates as a thinking partner and design adviser with senior leaders, creating and hosting innovative forums for strategic dialogue on critical organizational and societal issues. Juanita's keynotes and seminars have attracted a broad range of leaders across sectors, including Fortune 100 companies and members of government, health, education, and community-based organizations in the United States, Latin America, Europe, and the Pacific Rim. As a Senior Affiliate with the MIT Sloan School's Organizational Learning Center (now the Society for Organizational Learning), Juanita participated as a member of the core research team with the MIT Dialogue Project and as co-faculty for SoL's Executive Champions' Program. She has served as a Research Affiliate with the Institute for the Future and is a Fellow of the World Business Academy.

David Isaacs is the president of Clearing Communications, an organizational and communications strategy company working with senior executives in the United States and abroad. He has collaborated with a wide range of corporate clients, including Alpha-Graphics, Hewlett-Packard, Intel, Kraft General Foods, Scandinavian Airlines Systems, and Sanofi-Aventis. David's not-for-profit work has included hosting World Café dialogues with the Institute for Noetic Sciences, Shambhala Institute, Society for Organizational Learning, and Alliance for Transforming the Lives of Children. David has served as adjunct faculty at the California Institute for Integral Studies, St. Mary's College of California, and the University of Texas at San Antonio Business School's executive MBA program.

Contact information: Partners in life and work, Juanita and David make their home on Tomales Bay, California, a pristine ecosystem north of San Francisco. They can be reached at inquiry@theworldcafe.com or at 415/383-0129.

The World Café community is made up of organizational leaders and others who believe in the power of "conversations that matter" to help shape the future. Leaders from business, government, schools and universities, health systems, and community-based organizations around the world have contributed their stories and discoveries, both to this book and to our mutual learning. There are now skilled Café designers and hosts available in many locations. To learn more, contact inquiry@theworldcafe.com or call 415/383-0129.

Berrett-Koehler Publishers

Berrett-Koehler is an independent publisher of books and other publications at the leading edge of new thinking and innovative practice on work, business, management, leadership, stewardship, career development, human resources, entrepreneurship, and global sustainability.

Since the company's founding in 1992, we have been committed to creating a world that works for all by publishing books that help us to integrate our values with our work and work lives, and to create more humane and effective organizations.

We have chosen to focus on the areas of work, business, and organizations, because these are central elements in many people's lives today. Furthermore, the work world is going through tumultuous changes, from the decline of job security to the rise of new structures for organizing people and work. We believe that change is needed at all levels—individual, organizational, community, and global—and our publications address each of these levels.

To find out about our new books,
special offers,
free excerpts,
and much more,
subscribe to our free monthly eNewsletter at

www.bkconnection.com

Please see next pages for other books
from Berrett-Koehler Publishers

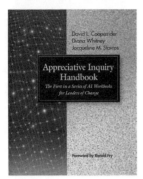

The Appreciative Inquiry Handbook

David L. Cooperrider, Diana K. Whitney, and Jacqueline M. Stavros

One of today's most popular change methods, Appreciative Inquiry (AI) has been used to undertake transformational initiatives in dozens of organizations, ranging from McDonald's to the U.S. Navy to Save the Children. The Appreciative Inquiry Handbook contains everything you need to launch any kind of AI initiative. It explains how AI works and provides sample project plans, designs, agendas, course outlines, interview guidelines, participant worksheets, a list of resources, and more.

Paperback • ISBN 1-57675-269-0 • Item # 52690-415 $45.00

The Appreciative Inquiry Summit

James D. Ludema, Diana Whitney, Bernard J. Mohr, and Thomas J. Griffin

The first book to provide a comprehensive practitioner's guide to the AI Summit—the preferred method when applying whole-scale change to large groups—The Appreciative Inquiry Summit provides step-by-step guidance for planning and running an AI Summit.

Paperback • ISBN 1-57675-248-8 • Item # 52488-415 $29.95

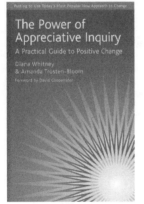

The Power of Appreciative Inquiry

Diana Whitney and Amanda Trosten-Bloom

The Power of Appreciative Inquiry is a comprehensive and practical guide to using Appreciative Inquiry for strategic large-scale change. Written by pioneers in the field, the book provides detailed examples along with practical guidance for using AI in an organizational setting.

Paperback • ISBN 1-57675-226-7 • Item #52267-415 $27.95

Berrett-Koehler Publishers
PO Box 565, Williston, VT 05495-9900
Call toll-free! **800-929-2929** 7 am-9 pm EST

Or fax your order to 1-802-864-7626
For fastest service order online: **www.bkconnection.com**

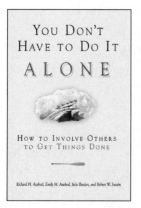

You Don't Have to Do It Alone

Richard H. Axelrod, Emily M. Axelrod, Julie Beedon, and Robert W. Jacobs

This book is the Swiss Army Knife on involvement—a comprehensive set of tool for getting the help you need. The authors lay out a straightforward plan for involving others to get things done, detailing a practical five-step process that will help you find the right people and keep them energized, enthusiastic, and committed until the work is completed.

Paperback • ISBN 1-57675-278-X • Item #5278X-415 $16.95

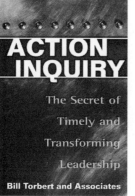

Action Inquiry

Bill Torbert and Associates

"Action Inquiry" is a fresh approach to learning leadership in the midst of action. This highly accessible process teaches us to exercise transforming power at key moments and more timely action in general.

Paperback • ISBN 1-57675-264-X • Item #5264X-415 $29.95

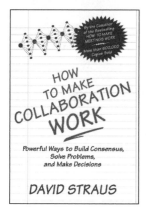

How to Make Collaboration Work

David Straus

In How to Make Collaboration Work, David Straus, a pioneer in the field of group problem solving, introduces five principles of collaboration that have been proven successful time and time again in nearly every conceivable setting.

Paperback • ISBN 1-57675-128-7 • Item #51287-415 $14.95

Berrett-Koehler Publishers
PO Box 565, Williston, VT 05495-9900
Call toll-free! **800-929-2929** 7 am-9 pm EST

Or fax your order to 1-802-864-7626
For fastest service order online: **www.bkconnection.com**